The guide to
LANGUAGES & CAREE

The Centre for Information on Language Teaching and Research provides a complete range of services for language professionals in every stage and sector of education, and in business, in support of its brief to promote Britain's foreign language capability.

CILT is a registered charity, supported by Central Government grants. CILT is based in Covent Garden, London, and its services are delivered through a national collaborative network of regional Comenius Centres in England, the National Comenius Centre of Wales, Scottish CILT and Northern Ireland CILT.

CILT Publications are available through all good booksellers or directly from:

Grantham Book Services Ltd
Isaac Newton Way
Alma Park Industrial Estate
Grantham, Lincs NG31 8SD
Telephone: 01476 541 080
Fax: 01476 541 061

the GUIDE to LANGUAGES and CAREERS

How to continue your languages
into further and higher education

- Degrees
- Diplomas
- Other qualifications

*By Ann King
with Gareth Thomas*

Centre for Information
on Language Teaching and Research

The views expressed in this publication are those of the authors and do not necessarily represent those of CILT.

Acknowledgements

The authors and publisher would like to acknowledge the following for permission to reproduce the photographs on the cover and throughout the book: University of Bath, Imaging & Photographic Unit; University of Exeter, Second-year students in the School of Biological Sciences.

The authors would like to express their gratitude to Ute Hitchin, their editor at CILT for all their careers publications over the last fifteen years, for her wisdom, experience, patience, and unfailing good humour.

Revised and updated edition published in 1999
First published in 1997
by the Centre for Information on Language Teaching and Research (CILT)
20 Bedfordbury, London WC2N 4LB

Copyright © 1999 Centre for Information on Language Teaching and Research

ISBN 1 903031 37 7

2004 2003 2002 2001 2000 1999 / 10 9 8 7 6 5 4 3 2 1

A catalogue record for this book is available from the British Library

All rights reserved. The purchase of this copyright material confers the right on the purchasing institution to photocopy the **Signposts** section and the **Checklists**, for their own use or for their students' use within the purchasing institution without any specific authorisation by the publisher. No other part of this publication may be reproduced, stored in a retrieval system, or transmitted in any form or by any means, electronic, mechanical, photographic, recording, or otherwise, without the prior permission in writing from CILT or under licence from the Copyright Licensing Agency Limited, of 90 Tottenham Court Road, London W1P 0LP.

Ann King and Gareth Thomas have asserted their right to be identified as authors of this work, in accordance with the Copyright, Designs and Patents Act 1988.

Printed in Great Britain by Copyprint UK Ltd

CILT Publications are available from: **Grantham Book Services**, Isaac Newton Way, Alma Park Industrial Estate, Grantham, Lincs NG31 8SD. Tel: 01476 541 000. Fax: 01476 541 061. Book trade representation (UK and Ireland): **Broadcast Book Services**, 2nd Floor, 248 Lavender Hill, London SW11 1JL. Tel: 020 7924 5615. Fax: 020 7924 2165.

Contents

Introduction: how to use this book   vii

Section 1	**Who needs languages?**	1
1	Employers do . . . and you do!	3
2	What are employers looking for?	7
3	In which careers are languages useful?	9
4	How do I prepare myself?	15
5	Who speaks what where?	17

Section 2	**Studying languages**	21
6	Learning languages post-16	23
	Checklist	29
7	Diploma courses with languages	30
	Checklist	33
8	Degree courses in languages	34
	Checklist	45
9	Languages of the European Union	46
	Checklist	53
10	Scandinavian languages	55
	Checklist	56
11	Russian and Eastern European languages	57
	Checklist	60
12	European Studies	61
	Checklist	63
13	Asian languages	64
	Checklist	67
14	Arabic, Middle Eastern and African languages	68
	Checklist	70
15	Linguistics	71
	Checklist	74

Section 3	**Studying languages with other subjects**	75
16	Institution-wide language programmes	77
17	Languages and business-related subjects (including accountancy)	78
	Checklist	86
18	Law and languages	88
	Checklist	96
19	Tourism, sport and leisure with languages	97
	Checklist	102
20	Engineering and languages	103
	Checklist	108
21	Science and languages	109
	Checklist	114

22	Information technology and computer science with a language	115
	Checklist	118
23	Food science and technology with languages	119
	Checklist	122
24	Agriculture, horticulture and other land-based subjects with languages	123
	Checklist	127
25	Preparing to become a teacher of languages	128
	Checklist	132

SECTION 4 Signposts to degree courses

		133
26	Studying for a degree in languages	135
27	Studying for a degree in languages with other subjects	144

SECTION 5 Studying and working abroad

		173
28	Studying in Europe	175
	Checklist	177
29	Work placements in Europe	178
	Checklist	182
30	Taking time out: the gap year	183
	Checklist	192

SECTION 6 Making your choice

		193
31	Finding a course	195
	Checklist	201
32	Getting in	202
	Checklist	206
33	Interviews and Open Days	207
	Checklist	211

Appendix: where to go for more help — a list of further resources

	213
General information	213
Specific subjects and career routes	214
Studying and work placements abroad	214
A year out/holiday jobs	214
Other useful publications	217
Free publications	217

How to use this book

It is no longer possible to reserve proficiency in foreign languages for an elite or those who acquire it on account of geographical mobility. It is becoming necessary for everyone, irrespective of training and educational routes chosen, to be able to acquire and keep up their ability to communicate in at least two community languages other than their mother tongue.

from *Teaching and learning: towards a learning society* (a White Paper published by the European Commission)

Over the last fifteen to twenty years, opportunities to study languages, and to include a language alongside another specialism in a further or higher education course, have grown enormously. When we were writing our first languages and careers publications in the 1980s, there was only a handful of degree courses in, for example, law or engineering, which included the study of a language. Now you can see from the Signposts tables in this book that the range of possibilities in these two subjects alone, and in many other subjects, including the sciences, is considerable. Indeed, the post-18 education scene, with regard to language learning and study abroad, has become quite complex and very rich in its provision.

The impetus for the explosion in the number of courses involving languages has come partly because of the new developments outlined in Chapter 1 — in particular, the internationalisation of world markets and the completion of the Single European Market. The co-operation on various aspects of education policy between EU member states has encouraged more student, teacher and youth mobility and exchanges; and students themselves and exchanges; and students themselves now demand more opportunity to continue a language, or to learn a new one.

And yet, in spite of the wealth of opportunities to do courses involving languages, the messages about what is on offer, and the advantages for both employers and employees of language competence, do not always get through to students. This is probably due in part to the complexity and breadth of provision.

It is important that these messages be heard. The rapidly evolving new Europe is very different from the old, and it needs a new generation of people, with new skills and new attitudes. Somewhere amongst those skills and attitudes, whatever one's field of employment, should be the ability to communicate in at least one or two other languages, the knowledge of cultures other than one's own, and a ready acceptance of other nations' differences. Some time ago, an article in the national press quoted the professor of management studies at a French business school as saying that an analysis of factors leading to the success of German, American and Japanese firms highlighted the significance of cultural factors (not just languages) in economic behaviour. He pointed to studies which show that executives working abroad, who are unaware of the intercultural aspects of business and management, have only a superficial contact with their foreign colleagues and return home quickly, often after costly setbacks and failures. Intercultural understanding is important and is one of the by-products of language study.

Young people in the UK, who are currently being educated and trained to a high standard in a whole range of different specialisms, will be in competition for jobs with other equally well qualified young people from other EU countries. One factor that could well be decisive with employers recruiting them in the new economic climate is their level of linguistic capability. How will British graduates and diplomates fare in competition with those of other nationalities who usually have a high level of competence in at least one, and often two, three or even more foreign languages?

We have written this book in order to raise awareness of the exciting range of courses and careers available, so that young people can make the right choices, and so that teachers and careers advisers can have more hard facts to back up the guidance they give on languages and careers.

The guide to languages and careers is designed to cater for a wide readership:

- **students of languages**, who we hope will appreciate a comprehensive directory of language courses and language-related courses in the UK, together with useful advice on, for instance, studying and working abroad, and taking a year off;

- **students of all subjects**, both pre- and post-16, who need to know the choices open to them, so that potential course and career opportunities are not lost to them;

- **teachers of modern languages**, so that they are well enough informed to be able to point their students in the right direction;

- **teachers of other subjects**, who are often asked by students to give advice on FE/HE courses, and who therefore need to know the options available;

- **careers teachers and careers advisers,** to keep them informed of newer developments in the field;

- **parents**, who we feel sure will value a guide to the ways in which their sons and daughters may choose to continue learning languages into further and higher education, and the benefits this can have in career terms.

The book is designed to be used on a number of levels:

Although very few people will wish (or need) to read it through from cover to cover, there are specific sections which are intended to be read more closely than others — in particular, the general introduction to the whole area of languages and careers in **Section 1 — Who needs languages?** — with its analysis of the views of employers, and an examination of the areas of employment where languages are often useful, sometimes essential. Pupils — all pupils — not just the more able linguists, need to be aware of these arguments; so do those who advise them on careers and course choice.

Section 2 — Studying languages is intended to appeal in particular to the specialist modern languages student, and it is sub-divided into courses at different levels — post-16 courses, diploma courses in FE and HE, and degree courses. Because post-16 and diploma courses do not **specialise** in languages, and because degree programmes are of their very nature specialist courses, the examination of degree courses in this section is further subdivided, with separate sections devoted to in-depth examinations of degree courses in each of a range of world languages. All these courses, whether of post-16, diploma or degree level, are linked to potential career destinations. The language student may wish to read the whole section — or may read one chapter which he or she feels is of most relevance, and then perhaps dip into one or two of the others.

Section 3 — Studying languages with other subjects is arranged in separate chapters, each dealing with a different subject/group of subjects or occupational area, and the related career possibilities. Students who are currently specialising in non-language subjects should be encouraged to look at this section — often the language qualification needed for entry to the diploma and degree courses described is no more than a good GCSE. Again, the chapters which would appear to be of most relevance can be read in some depth, whereas other chapters may be skim-read, or even ignored if they do not appeal or require the study of subjects of which the student has little or no experience. For the purposes of this publication, which is concerned with linking languages with careers, the 'other subjects' highlighted are almost exclusively subjects which are vocational or semi-vocational in nature, with only passing references to joint honours, combined honours, and modular schemes which, of course, allow languages to be combined with almost any other subject at a university or college somewhere in the UK.

Section 4 — Signposts contains a range of useful tables which will allow the adviser or researcher to pick out, almost at a glance, the institutions which offer a particular degree course with a language, or with study abroad, as well as the range of languages which may be studied.

It has not been possible to tabulate HND and other diploma courses in this way because the range of different course titles is so wide, the institutions at which they are offered so many and various, and the range of languages offered and the levels to which they can be studied so frequently changing in response to demand and other circumstances. There is an examination of these courses in other parts of the book, in Section 3, in particular. **Signposts** tables may be photocopied for individual use or for display purposes.

Sections 5 and 6 provide a wealth of practical information and advice on studying and working abroad, including a range of things to do in a year out; the factors to consider in choosing a course and an institution at which to study; and the procedure for applying for a place, including interviews and open days.

The **Appendix** at the end provides a list of further resources under a number of headings: general information on courses and institutions; information about specific subjects and career routes; studying abroad; a year out and holiday jobs; other useful publications; and free publications.

A feature of the book are the **Checklists** at the end of each chapter. These summarise the main points, and can be read through after reading the chapter, to act as a reminder; or they can be read first, as part of a skim-reading process, to enable the reader to identify relevant sections to be read in greater depth. Since they summarise the main points in the book, they are potentially useful as hand-outs and display items. For this reason they, too, may be photocopied.

Ann King
Gareth Thomas

Section 1

Who needs languages?

Employers do . . . and you do!

What are employers looking for?

In which careers are languages useful?

How do I prepare myself?

Who speaks what where?

Employers do . . . and you do!

Talking English louder is not enough . . . There has been a gradual awakening on the part of British business at least to the disadvantages of not understanding the mentality of the customer and speaking his language.

Sir Peter Parker, Industrialist

If you have enjoyed learning languages and want a career that involves working or living abroad, or even if you want to use your languages as part of your job but don't necessarily want to go abroad, there are more and more jobs where languages are needed and speakers of other languages are valued. This growing need for people with language skills is attributable to a number of fairly recent developments, all of which have implications for you and your future career:

- changes in technology;
- change in Europe;
- increasing internationalisation;
- advances in transport systems.

Technological change

We are living through a period of enormous technological change. New developments in information technology and computer applications, many of them revolutionary just a few years ago, are now part of our daily lives, even in the home — such as fax machines, personal computers, high speed telecommunications, computerised banking and booking systems, electronic transfer of funds, viewdata information sources, the use of office computer systems for dealing with accounts or contracts, electronic mail, and conferencing via satellite links. All this means that business practices have been transformed because people can now have close and virtually immediate contact with colleagues and clients across the world, without moving out of their offices or their homes. Transnational deals can take place without the need for travel and written correspondence is no longer dependent upon the vagaries of postal systems. International business, which used to be more or less restricted to large companies, is increasingly becoming a possibility for quite modest organisations. The result of all this is that markets have become globalised because communications are now so sophisticated.

What this means for you

There will be more and more opportunities for you to work with an organisation which has dealings with parent companies, subsidiaries, suppliers or clients in Europe, or indeed much further afield — and therefore it is getting more and more likely that your languages will be an important asset both to you and to your employers.

A changing Europe

In the twenty-odd years since the UK became a member of the European Community, the pace of change, both political and economic, has been dramatic. The EU has also grown greatly in the area it covers. In the beginning there were six, then nine, ten, twelve, and today fifteen member states — in addition to the UK these are Belgium, Denmark, France, Germany, Greece, Ireland, Italy, Luzembourg, the Netherlands, Portugal, Spain; and since 1 January 1995, Austria, Finland and Sweden. And now the EU has committed itself to further enlargement, to take in the applicant countries from central and eastern Europe.

The founding agreements of the EU have been

revised three times since the Treaty of Rome began, by outlawing discrimination based on nationality in matters connected with the free movement of workers: the Single Act in 1987, the Maastricht Treaty on European Union in 1992, and in 1997 the draft Treaty of Amsterdam, which contains new rights for citizens, including the extension of freedom of movement and employment within the European Union.

One of the consequences of this is that you now have a right to go to another member state to work, and are entitled to the same treatment as nationals of the 'host' country in matters of pay, working conditions, taxation and trade union rights. This applies to all types of employment, with the exception of certain restricted jobs in the public service.

There do remain some practical barriers, however. A major problem at present for those wanting to work abroad is that other member states have their own specific requirements in terms of qualifications needed for skilled and professional posts. The European Economic Area Agreement of May 1992 has helped to remove this obstacle by providing for the mutual recognition of professional qualifications throughout the EEA, but acceptance of this has not been particularly rapid in some areas.

There were initially a number of directives issued, with the intention of harmonising the basic training for the professions across the member states. This made it easier for doctors, dentists, nurses, midwives, vets, pharmacists and architects to work freely within the EU, but progress in this was slow — for example, the agreement on the harmonisation of architects' qualifications took twenty years! As a result, a more 'blanket' approach was seen to be required, and an agreement has now been reached which obliges member states to recognise qualifications from elsewhere in the EU which have been obtained after the successful completion of at least three years' degree level and/or professional training. This means that 'free movement' now applies also to accountants, lawyers, teachers, engineers, surveyors, physiotherapists, and many others.

So if you want to exercise your chosen profession in another member state, you should be able to do so. But of course you will need to be proficient in the languages of the countries you choose to work in — as this advertisement from a major German company indicates:

> . . . **engineering and science graduates [and] those graduating in other disciplines such as economics with engineering, business administration, economics and computer science . . . from other European countries have good prospects of joining the Daimler-Benz Group if they have a knowledge of German.**

Those who have had between three and five years' practical experience of a trade or profession can purchase a 'Certificate of Experience' issued by the Chamber of Commerce on behalf of the DTI, which allows their experience to be recognised in other member states. This applies to retailing, the hotel and catering trade, the construction industry, hairdressing, and insurance, for example, as well as to self-employed work in transport and travel agencies.

The EU has, over recent years, initiated and supported generous programmes of co-operation between member states in the field of education and training. Most of the transnational study schemes in higher and further education have been made possible through European Action Schemes, which have been designed to m eet the education and training needs of students within the EU, and to facilitate the movement of students between member states — and, in certain programmes, have included Iceland, Norway and Liechtenstein as well.

These Action Schemes have evolved over the years, and there are now two major ones which provide funding to promote academic and vocational qualifications throughout the EU:

Socrates

This programme promotes cooperation in the field of education, and includes ERASMUS (the Action Scheme concerned with the mobility of HE students) which last year provided for 160,000 EU students to spend a fully recognised part of their course of study in another EU member state (or in Iceland, Norway or Liechtenstein).

Under ERASMUS you could be given a grant to go towards the extra expenses involved in studying abroad for a period of between three months and a year. These could include, for example, travel expenses, appropriate language training, and contributions to make up the extra costs of living and accommodation abroad. You would not lose any part of any LEA grant you received, or your eligibility for a loan under the UK government scheme. And you would not pay any fees at the other European host institution.

Leonardo da Vinci

This programme is designed to complement vocational training policies in individual member states. It can provide opportunities for higher education students, and recent graduates, to undertake periods of up to twelve months' industrial training within companies in other member states. You would not necessarily receive a salary — that is up to individual employers — but you would receive a contribution towards language tuition, and expenses such as travel and subsistence. You cannot apply personally for funding, but your university or college should be able to help you arrange this.

What this means for you

The European Union has in effect become one huge multinational, multilingual job market, so that a job in Cardiff or Coventry will be as European as one in Copenhagen or Cologne. This gives you wonderful opportunities, but you should also remember that just as you can go to France or Italy or Portugal to look for work, so young people from Spain, Denmark or Greece are able to come to the UK to do the same thing. You may be just as well qualified as they are professionally, but they may well be better qualified than you linguistically. To take full advantage of the challenges that the Single Market has brought, it would pay you to think seriously about developing the necessary language skills. You may find yourself in competition for jobs with someone from Germany or the Netherlands who can speak three or more languages! The policy of free movement of labour does not mean that work is easy to find, and it would be sensible to prepare yourself as well as you can for your future career.

Fortunately, the Community Action Programmes have helped to bring about enormous changes in further and higher education and training, with the result that you have a wide choice of courses and schemes available to you which allow you to study or undertake training or work experience in other member states, often as part of a British degree or diploma course, many of which enable you to get foreign qualifications as well as British ones. And a significant number of universities and further and higher education colleges can offer you a course which will allow you to gain a professional or vocational qualification at the same time as learning a language.

The Single Market has finally brought home to most British commercial and professional organisations that they need staff who can communicate with their business partners abroad in their language, rather than expect the rest of the world to speak English. This situation is obviously one which you, if you are looking for a career where you can use your languages, should try to exploit.

Increasing 'internationalisation'

However important the changes in Europe have been, to confine our sights to Europe alone would be to 'think small'! British industry and business are having to adapt to an increasing international environment — one that extends beyond Europe. Transnational mergers are on the increase, and not just amongst the large manufacturing firms. The result of British companies merging with, or being acquired by foreign ones, and of foreign firms coming under the control of firms in the UK, is that it is no longer just senior personnel who will be working in an international context, but clerks in high street banks and building societies, or operatives on factory production lines.

Growing international business, and the regulations needed to control it, mean that many jobs which have been seen as purely domestic are now taking on an international flavour. For example, the last decade has seen a growth in large firms of international accountants who audit the accounts of multinational companies in their many branches throughout the world. And international law, including company law, is another area which is growing in response to the needs of the international marketplace.

What this means for you

> The internationalisation of business and industry means your chances of having an international career are increasing. It means, too, that people for whom this is not an aspiration may well find that in the future they will need to use languages as part of their jobs. And not just European languages — Japanese car manufacturers have set up factories in the UK, and British accountants, lawyers and engineers, for example, are working in Asia and the Middle East.

Advances in transport systems

Communications and travel on a global scale are continually improving. This is particularly true within Europe. The possibility of getting fairly rapidly from A to B within the EU is now in place, or very nearly so. Air traffic is particularly busy in the London-Paris-Frankfurt triangle, and new transport developments are making train and road travel just as fast and practical. The EU has drawn up plans for the funding of major European infrastructure projects to support trade within the new Single Market, as well as a blueprint for high-speed train networks to be created by 2010.

More recently, the opening of the Channel Tunnel has in reality made England, Scotland and Wales a part of Europe — a peninsula joined to the mainland, no longer 'cut off' by the sea. Both goods and passenger traffic (but especially the latter) between the UK and the rest of Europe are increasing dramatically.

What this means for you

> These advances make it possible for you to widen your horizons and to consider a career outside the UK, or one which involves travelling around.

What are employers looking for?

All the signs point to the fact that languages are going to be more and more important in career terms. British employers are becoming increasingly aware that they need people at almost every level of their organisations who can use languages as part of their job, whether in a professional or a social context.

So, it can be a definite advantage to equip yourself with several skills which will be useful to you in your career. If you have enjoyed learning languages at school, you would be very wise to continue with a language and/or start a new one.

There are also going to be increasing opportunities for people to move freely between countries as a normal part of their working life. In many companies languages are important at every level of the organisation, and from a business point of view it makes good commercial sense to speak the customer's language — as Willy Brandt, a former German Chancellor, put it:

> *If I am selling to you I will speak English, but if you are selling to me, dann müssen Sie Deutsch sprechen.*

You are far more likely to gain your customer's respect and be able to play a controlling part in business negotiations if you are able to communicate directly in his or her own language.

But being able to speak another language is only part of the picture; there are some other important factors:

- Languages on their own are not enough.
- Which languages are 'useful'?
- Understanding other lifestyles.

Languages on their own are not enough . . . .

If you want to make a career for yourself, earn a reasonable salary and have a good chance of promotion, you need to link your proficiency in languages to another specialism, like business studies, secretarial training, marketing, tourism or hotel management, science, engineering . . . Unless you intend to do a job which is directly related to languages, such as translating, interpreting, or teaching languages, the language(s) you can offer a prospective employer will almost certainly not be the main reason for your landing the job.

But an ability to speak another language could well be the deciding factor between you and another candidate for that job you want so much. Even if you do not get to use your linguistic skills very much in your first post, they could prove to be a real bonus later on, especially for subsequent promotion within the company.

Which language?

In the business world it depends where you are working — the preferred language for trade is the customer's own language. This is illustrated by the true story of the Dutch businessman who could speak six languages and when asked which of these he used in his business dealings, replied that he used whichever gave him commercial advantage at any particular time. It is obviously useful to be so proficient!

The languages most people study at school — French, German and Spanish — are still increasingly needed, but a recent study found that British business primarily needs to employ speakers of German, Japanese and Italian in order to do well with exports.

Spanish is in demand, as much for trade with Latin America as for dealing with Spain itself. Arabic is needed by those who work in the oil trade, and for political or media purposes because of the strategic importance of the Middle East.

French is frequently in demand by employers, although there is a preponderance of speakers of French, since it remains the most widely taught language in UK schools.

There is, of course, an argument that if you speak one of the less commonly learnt languages — Dutch, Scandinavian languages, Portuguese, modern Greek, Russian, Chinese, for example — you could have a rarity value in the job market.

This does not mean that the language you are learning now may be the 'wrong' one! Far from it. In learning your French, German or Spanish, you have also learned how to learn a language, so that acquiring a new one is likely to be relatively easy for you, provided that you are prepared to put in the hard work! There are plenty of higher or further education courses which offer you the possibility of learning a new language, either on its own or in combination with another subject. And many companies provide language training for their employees, because they see it as crucial to their economic success, with the result that they may employ you on the strength of your French, knowing that they can help you to add Italian or Japanese when the need arises.

Understanding other lifestyles

An important by-product of your language studies is a developing appreciation of other people's differences. This cultural awareness is valuable in two ways — as part of your wider cultural education, and as a highly important career asset.

All communities take a pride in their customs, their way of seeing the world, their way of expressing themselves in language (written and spoken), in art, in music, and in their day-to-day living. This is what constitutes culture. Europe today displays enormous cultural diversity, with its 45 different native languages in everyday use, the attachment of its component member states to their own structures and traditions, and the fierce independence of many of its smaller cultural groups, like the Catalans, the Basques or the Bretons. And Europe is a microcosm of the world. Most people you meet on your travels abroad will want you — perhaps often expect you — to show an interest in the differences between your culture and theirs. They will certainly be delighted if you do so!

This cultural understanding can be of great benefit in your career, as a complement to your language skills, both to you and any organisation which employs you. This is because, in order to work successfully abroad, you need also to have an appreciation of ideas, traditions, customs and lifestyles which are often very different from your own.

When you work in another country, you need to get used to different ways of working. The social aspects of your work, too, are as important as the purely professional ones: you may not get very far, or enhance your company's reputation, if you are not open to cultural differences — you could appear rude, you might even seriously upset people.

An understanding of foreign customs and lifestyles is particularly important if you want to work abroad in marketing or selling. A really accurate knowledge of what your potential customer feels, and thinks, and aspires to, is crucial to success in this field.

There are many ways of entering the culture of another community, but none so efficient as understanding (and even better, speaking) its language, because then and only then are the intricacies of that culture revealed in all their complexity. As a student of languages you will be extremely privileged, since you will have a head start!

In which careers are languages useful?

A language is just a means of communication, and it needs to be allied to other qualifications and personal attributes if you are going to be successful in the job market. This view is endorsed by a London recruitment consultancy:

> . . . we interview between 600 and 700 linguists a year, and receive CVs from another 1,200, some of whom still think that having a degree in modern languages will be their passport to riches and success. Unfortunately the reality is that the commercial world demands additional, complementary skills.
>
> The Language Business, quoted in *Language Matters*

Other parts of this book go into detail about specific careers and deal with topics such as degree and diploma courses with languages, study abroad and 'year out' opportunities, but what follows here are a few examples of employment sectors where languages have been found to be important and useful.

Retail sector

> All candidates must be able to communicate fluently in English and, for positions on the continent, at least one of the following languages: Dutch, Flemish, French, Spanish.
>
> *Job advertisement for Marks & Spencer plc (graduate recruitment)*

There are all sorts of jobs in the retail sector which involve working abroad, sometimes in more than one country. Marks and Spencer have opened up branches in mainland Europe and across the world, as have other shops which are familiar to us, like Laura Ashley and Body Shop. Buyers and merchandisers travel the world attending food fairs, book fairs and fashion shows in search of new lines; marketing experts devise new advertising strategies tailored to the needs of local populations, and to do so they need an appreciation of foreign cultures and lifestyles in addition to a knowledge of languages.

Tourism

It is obvious that an ability to speak at least one foreign language is crucial if you are going to travel abroad as part of a job in the tourist trade. But at home, particularly in the tourist centres and festival venues, there is a need for speakers of a wide range of languages to assist foreign tourists in shops, hotels, tourist offices and so on. In Edinburgh, for instance, which attracts people from all over the world to its annual festival, the managers of a large department store have made sure that they know which members of their staff understand and speak which languages:

> Jenners Department Store, Edinburgh, keeps an annually updated list of all shop assistants speaking any language other than English . . . so that whenever a problem arises the relevant assistant can be contacted. Languages currently available include French, German, Italian, Greek, Danish, Norwegian, Swedish, Dutch, Polish, Russian, Spanish, Turkish and Arabic.
>
> *from 'Lost for Words', a report published by the British Tourist Authority*

Often only a relatively modest level of language proficiency is required here — we are not talking about language 'experts'!

Transport

> British Airways . . . aims to provide training for as many of its 6,000 cabin crew (including those on domestic flights) as possible in French, German, Italian and Spanish. BA has also begun training in Japanese and, after market research, is considering extending this to Portuguese, Arabic, Mandarin and Cantonese.
>
> *from 'Lost for Words'*

It is fairly obvious that an airline would want its cabin crew to deal sympathetically with the needs of its many customers from all over the world — which means being able to speak to them in their own languages.

It might surprise you more to learn that some train drivers need to learn French. But when you hear that the drivers concerned are the ones who take the high speed trains through the Channel Tunnel, it is not so surprising. As the trains go between London and Paris or Brussels without changing crews, so the drivers, as well as customer service personnel, have to learn sufficient French to be able to do their jobs efficiently and safely.

Public relations

> " On graduating she worked first in International Marketing, then at Sky Television in public relations. After this she moved to the GB-USSR Association where she co-ordinated the British Month in Kiev. The success of this major event no doubt contributed to her being offered her current post as Moscow Office Director of the British Soviet Chamber of Commerce.
>
> *University of Northumbria at Newcastle prospectus* "

This young woman had done a degree course in German and economics, and had also done Russian from scratch at university. She added public relations and marketing skills to her language qualifications by gaining on-the-job experience, and was thus well placed to apply for the Moscow post.

Mapping out a career in this way is important — remember, linguistic ability on its own, although very useful, is hardly ever a sufficient qualification for a job.

Banking

> " I joined the International Division of the National Westminster Bank and spent several weeks 'in the classroom' learning the basics of banking. I then spent five months as a Marketing Officer on the team of an International Accounts Executive . . . After fifteen months with NatWest I was promoted to Assistant Manager and given a post as Personal Assistant to the Senior International Executive for the UK.
>
> *St Andrew's University prospectus* "

This person joined the bank with a degree in French and German and then, to provide her with the relevant banking qualifications, the bank trained her on all aspects of the job during her first fifteen months with them.

All of the British high street banks have international divisions and branches throughout the world. Barclays Bank plc has offices in 77 countries, for example.

There is often a need for speakers of foreign languages in London branches and other tourist centres in this country, and some employees are sent to work in branches in Paris, or other major European cities, on the strength of their proficiency in languages.

Senior employees (a position you should arrive at eventually!) can get more prestigious overseas postings provided that their level of linguistic expertise is high, as this excerpt from a recent advertisement illustrates:

> A multinational banking group with head offices in the United Arab Emirates wishes to fill a vacancy shortly at the most senior level . . . a high level of fluency in spoken and written French and English is a necessity, and knowledge of Arabic will be most beneficial.

Information technology

> " After completing my studies (BA degree course in English with French) I accepted the post of trainee Business Systems Analyst with a very large British company. I spent two years designing, developing and implementing new computer solutions and was then offered my present position which is Systems Consultant with a German owned, internationally expanding software house. My French, of course, was instrumental in my obtaining this post in a company where every employee can speak at least two European languages.
>
> *from Edge Hill College prospectus* "

Here is another example of someone who has completed a higher education course in languages and then gone on to work with a firm as a trainee in order to get specific qualifications. Although post-18 courses in further education tend to be vocationally oriented, you do not have to think exclusively in career terms when you choose a higher education course. It makes good sense to choose a subject you are good at, and enjoy, because then your chances of doing well are likely to be increased — and employers like to recruit successful people.

Of course other routes into a job such as this would be for you to choose a specialist course in computer science, and then brush up on the language you did at school — or learn a new language; or you could do one of the many courses which combine the study of computer science/information systems with a modern language (see Chapter 22).

Accountancy

> " When I joined Peat Marwick I was promised an opportunity to travel, so I could use and develop my language skills (she had done a degree in Spanish with French and Portuguese), and in my second year with the firm I went on a working mini-tour of France, reviewing the results of chemical installations in France, Belgium, Italy and Spain which were part of a major international chemical group . . . Last year I commuted to Paris for three months, assisting in the acquisition of a French electrical retail company quoted on the London Stock Exchange.
>
> *from University of Hull prospectus* "

This person went into accountancy after a university modern languages course, and although it is perfectly possible to make a career for yourself as an accountant without first getting a degree, the demand for graduates is strong now, and graduates tend to progress more rapidly in their careers.

Business consultancy

> Graduates can be from any discipline, but must be European nationals and fluent in at least two European languages including English. Successful applicants will be required to join one of our European offices for two years before returning to an office in their home country. With Andersen Consulting you will have the opportunity to work with major national and multi-national clients ranging from financial services, industrial and consumer products to the Government and other public services . . .
>
> *Job advertisement for Andersen Consulting*

From this you can see that the actual subject you study for a degree is not that important. Many firms are on the look out for graduates because they believe that a graduate is someone with a high level of intelligence, commitment (it takes commitment to go on studying for three or four years), and the flexibility to adapt positively to the challenges ahead.

Secretarial work

There are several routes to a career as a secretary or personal assistant where you can also use languages, and perhaps travel. One of them, obviously, is to do a secretarial diploma course, particularly a bilingual secretarial course; another is to get a degree first — in any subject — and then do a postgraduate course in secretarial skills.

There are plenty of secretarial and bilingual secretarial courses available at further education colleges and private colleges, as well as in higher education institutions. Secretarial courses have changed significantly over recent years, and course titles reflect this. If you want a degree course in secretarial skills, you could be choosing from titles like 'Administrative Management' or 'Office Systems Management' or 'Office Information Technology', and many of these courses include the study of languages.

A glance at job advertisements will show you that languages are an important asset in this field, as for example in these extracts from national newspapers:

> . . . a bright young secretary/PA with good shorthand/typing, preferably French or German, and some experience . . .
>
> . . . bilingual secretary for lively division of prestigious art company . . .
>
> Vice President of international company needs French, Portuguese or Spanish speaking PA.
>
> . . . PA to MD . . . Fluent German and another European language would be desirable.
>
> An experienced PA with fluent Japanese is required to work for the General Manager of a small financial company.

Marketing/Sales

> " On graduation (from a degree course in German and English) she applied through a London agency for work and found herself being interviewed by Burberry's. During her first year with them she worked on customer liaison, dealing with buyers in Germany, Switzerland, Austria and France, using her language skills every day. . . . At the end of her second year she was headhunted by Aquascutum to be their European Sales Manager . . .
>
> *Oxford Brookes University prospectus* "

A real success story which must owe a lot to the personal qualities of the young woman concerned, although her languages were obviously an important factor.

Someone else who had done a language degree, this time in French, and who wanted to carve out an international career for himself, consciously joined an international company as a marketing trainee:

> " There are few companies that will send you to far off places within four months, but after a whirlwind introduction to business and to Coats UK, it's off to the joys and perils of any of five continents. This is true international business: the USA in my first year, Brazil in my second, with three weeks to learn Portuguese in between.
>
> *St Andrews University prospectus* "

The fact that he learnt Portuguese for his trip to Brazil in three weeks is an example of something we said earlier (see 'Which language' on p7): that if the job you do requires you to speak a language you are not proficient in, your employer will often arrange for you to have intensive training. This is relatively hard work, depending upon how similar the new language is to the one you have already studied, but it is made a lot simpler by the fact that you already understand what learning a language is all about.

Law

> She spent her year abroad at the Law Faculty of the University of Heidelberg. On graduating she went to Chester College of Law, and after two years' articles, she qualified as a solicitor. She then spent ten months in Germany on the DAAD young lawyers' programme and is now working for a firm of solicitors in the City, dealing largely with German clients.
>
> *University of Wales College of Cardiff (School of European Studies) prospectus*

This shows you that in the legal profession you cannot break into an international career quite as quickly as you can in some of the examples above — legal training is necessarily lengthy, and therefore quite a costly business — but after a four-year degree course in law and German, and another three years' training, this person has clearly got an exciting and well-paid post.

There are more branches of the legal profession in which languages are an advantage — international law practices and multinational companies, as well as quite small legal practices and companies, increasingly find themselves dealing with and on behalf of clients who have interests abroad.

Teaching

A significant number of modern language graduates take up teaching careers in schools, colleges and universities. Some choose to teach English as a foreign or a second language, for which a Teaching English as a Foreign Language (TEFL) or a Teaching English as a Second Language (TESL) qualification is most useful, and often necessary.

Sometimes the experience of the year abroad as part of a degree course exerts an influence on career intentions, as here:

> She graduated with a degree in French, having spent her third year as an English language teaching assistant in a lycée in Le Mans, France . . . for two years she worked in Portugal, teaching English as a foreign language. Since then she has been employed as a teacher of English as a foreign language at an English university.
>
> *University of Newcastle prospectus*

Science and engineering

> I was sponsored throughout my degree (in Environmental Sciences) by Carlisle City Council and after graduation I returned there as an Environmental Health Officer . . . My current position (with the Institution of Environmental Health Officers in London) takes me all around the UK and sometimes Europe . . . A great deal of my time is taken up formulating responses to Government and EC proposals.
>
> *University of Salford prospectus*

Because of the globalisation of business and industry, there is a growing need for engineers, technologists, scientists, construction workers and others, for whom proficiency in a language has not perhaps been important until now, to be able to communicate effectively with colleagues in other countries, particularly with site and factory workers who may not be able to converse in any language other than their own.

> **Successful candidates will have an engineering or science degree or have a technical background . . . A decided asset would be fluency in a European language . . .**
>
> *Job advertisement for a management post with a multinational corporation*

Work with ethnic communities

So far, we have concentrated mainly on learning languages in order to work abroad, or perhaps to help tourists who come to the UK, but those of you who already speak one of this country's community languages have a very useful qualification to add to your CV — particularly if you see yourself eventually working in social work or a related career such as health care, child care, youth work, education, legal aid, immigration law, welfare and community development:

> You will have a Social Work qualification or a degree and relevant Social Work experience... Working knowledge of at least one of the main Asian languages is essential.
>
> *Advertisement for Social Services Development Officer with Black and Asian Communities*
>
> Your responsibilities will include interviewing and advocacy on behalf of clients, research, case follow-up, client referrals, client representation at tribunals/court, and general administration... Applicants must have an awareness of issues relating to the Asian Communities together with fluency in two of the following: Hindi, Bengali, Punjabi, Urdu or Gujerati.
>
> *Advertisement for Citizens' Advice Bureau Specialist for Asian Community*

You would need the relevant specialist qualifications and/or practical experience, of course, but a knowledge of cultural diversity and an ability to relate to, and speak to members of multi-cultural communities are important skills which are in demand, particularly where non-English speakers need interpreters to enable them to put their case, to obtain specialist care, or to exert their legal or other rights.

Overseas aid work

Charities and aid agencies recruit salaried employees, and it is usually necessary, or at any rate desirable, for those who go to work overseas to have some capability in a foreign language:

> Effective communication skills (including fluency in English) are essential. A good knowledge of French would be advantageous.
>
> *Advertisement for a job with an aid agency working with poor populations in Africa*
>
> The successful applicant will have excellent organisational and administrative ability, and possess strong communication and interpersonal skills... Previous experience of living in China and a knowledge of the Chinese language would be a distinct advantage.
>
> *Advertisement for field officer for voluntary service overseas*

There are openings abroad, too, for nurses and other health care workers. Again, some knowledge of relevant languages would obviously be desirable. For the examples below Spanish (for Bolivia), Portuguese (for Brazil) and French (for Mali) would be useful; you would not be required to know the local languages or dialects before you went, of course, but you would no doubt acquire a working knowledge of them while you were there!

> *Bolivia*
> Nurse to work with campesino community in Cochabamba to develop activities for health education, and train local agents and a Quechua-speaking counterpart.
>
> *Brazil*
> Health workers to work with local health teams in the interior towns of Amazonas.
>
> *Mali*
> Nurse/midwife to join the maternity team of Timbuktu health centre, and help develop its health education work.
>
> *Advertisement from a recruitment agency specialising in medical posts in Latin America and West Africa*

How do I prepare myself?

How good at languages do I need to be?

Although higher level qualifications are becoming more and more sought after by employers, some of the examples above do not require you to have a particularly high level of language proficiency — your school-level language skills are often enough.

Not all of them require you to have degree level qualifications — there are jobs with, for example, banks, tourist agencies, shops, and transport firms, where advanced academic qualifications are not necessary, but where languages are often useful.

Career plans

If you are keen to work abroad, but a degree course is not for you, then you could look for a job with a firm that is expanding into Europe, or with a multinational company. You could also consider a job with the European Commission which employs both graduates and non-graduates.

However, in future, it is likely that there will be more career openings for the highly skilled and the well qualified, both academically and professionally. Opportunities for graduates, diplomates and professionals are likely to be better than for those with lower qualifications.

With this in mind, you would be well advised to aim for the best qualifications you can, and if you want a career where you can use languages, there are a number of options available to you in higher education which will enable you to enhance your strengths, interests and aptitudes:

- modern language degree or diploma courses;

- combined degree or diploma courses which include a language;

- degree or diploma courses which involve study or work-experience abroad, and often give you a foreign qualification as well;

- degrees leading to professional qualifications, e.g. law, medicine, dentistry, engineering, architecture, which can open up careers abroad;

- supplementary language courses which are often available on a voluntary basis at HE institutions, or as an optional part of a course;

- degree or diploma programmes which allow study abroad to be accredited as part of the final qualification.

All these possibilities are explored in detail in other parts of this book.

What to do now

Much of what we have said here concerns decisions which may seem to you a long way off. There are, however, several things you can do now (as well as taking advantage of your educational opportunities) which will perhaps open up more opportunities for you later on:

- If you are able to do so, make the most of school/college visits abroad, as well as family holidays. Any experience abroad, however brief, adds that little bit more to your knowledge of other cultures and countries, and gives you an opportunity to practise your language skills.

- Read as much as you can in the language(s) that you want to specialise in. It can be light reading — magazines perhaps, even just snippets, but make sure that you read with a purpose, making a mental or a written note of expressions and phrases you want to remember.

- Read as much as you can about what is going on in the world, and particularly about the country/regions you might like to work or live in eventually.

- Take opportunities to listen to foreign radio or to watch TV programmes in foreign languages.

- Make the most of your holidays by getting some relevant work experience . . . perhaps abroad.

All these can help you to take your first steps along the path to a career with an international flavour . . . and will also stand you in good stead for when you have interviews for a place at a university or college, or eventually for a job.

Who speaks what where?

The European Union

The European Union has its origins in treaties and agreements drawn up in the years immediately after the end of the Second World War (1939–45), inspired by the need for joint action to ensure that the millions of deaths, the devastation, and the severe economic depression caused by the nations of Europe fighting each other in two world wars never occurred again.

It began with six members in 1958 — France, West Germany, Italy, Belgium, the Netherlands and Luxembourg — and now has a membership of fifteen, with the addition of the UK, Denmark and the Republic of Ireland in 1973, Greece in 1981, Spain and Portugal in 1986, and Austria, Finland and Sweden in 1995.

The European Union has put in place special action programmes to provide money to open up opportunities for students to travel, study and/or gain work experience in another member state (see pp4–5). You now also have certain rights under EU rules: the right, in general, to have your qualifications recognised in another member state; the right to look for work and take up employment in any other member state without a work permit; if you do go to another member state to work, the right to the same terms and conditions of employment as nationals of the 'host' country; and the right to be allowed to set up your own business anywhere within the EU.

There are eleven official languages of the EU — Danish, Dutch, English, Finnish, French, German, Greek, Italian, Portu-guese, Spanish and Swedish. Although in practice most everyday business at the European Commission in Brussels, and at the European Parliament, is conducted in either French or English, all official documents are translated and all meetings involving national officials are simultaneously interpreted into all eleven official languages. The Commission, the Parliament, the Court of Justice and the Council of Ministers are major employers of linguists — together they constitute the largest employer of translators and interpreters in the world. The Commission itself employs about a third of its thousands of employees on interpreting or translating between the eleven official languages.

Discussions are under way about extending the boundaries of the EU eastwards to take in the Baltic States and the six former Soviet republics in Europe. One of the implications of enlargement would be the very large increase in official languages. A case has been made to reduce the number, perhaps just to English, French and German (which are also the languages most widely used in the EU for business purposes), although there would understandably be opposition to this from other member states, particularly Italy and Spain.

European languages

Language	Where spoken	Official language UN	Official language EU
French	France; parts of Belgium, Switzerland & Canada (Quebec); Luxembourg; some African countries	✓	✓
German	Germany; Austria; parts of Switzerland & E. Belgium; Luxembourg; Liechtenstein		✓
Italian	Italy; part of Switzerland		✓
Spanish	Spain; most of S.America; Mexico	✓	✓
Danish	Denmark		✓
Dutch	Netherlands; part of Belgium (Flemish)		✓
Finnish	Finland		✓
Greek	Greece; part of Cyprus		✓
Norwegian	Norway		
Portuguese	Portugal; Brazil		✓
Russian	Russia; Ukraine; Belarus and other former Soviet republics; widely understood in E.Europe	✓	
Swedish	Sweden; part of Finland		✓
		English is an official language of both the UN and the EU	

Oriental and African languages

Language	Where spoken	Official UN language
Amharic	National language of Ethiopia	
Arabic	Middle East; Egypt; parts of N.Africa	✓
Bengali	Bangladesh; W.Bengal; UK Asian community	
Burmese (Myanmar)	National language of Burma (renamed the Union of Myanmar in 1989)	
Chinese	China; Hong Kong (Cantonese)	✓
Gujarati	Gujarat (on NW coast of India); Gujaratis also live in Bombay, and in UK, USA and E.Africa	
Hausa	One of the principal languages of Nigeria; important language in Niger, Ghana and Cameroon	
Hebrew	Israel; used for various purposes by Jews worldwide	
Hindi	National language of India; UK Hindu community	
Indonesian (a variety of Malay)	Indonesia	
Japanese	Japan	
Korean	Korea	
Malay	Malaysia; parts of Indonesia	
Panjabi	State language of the Indian Panjab; UK Pakistani and Sikh community	
Sinhalese	National language of Sri Lanka	
Somali	Somalia; Somaliland; Djibouti; Ethiopia; Kenya	
Sotho	Lesotho; also spoken in S.Africa	
Swahili	Most of E.Africa	
Tamil	State language of Tamilnadu (formerly Madras) in India; N.Sri Lanka; also parts of Malaysia, Mauritius and Fiji	
Thai	Thailand	
Turkish	Turkey; part of Cyprus	
Urdu	National language of Pakistan; one of the official languages of India; widely spoken in UK by Muslims from Pakistan and N.India	
Yoruba	One of the principal languages of Nigeria; also spoken in the Republic of Benin, Ghana, Togo, Côte d'Ivoire, as well as in parts of Brazil and Cuba	
Zulu	S. Africa (one of the nine Bantu languages spoken there)	

Section 2

Studying languages

Learning languages post-16

Diploma courses with languages

Degree courses in languages

Languages of the European Union

Scandinavian languages

Russian and Eastern European languages

European studies

Asian languages

Arabic, Middle Eastern and African languages

Linguistics

Learning languages post-16

What choice do I have?

All sorts of exciting choices start opening up for you between the ages of sixteen and eighteen. Broadly speaking, you have the choice of whether to stay on in full-time education in order to gain further qualifications, or whether to leave, get on to a training scheme, or look for a job.

If you do decide to carry on studying, you have the choice of getting your qualifications in the sixth form of a school, in a sixth form centre, or at a further education college. You can even follow a part-time course — either in the evening, or on a day-release basis from work.

Then, of course, there is the choice of what courses you take — not just the subjects you would like to do, but the type of course you want to do. Do you want a course which allows you to adopt a more practical approach to your learning, and leads to a vocational qualification, or do you want the more academic approach of 'A' levels or Scottish or Irish Highers?

And when you are choosing your course, you will need to bear in mind where you want your post-16 education to lead you.

Do you have a specific career in mind? Then you need to choose your course accordingly.

Do you want to go on to higher education — a diploma or degree course at a university or a college of higher education, perhaps? Then you will have to bear in mind the qualifications you will eventually need in order to get on to a particular course.

You should do a bit of research and consult careers advisers as to what subjects you ought to study, and what levels of qualifications you will need.

Will GCSEs or SCE Standard grades be sufficient in some subjects?

Which subjects will you need to have studied at a higher level?

But don't think too narrowly about a future career or a future course. You are quite likely to change your mind in the next couple of years!

It is also impossible to predict the precise nature of your future working life these days, because of all sorts of factors, especially new technological advances and scientific discoveries, which are revolutionising many industries and changing the nature of work and the types of jobs which are available.

These days it is more important than ever that the choices you make at this stage do not close down your options in the future. Even if you feel you are quite confident now about one particular career route, you ought to make sure that you have some alternative avenues open to you in case you have to change your plans. You will have a definite advantage if you equip yourself with several skills — a language among them — and are willing and able to learn more as new circumstances emerge in your adult life.

What are the best jobs to go into?

The best job is one that suits **you**. People will tell you that a good salary and excellent chances of promotion are important. They are, but you must take into account your own strengths (and weaknesses!), and your interests and enthusiasms. Try to think about what you might want out of a career, and ask yourself some of these questions before you link your decisions about your future life to the choice of a post-16 course:

What do I want out of a career?

- Do I want security, or a job which offers me a challenge?
- Do I want a career which gives me opportunities to travel, or would I prefer to settle down, and have a job which allows me to devote time to family life?
- Do I want to be given lots of responsibility?
- How adaptable am I?
- How good would I be at working under stress and to strict deadlines?
- Do I eventually want to be the boss, or would I prefer others to take decisions for me?
- Do I want to work with people? On my own? In an office? Out of doors? In a large organisation? From home . . ?

Choosing the right course

Once you have made the decision to apply for a post-16 course, you need to choose one which will suit you. How much choice you have here really depends upon where you live, and how many schools and colleges there are in your area offering post-16 education. The range of courses available to you can also depend upon the size of those schools/colleges — larger institutions can usually offer a wider range of options (although a large college may not suit you for other reasons — only you can know what's best for you!).

When you pick a course you need to have these questions at the back of your mind:

What sort of course am I looking for?

- What am I good at? . . . not so good at?
- Do I want a course which will prepare me for work?
- Do I have a favourite subject which I want to study further?
- Do I want a course which will stretch me intellectually?
- Would I prefer a course with some practical work? . . . with a lot of practical work?
- Have I looked into studying subjects I have not had the chance to do before?
- Do I want a course which has a single once-and-for-all exam at the end of it?
- Or would I do better under a continuous assessment system? A modular system, perhaps, where I can build up credits towards my final result as I go through my course?
- Are there any 'minor' or short courses I can do alongside my main programme of study — like word processing, computing, a language — which could be useful to me in my studies or my career?

Making sense of what's on offer

Nearly all courses on offer these days are geared towards nationally recognised qualifications. Here are some of the titles you will have to choose from:

'A' levels

GCE Advanced levels are well understood by employers and universities as an indication of potential and achievement. They offer an ideal route to higher education and/or a profession. You choose individual subjects, and so you can pick a balance of subjects to suit your tastes and your career aspirations; you could also choose a mix of science and arts subjects, so you could, for example, keep a language going if you wanted to become a scientist, an engineer, a lawyer . . . and thus give yourself more career opportunities later on — like being able to travel in your work, or to work abroad.

At the moment, the majority of those intending to go on to a degree course study three 'A' levels, and a few find they can manage four. Most 'A' levels have an end-of-course examination; some have a coursework component; some are modular so that you get results of individual study units as you progress through the course. These examinations will change in September 2000.

'AS'

Advanced Supplementary courses will become Advanced Subsidiary courses in September 2000. They will be worth 50% of an 'A' level and be considered halfway to an 'A' level qualification.

Higher Still

In Scotland many students take between three and five SCE Higher Grades rather than 'A' levels. Highers are taken at age seventeen/eighteen, and are the standard entrance qualification for four-year Scottish university courses. English universities, where most courses last three years, often require a further Scottish qualification — the new Advanced Higher — which is taken in the sixth year of secondary schooling, after passing Highers.

Vocational qualifications

There is a wide range of vocational courses, leading to diplomas and certificates, which provide preparation and training for specific areas of work. Diplomas include more units than certificates; diplomas usually take two years of full-time study, and certificates two years of part-time study.

A National Diploma is considered as the equivalent of two 'A' level passes. It can lead on to employment, or to a Higher National Diploma (HND) in the same subject area at FE/HE college or university; and a National Diploma with very high grades can be acceptable as an entrance qualification to a degree course in a related subject area.

You are assessed by a combination of continuous assessment and final exams.

GNVQ

General National Vocational Qualifications are vocational courses designed to lead on to employment or to further study.

There are three levels of GNVQ; the third level — Advanced — is the equivalent of two 'A' levels and will usually take two years to complete. GNVQs do not train you for any specific job but provide you with a broad knowledge and understanding of a particular vocational area. A GNVQ course also helps you to develop skills which will be valuable in a career (like information technology, communication, and working with figures); and you do additional study units which enable you to make your GNVQ match your own personal requirements by choosing from a range of specialist options (depending upon what courses an individual school or college can offer) — so if you were doing an Advanced GNVQ in Leisure and Tourism, for instance, you might be able to choose options in canoeing and sailing, or in sports studies, or horse studies, or environmental conservation.

A GNVQ can provide you with the necessary entrance requirement for a higher education course in a related subject area, although you might find that, if it was a degree course you wanted, you would need to get a distinction, as well as a further qualification like an 'A' level or an 'AS' — there is time available on an Advanced GNVQ programme to study an 'A' level.

GNVQs are assessed by a combination of continuous assessment and final exams.

GSVQs

GSVQs are the Scottish equivalent of GNVQs (see above).

IB

Some educational institutions — usually European or international schools — run course programmes leading to International Baccalaureate qualifications. The IB is an examination package which takes the place of both GCSE and 'A' level exams, and in which a range of subjects are studied at either Higher or Subsidiary level. Because of the number of subjects they take (estimated to be the equivalent of about 4.5 'A' levels), IB students have to work hard, but are able to keep their post-18 options open as long as possible. All IB students have to study at least one foreign language.

The IB is internationally recognised as a qualification, and many UK universities and colleges of higher education set their entry requirements in terms of the IB as well as 'A' levels, Highers, GNVQs and GSVQs.

Will languages be useful to me in my career?

At present it is mainly senior managers and sales personnel who travel abroad, but it is not just these people who need to be able to use languages. Very often the people who have the most contact with foreign language speakers, and therefore the greatest need to be able to understand and speak languages themselves, are those working in administration and secretarial departments. These people have to read and understand letters and faxes from abroad; they have to be able to write in a foreign language so that intelligible letters, faxes and e-mail communications can be sent to foreign colleagues and clients; they have to receive foreign visitors from abroad; and they have to be able to communicate effectively over the telephone with foreign colleagues and clients. Every bit as important to the company as someone higher up the organisation, if not more so, is the person who answers the telephone to a foreign client who speaks little or no English. This may perhaps be the client's first contact with the company, and if the wrong note is struck, or if communication cannot take place, that client's business will have been lost.

This sort of argument does not escape employers, and they will often pay more to get an employee who is able to speak a language.

I want to include a language in my course

School sixth forms, sixth form centres and FE colleges offer the sixteen-year-old school leaver language courses of all kinds — for example, short modules which you can study as an optional 'extra' to your main course; courses which help you to use language effectively for communication purposes, and where writing the language may be optional; courses which enable you to develop language skills within a business context; GCSE language courses (add another language to your CV?); and, for those who want to specialise in languages, 'A' level or Scottish Higher Still programmes where you can take one or more languages.

Not all of the courses are assessed by one end-of-course examination. Some of them are assessed by continuous assessment plus an exam; others by assignments only; and some of the shorter courses are competence-based, with a certificate being awarded after the successful completion of a certain number of hours of study.

... a language with 'A' levels or Scottish Higher Still programmes

Many students who have done well at languages want to take them further and study them to a higher level. If you recognise yourself here, then you could opt for an 'A' level programme, or Scottish Higher Still if you live north of the border. And if you really want languages to play a major part in your future career, it might be a good idea to choose to study two languages. Don't worry if you have only done one language up to now — there are quite a few places which will let you do a 'new' language (Spanish, perhaps, or Italian or Russian . . .) as a beginner, and get you to 'A' level standard in two years.

Or if you don't see yourself as a language specialist, take another look at **Section 1 — Who needs languages?** and at the other chapters in this section on **Studying languages . . .** to see how useful languages can be in a career and how many higher education courses there are in which you can combine a language with another specialism. Most degree courses will only specify two subjects at the most which you will have to have studied to 'A' level (or equivalent) — why not make your third subject a language? And if you have the opportunity (and the ability) to do four 'A' levels, then a language could certainly figure somewhere in your course.

If you are planning to do an 'A' level programme and want to include a language course, but do not want to do as much as an 'A' level in a language, then find out if the school or college you want to attend offers a non-'A' level language course which you can do alongside your main subjects. Although the range of courses on offer differs from institution to institution, there are courses available which enable students to develop an ability to use languages effectively for practical communication. The languages most widely available are French, German and Spanish, but sometimes there are others, like Italian, Russian or Japanese. There are usually different levels of course available, so you can choose a course according to your ability and previous knowledge; or you could start a new language from scratch, either a GCSE course which you could probably complete in a year, or a vocationally oriented one like a Certificate in Business Language Competence.

If you didn't get an A–C pass in a language at GCSE, you could consider retaking — it would be a pity to pass up an opportunity of getting a useful qualification in a subject you had spent about five years on already. Or if you really think you have had enough after five years, why not consider learning a new language? Again, you could do a GCSE course, or a certificate course (Business Language Competence), or Foreign Languages at Work (FLAW) perhaps, or a language module as part of a vocational course.

... a language with GNVQ/GSVQ programmes

There are three levels: Foundation, Intermediate, and Advanced in GNVQ; Level I, Level II and Level III for GSVQ, which is the Scottish equivalent of GNVQ.

Foundation level is equivalent to GCSE and usually takes one year.

A GNVQ Intermediate also usually takes one year and can give you a leg up on to an Advanced GNVQ programme. There are no formal entry requirements for the course, so if you have not done too well at school, this might be a route you could take into further education, and even higher education, rather than retaking your GCSEs.

To get on to a GNVQ Advanced programme, you would normally need to have passed four GCSEs at grade C or above; or a GNVQ Intermediate in appropriate subjects.

GNVQs/GSVQs have been specifically designed to give students a more academic progression route than a purely vocational course to further training and employment, and a more vocational route than 'A' levels or Highers to further and higher education.

There are GNVQ/GSVQ courses available in a range of vocational areas, like:

- business;
- leisure and tourism;
- media: communication and production;
- health and social care;
- engineering;
- science;
- hospitality and catering.

Within your chosen area, you will study a range of mandatory units, and do work in core skills (communication, numeracy and information technology). You will also be able to choose from a selection of optional units, assessed by project and assignment work, which can include language studies.

The languages available at most schools/colleges are French, German or Spanish, more often than not, but units are in fact possible in a very wide range of languages, such as Arabic, Bengali, Cantonese, Chinese, Dutch, English as a second/foreign language, Gujarati, Hindi, Italian, Japanese, Panjabi, Russian, Urdu, Irish and Welsh. They are usually offered at beginners' and non- beginners' levels. There are often 'European' options you can do, too — like business within Europe.

The flexibility of the scheme means that in theory you can tailor your GNVQ programme to your personal requirements by 'mixing and matching' modules and courses from other areas of the school/college curriculum. Of course, no institution can offer an unlimited range of possibilities, so what you can choose to do will be dependent upon what is available. However, you should be able to combine GNVQs with 'A' levels and GCSEs (possibly to make yourself more viable for higher education), and you should be able to include a language somewhere in your programme.

So when you discuss your GNVQ/GSVQ programme with the school/college you want to attend, think seriously about keeping a language going, or starting a new one, and ask if you will be able to add a short language course (like one of those mentioned above), or a GCSE in a language, or even a language 'A' level.

...a language with vocational programmes

There are NVQ (SVQ in Scotland) vocational courses in a wide range of subject areas in colleges of further education throughout the UK.

On an NVQ/SVQ programme you would do a certain number of compulsory core modules and be able to choose from a range of optional modules. You can be offered a language as one of these options (usually French, German, or Spanish) which can be taken at different levels to suit your own individual language ability. You could possibly fit in the study of more than one language if you wanted to.

...a language with a secretarial course

Many secretarial or administration courses, and courses in other vocational areas like accountancy, give you an option of doing a language as part of your programme. In some colleges you can take other courses alongside your main programme, so you could choose whatever seemed most suitable for your career needs — anything from a short course to a GCSE or an 'A' level. For more information on secretarial courses with languages consult **Chapter 17 — Languages and business-related subjects.**

Can I study a language once I have started work?

Yes, you can. FE colleges and some schools put on evening classes in languages, and sometimes classes during the day. A few colleges put on weekend courses.

Get in touch with your local college(s) to see what there is on offer to suit you. Or your local library will have details of evening classes available in your area. If you live in London, there is a publication which lists courses in London: it is called *Floodlight* and you can get it from newsagents.

Will I have to pay tuition fees?

Generally speaking, UK students under nineteen, or those who are registered unemployed, do not have to pay any fees for full-time courses.

If you find that you are required to pay fees, get in touch with the college finance department who may be able to arrange for you to pay in instalments, or find out if you are eligible for a reduction in fees. They may also be able to put you in touch with your local Training and Enterprise Council who can occasionally help by finding you some money.

Learning languages post-16
Checklist

1	Don't think too narrowly about your future career — you should try to keep as many options open as possible. Equip yourself with a range of skills — including a language — which will be useful to you in your working life.
2	If you want to go on studying after the age of sixteen, you have, broadly speaking, the choice of courses which are academic in nature ('AS' level, 'A' level, Scottish Higher/Advanced Higher, IB), ones which are vocational (NVQ, SVQ), and ones which are a combination of the academic and the vocational (GNVQ, GSVQ).
3	Since a language is likely to be very useful to you in career terms, you should think seriously about keeping a language going, or starting a new one.
4	If you want languages to play a major part in your career, then you should consider doing an 'A' level or a Higher Grade in a language — or even in two languages.
5	If you intend to specialise in something other than languages, don't think that an 'A' level or Higher Grade language course is not for you — there are plenty of careers where a high level of foreign language proficiency is required, and degree courses in a whole range of specialisms which include the study of a language.
6	Or you might consider doing a GCSE language course, or a more vocationally oriented language course, alongside your 'A' levels or Highers.
7	You can do a language as an option in GNVQ/GSVQ, NVQ/SVQ, and some vocaional programmes.
8	If you decide not to stay on in full-time education, part-time language courses are available at evening classes, or during the day, or even perhaps at weekends.

cilt

Diploma courses with languages

Languages for a career

If you are looking forward to using languages as part of your career, and perhaps travelling abroad as well, you should have plenty of opportunity these days, provided of course that you equip yourself with suitable qualifications.

Being able to speak a language is only half the picture. You need languages **plus** other qualifications, unless you are prepared to earn your living doing seasonal work in a holiday resort, casual labouring or some other job which offers few long-term prospects. If you want to make a career for yourself (even though your career direction might change several times during your working life), if you expect to earn a reasonable (at least!) salary, and to have a good chance of promotion, you need to link your proficiency in languages to another specialism, like business studies, secretarial training, marketing, tourism or leisure management.

Where can I get these career qualifications?

There are opportunities to do a course which will prepare you for a career at:

further education colleges, which offer a range of vocational courses leading to professional qualifications, usually according to local demand;

colleges/institutes of higher education and many **universities,** which offer diploma courses as well as degree courses, most of them leading to a Higher National Diploma, and a few to a Diploma of Higher Education, or a college/university diploma (which is an internal award, often running concurrently with an award from an outside body).

Higher education diploma courses attract a mandatory grant, just like degree courses, and you apply for them through the UCAS scheme.

Most higher education institutions now have in place a very flexible academic structure which would allow you to use an HND course as a stepping stone to the third year of a degree course in a related subject. In fact, significant numbers of successful HND students transfer to degree courses when they are either part way through or at the end of their course.

What qualifications do I need . . .

. . . to get on to an HND course?

The short answer is, lower grades than you would need to get on to a degree course. The usual requirements are:

- a National Certificate or Diploma in an appropriate occupational area; or
- a GNVQ/GSVQ in an appropriate subject/area; or
- one or two passes (usually two) at 'A' level (or equivalent) in appropriate subjects — the actual grades vary from course to course and from institution to institution, but it could be anything from one E to BD/CC.

There are many jobs for which employers will only recruit graduates. But having said that, the record of employment of diplomates from Higher National Diploma (HND) courses is very good.

. . . to do a DipHE?

'Freestanding' DipHE courses are not widely

available. They are often intended as a good route into higher education for more mature applicants. The entry qualification is likely to be two, perhaps three, good 'A' level passes (or equivalent), with the possibility of discretionary entry for mature applicants (in other words, relevant experience is counted instead of formal qualifications).

A DipHE course takes two years if you follow it on a full-time basis, but if it suits you to be a part-timer, it would take three years. In practice, what tends to happen is that students registering for a degree can often withdraw, if they need to, from their degree course after two years with the award of a DipHE.

Modular programmes

Higher education institutions, which have adopted a flexible approach to their curriculum, offer modular programmes on which you can get a certificate after one year's successful study, a diploma of higher education after two, and a degree after three. In terms of modules, for example, on a three-year full-time course leading to an honours degree, a certificate can be achieved by passing nine modules, a diploma by passing eighteen, an 'ordinary' degree by passing 23, and an honours degree by passing 27.

On a modular programme you can make up your own 'customised' course by choosing from a menu of modules. You could do a single subject course, or could put together a joint course, for example, Spanish and tourism, or French and fine art.

Can I do a language with a course which will be useful for a career?

Yes. There is a possibility of doing language modules on most diploma programmes — and these cover a very wide range of occupational areas.

There are National Diploma/Certificate and Higher National Diploma/Certificate programmes in the following broad areas:

- agriculture and land-based occupations;
- art and design;
- business;
- caring;
- catering and hospitality;
- computing;
- construction and the built environment;
- distribution;
- engineering;
- information technology;
- leisure studies;
- manufacturing;
- performing arts;
- science.

Names of actual courses vary from institution to institution, depending upon the emphasis put on different parts of the course and the types of modules that the institution decides to offer. For example, a course leading to an HND in business studies might be called something like European Marketing and Business Studies at one place, or European Business with Languages at another; it might just be called Business Studies — but still provide opportunities to do a language. For more details about diploma courses in most of these occupational areas, see **Section 3.**

I want to combine a language with secretarial training

If you want to do something in the secretarial line, there are any number of executive linguist and bilingual/trilingual secretarial courses in FE colleges, colleges of higher education and some universities. All of them will give you the necessary information technology skills as well as a very high level of proficiency in at least one foreign language.

The principal examining bodies for secretarial and administrative programmes are the Royal Society of Arts (RSA) and the London Chamber of Commerce and Industry (LCCI). As well as FE and HE colleges, private (and therefore quite expensive) secretarial colleges run a variety of courses leading to the examinations of these national bodies for those who want to train for secretarial and personal assistant posts. Many of them offer language tuition as well. See the chapter on 'Languages and business-related subjects' in **Section 3** for more details of secretarial courses with modern languages.

What languages could I study?

The languages which are on offer are usually French, German and/or Spanish. At some places you might be able to do other European languages; and at a few Japanese, or community languages like Panjabi or Urdu might be on offer.

The availability of individual languages, and the level to which you would be able to learn them, is really a matter for individual institutions and what they are able to provide. Large institutions like universities and some colleges of higher education are able to offer tuition, often in a wide range of languages, through their language centres; smaller institutions may only be able to offer specific languages subject to demand — and demand is likely to vary from year to year. So you must get hold of prospectuses and course details in order to find out what languages you can do where. And you may need to contact any institution you are thinking of going to, in order to discover the true picture.

Diploma courses with languages
Checklist

1. If you want to use languages as part of your career, you will need to link your languages to some other specialism.

2. Colleges of further education and higher education, and some universities, offer a range of diploma courses, mainly vocational in nature.

3. If you chose to do an HND or a DipHE, you would be eligible for a mandatory grant, just like students doing a degree course.

4. Often an HND can lead on directly to the third year of a degree programme in the same subject/occupational area.

5. An HND has a lower entry requirement than a degree in terms of 'A' level (or equivalent) grades.

6. Flexible academic structures at some higher education institutions mean that it is possible to withdraw from a degree course after two years' successful study and be awarded a DipHE.

7. Continue your education as far as you are able, so that you become as highly qualified and skilled as you can: there are likely to be restricted job opportunities for the unskilled in the future.

8. It is possible to do language modules on most diploma programmes.

9. Language tuition is very often available to those doing secretarial training.

10. Executive linguist and bilingual/trilingual secretarial courses train their students to a very high level of linguistic proficiency.

11. The languages generally available are French, German and Spanish.

12. The range of languages available will depend largely on individual institutions.

Degree courses in languages

There are thousands of first (or undergraduate) degree courses for you to choose from and, provided that you don't want to do something really unusual, there are hundreds of higher education institutions in the UK at which you can choose to study.

Degree courses give you the opportunity to pursue your scholarly interests at the same time as getting a valuable career qualification, either by:

- studying to much greater depth a subject you have enjoyed and done well in at school; or by
- taking up a new subject; or by
- choosing a career-oriented subject like computer science, journalism, management studies, or media studies; or by
- studying a combination of two or more subjects, perhaps one you have done before, and something new; or by
- combining a subject with a vocational specialism (French and business studies, perhaps, or geography and tourism); or by
- following a course which leads to professional qualifications, like engineering, medicine, law, hotel management, perhaps.

First degree programmes generally lead to the award of a **bachelor's** degree, for example . . .

- BA Bachelor of Arts
- BEng Bachelor of Engineering
- BEd Bachelor of Education
- BSc Bachelor of Science
- LLB Bachelor of Laws

. . . although there are:

- some four-year science or engineering first degree courses which lead to a master's degree — an MSc or MEng (via a BSc or BEng award at the end of the third year of study);
- first degree courses in non-science subjects in some institutions, notably the older Scottish universities, which lead to the award of an MA (Master of Arts);
- courses at Oxford and Cambridge universities which lead to the initial award of a bachelor's degree, but provision is made for it to be converted to a master's degree after a couple of years.

How long does a degree course take?

Usually three years, and often four years at Scottish universities. Specialist courses, like medicine or veterinary medicine, for instance, take longer than three years.

Most modern language courses take four years; this is because a year abroad is included — time which is usually spent studying or doing work experience in a country where the language you are studying is spoken.

Recently, however, it has become possible at some institutions to study part-time, generally over a period of four to five years, or to do an accelerated programme in just two years (without the long summer vacation). Such courses tend to be more popular with mature students who need to fit in the demands of a family or a career. However, if you do a part-time course, you are usually responsible for paying your own fees.

What do terms like 'joint honours', 'modular' and 'CATS' mean?

There are several different types of degree course on offer at universities and colleges of higher education, depending upon the course structure, and several terms used to describe them which may be new to you. You will need to become familiar with them if you are going to find your way around the prospectuses and other careers literature:

Single honours courses

involve the study of one subject, often with a subsidiary subject (sometimes called a 'minor' or 'ancillary' subject) in the first and perhaps second years.

Joint honours courses

involve the study of two subjects which have equal weighting throughout the course. In a joint honours course, therefore, you could study two languages to equal level; or choose a more or less related pair of subjects, for example politics and Russian, French and linguistics; or choose unrelated subjects, like German and chemistry.

Combined honours courses

involve the study of two, three or four subjects during the first year. You can normally choose two in which to specialise later in the course. This category includes general arts/combined arts/humanities courses, the range of which varies from institution to institution. Combined honours courses are similar to . . .

Modular courses

which are courses divided into units or 'modules', allowing you to build your own study programme on a termly, half-yearly or yearly basis. You can choose related or unrelated subjects, specialised or more broadly-based ones, single or double modules, reflecting your own academic and vocational interests. There is usually very little or no integration between the subjects, and each module is taught and examined separately. However, there is someone on hand to help you make a sensible choice so that your overall degree programme has some coherence.

Sandwich courses

allow you to combine your study with periods of work experience or training (usually paid!). Sandwiches can be 'thin' or 'thick':

A **thin sandwich** includes relatively short periods of work placement, usually of three months' or six months' duration, throughout the period of a four-year course.

A **thick sandwich** will involve a full year's work placement, usually in the third year of a four year course. Some language courses, or joint language and business studies courses, where the year abroad is spent on a work placement rather than on an approved course, are of the thick sandwich type.

A sandwich course can be 'college-based' or 'industry-based'. If you are sponsored by a company, your course is 'industry-based' and you will do your work placement with the sponsoring company; if you do not have a sponsorship, your course is 'college-based' and your university or college will help you to find a placement. **Sponsorships** are more usually available to science and engineering undergraduates, but there are some available to students of other disciplines. There are published lists of firms offering sponsorships which are usually available from careers officers or in careers libraries. There is also a useful book, *Sponsorship for students*, which is listed in Section 5 of the **Appendix.**

CATS

or **Credit Accumulation and Transfer Scheme,** is a system in operation in an increasing number of institutions. This is where a course is broken up into modules, each having a 'credit value', and you progress through your course, accumulating credit points as you pass each module, until you have enough credits to make up a degree.

This system also has the advantage that you can get credit for partial completion of your course if for any reason you have to drop out part way through; and then you can pick up your studies again at the same institution, or even at another one, at a later date, without having to start all over again. You would be eligible for a Certificate of Higher Education if you left after successfully completing one year; and a Diploma of Higher Education after a successful second year.

The CAT system is compatible with other credit accumulation schemes used elsewhere, for example the **SCOTCAT** system in Scotland, the **ECTS** (European Community Course Credit Transfer Scheme) within the European Union, and the **semester** system in the United States. These schemes therefore allow students to move more easily between institutions, either at home or abroad, carrying their credits forward with them. In theory, you could study for a degree at several different institutions; in practice, doing a sort of 'patchwork' degree all over the place would perhaps not be a very good idea. There would, however, be very real advantages for you in the scheme if you wanted:

- to modify an existing degree course by omitting one or two modules and studying modules from another course — taking a business studies, or a computing module as part of a languages degree, for instance; or a language module as part of another degree course;
- to construct your own 'customised' degree programme by taking modules from a range of degree courses on offer in an institution (such a programme would have to be approved by the institution, of course — you don't have a completely free hand to put together whatever you wish!);
- to study abroad for a period of time — usually anything from three months to a year — and have the work you have done accredited as part of your degree;
- to do a degree course which is closely linked to a National Diploma or another professional qualification which you have already successfully completed — it could be possible to cash in your credits towards the degree award;
- to alternate your study with your other commitments — earning your living or raising a family, for instance.

A word of warning though — you would need to check with any authority which provided you with a grant if you wanted to change either your course or your institution.

Franchised courses

are ones where part of the programme — usually the first year — is offered by a college of further education as a 'feeder' for the parent university. The course is carefully monitored by the parent university and is therefore a genuine degree from that university — but such an arrangement does not really provide you with the full university experience, particularly as regards the social life, and possibly also as regards the library and study facilities. It could help you, however, if the FE college is near your home and if for any reason you would find it inconvenient or too expensive to move away from home.

Should I choose a career-oriented course to make sure of a good job?

Opportunities to combine a language with a degree course in a vocational subject like law or engineering, or with a semi-vocational one like business studies or computer science, have increased over recent years. But you should not think that the only way to get a good job when you leave higher education is to choose a course linked exclusively to a possible future career.

When you make **your** choice of a degree subject you should remember that, unless you intend to go into one of the professions, your degree specialism is not always particularly important to a potential employer, as these employers' comments from recent editions of the AgCAS (Association of Graduate Careers Advisory Services) publication *What do graduates do?* testify:

> The subject itself doesn't matter, but we are looking for excellence within it ... As long as you have the right sort of mind and outlook we'll teach you to do the job.
>
> *BMP DDB Needham*
> *(a major UK advertising agency)*

> Your personal qualities are far more important to us than your degree discipline. What matters is your ability to harness your talent so you can progress rapidly in the firm and take on responsibility at an early stage. We look for people with drive and maturity who are strong intellectually and have good skills with people ... Foreign languages and IT are a bonus.
>
> *Touche Ross (an international firm of chartered accountants)*

> We look for people who can demonstrate initiative, leadership, problem-solving skills, an ability to work with others, creativity, innovation, priority-setting skills, and for our technical areas, technical excellence. With the exception of specific areas within research and development and engineering, we do not have a particular degree discipline in mind when we recruit.
>
> *Procter & Gamble Ltd (a major international manufacturing company)*

> Combined studies graduates applying for scientific jobs need to have complementary subjects rather than a diversity. Some of our jobs are diverse on the non-technical side, such as operations management which covers customer complaints, administration, use of computers and managing work study. Here an arts background plus business and computing skills would be ideal.
>
> *Severn Trent Water Ltd*

> Graduate recruitment to Unilever is the major source of senior management in our business. We recruit into every major industrial function and while would-be engineers and scientists need to have studied specific degrees, graduates of any discipline join us in marketing, sales, finance and personnel. We are more concerned with the skills and achievements that have been collected during your education ... Intellectual ability is taken for granted (your degree tells us that), but you will need to be able to operate effectively in teams, supporting and motivating others.
>
> *Unilever (an Anglo-Dutch multinational company)*

Employers make a considerable investment in their graduate recruitment practices because they are keen to attract the best of each year's crop of higher education leavers, and although quite a few of them will be looking for graduates with a particular specialism, the comments above will show you that the subject you do for your degree is not always important — what matters are your own personal qualities and the fact that you have the intellectual capacity (and staying-power) to have studied at degree level for three or four years.

Why do employers recruit graduates?

The reason companies recruit graduates for certain posts — usually management posts — is that they need highly intelligent people with the creativity and flexibility of mind which study at this advanced level can bring, plus a range of skills which enable you to:

- communicate well (both orally and in writing);
- prioritise and make decisions;
- solve problems;
- operate as a member of a group or team;
- manage your own time and meet deadlines.

And employers will expect you not just to be able to talk about these skills but to show some evidence that you actually have them. Some of them — like communication skills and problem-solving — are likely to form part of your degree course, but the others often come with the experience of working with others and of organising things — and here a whole range of your extra-curricular interests and activities could come into play, like for instance your being a committee member of a club, a member of a sports team, a participant in amateur dramatics, or an organiser of a party or an event. Relevant work experience can also encourage the development of these skills. If the course you choose does not include a work placement, it might be worth your while to gain some relevant experience during your university vacations. Employers are not just interested in your formal qualifications, they are also interested in your CV.

The class of your degree, too, will no doubt be important to a prospective employer — see the comments made by BMP DDB Needham above. Companies will be interested in how well you have done in your studies because they will, quite simply, be looking for the best!

And since it is more likely that you will be successful in your degree if you are well motivated and enjoy what you are doing, then you would be well advised to choose a subject which you think you are going to enjoy and are likely to be good at. It is not really sensible to force yourself to do something which you don't really like only because you think it may open up opportunities to you later on.

It is also worth remembering that employment trends change, so it is usually a mistake to choose a specific degree subject because the employment take-up for that specialism appears to be particularly good at the moment. By the time you graduate the situation may have changed!

Can I predict what sort of a career I will have?

Not really. In his book *The Age of Unreason* the much respected expert on management development and patterns of employment, Charles Handy, highlights the enormous pace at which everything in the world today is changing, and has a lot to say about the impossibility of predicting what sort of careers we will have over the next thirty years or so:

> *Thirty years ago I started work in a world-famous multi-national company. By way of encouragement they produced an outline of my future career — 'This will be your life', they said, 'with titles of likely jobs.' The line ended, I remember, with myself as chief executive of a particular company in a particular far-off country. I was, at the time, suitably flattered. I left them long before I reached the heights they planned for me, but already I knew that **not only did the job they had picked out no longer exist, neither did the company I would have directed nor even the country in which I was to have operated.***
>
> *Thirty years ago I thought that life would be one long continuous line, sloping upwards with luck. Today I know better. Thirty years ago that company saw the future as largely predictable, to be planned for and managed. Today they are less certain. Thirty years ago people thought that change would mean more of the same, only better . . . Today we know that in many areas of life we cannot guarantee more of the same, be it work or money, peace or freedom, health or happiness, and cannot even predict what will be happening in our own lives. Change is now more chancy, but also more exciting . . .*
>
> From *The Age of Unreason* by Charles Handy (Business Books, 1989; Arrow Books, 1990)

Does it matter which subject I choose?

Perhaps not. The actual career destinations of graduates leaving institutions of higher education is, in very many cases, quite unrelated to the subject they have studied. Modern foreign language graduates enter a very wide range of jobs, both in the UK and abroad. A significant number take up a career in teaching — either abroad, where they teach English as a foreign language; or they take a one-year Postgraduate Certificate of Education (PGCE) course prior to teaching in the UK. Some go into jobs where their languages can be of direct relevance — for example with multinational companies, in the immigration service, with travel firms, or as translators or interpreters; a very few become *stagiaires* (trainees) with the European Commission (see p52). But the vast majority go to work in banking, insurance, accountancy, or as trainee managers in finance, marketing, personnel or sales departments of companies, where their knowledge of languages is perhaps not important to them in their first appointment, but could be a real benefit, both to their company and to them, in subsequent jobs.

Here are the most recent statistics from *What do graduates do?* (published annually by Hobsons, but now discontinued) which show what the 1995 modern languages graduates went on to after getting their degrees, as well as the courses and jobs which the 1994 graduates entered:

Type of work (1995)

Men	523	
Women	1,373	
Total	**1,896**	
A Managers and administrators		27.5%
B Teaching professionals		3.5%
C Business and financial professionals		3.3%
D Business and financial associate professionals		2.7%
E Literary, artistic and sports professionals		4.4%
F Other professionals, associate professional and technical occupations		5.2%
G Clerical and secretarial occupations		29.1%
H Personal and protective service occupations		6.1%
I Sales occupations		11.8%
J Other occupations		5.5%
K Unknown occupations		0.9%

First destination (1995)

Known first destinations (1995)		
Men	1,029	
Women	2,795	
Total	**3,824**	
Total number graduating	**4,417**	
a in UK employment		49.6%
b In overseas employment		12.3%
c Studying for a higher degree, diploma, certificate (including PGCE), or professional qualification in the UK		21.5%
d Other further study or training in the UK		1.3%
e Further study or training overseas		1.3%
f Not available for employment, study or training		4.9%
g Believed unemployed		7.5%
h Seeking employment or training but not unemployed		1.6%

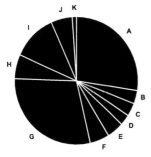

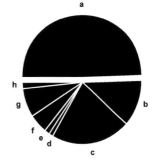

key points

- Nearly a quarter proceeded to further study or training
- Nearly half were in UK employment, and a further one in eight found jobs overseas
- More than a quarter of those in UK employment were working as managers or administrators

> **Examples of courses and jobs entered by (modern languages) graduates in 1994**
>
> FURTHER FULL-TIME STUDY
> **MPhil:** East German Literature
> **MA:** European Political Culture; Theatre and Film Studies, Tourism Management; Translation
> **MSc:** Information Technology
> **Certificates and diplomas:** Bilingual Secretarial; Bilingual Business Admin; Education (PGCE); Modern Language for Exports; Language Studies; Law (CPE)
>
> EMPLOYMENT
> **au pair:** France; Germany; Italy
> **banking trainee:** Bank of England; Bilbao Vizcaya Bank, Jersey; Deutsche Morgan Grenfell
> **bilingual sales administrator:** Regency International
> **business analyst:** PA Consulting Group
> **chartered accountancy trainee:** Coopers & Lybrand; KPMG; PW
> **civil service executive officer:** Immigration & Nationality Dept
> **clerical work:** Alfred Marks; American Express; Brann Direct
> **export administration/sales:** AB Connectors; Refensa Ltd
> **graduate trainee:** Mars confectionery
> **insurance broker:** Sedgewick
> **journalist:** Reuters
> **lecturer:** Bolton College; West Kent College
> **management accountancy trainee:** Evans Medical Ltd
> **management trainee:** British Airways; NFC
> **marketing trainee:** AT&T, Germany; Tate Bramald Consultancy
> **market research:** Marketpower Ltd; NOP Market Research
> **media analyst (for Eastern Europe):** Kagan World Media
> **PA/secretary:** Procter & Gamble; Sunday Mirror
> **PR/marketing trainee:** Write Image
> **personnel officer:** Eurocentres; Royal Insurance
> **publishing — assistant editor:** Financial Times
> **retail management trainee:** Marks & Spencer, UK & France
> **systems analyst:** Visa International
> **teaching English:** Germany; Japan (JET Programme); Poland; Russia; Spain
> **tour guide:** Blenheim Palace
> **tour operator representative:** Eurocamp, Venice; Saga Tours; Thomson Tour Operators
> **translator:** GCHQ; Hoffmann LaRoche, Basle
> **travel assistant:** London Tourist Board
> **voluntary work:** VSO, China

Are there plenty of jobs for graduates?

Not plenty, but there has of late been a welcome upturn in the number of graduate vacancies available. Not only the large companies, but more recently small and medium-sized firms as well, have begun to recruit more graduates.

You will see from the figures above that many modern language graduates in 1997 obtained permanent jobs in the UK. Although this is lower than the figure for **all** graduates, it can be partly explained by the fact that a significant proportion of modern language graduates go to work abroad on a permanent or temporary basis.

In fact, the number of unemployed modern language graduates is lower than the overall number of all graduates unemployed, so the outlook is quite bright for those with modern language degrees, particularly since language proficiency is likely to enhance anyone's job prospects, whatever their degree specialism.

It should be said, however, that a language qualification only really becomes a winner in the job market when you have some other area of expertise alongside it. This might be management training, a teaching qualification, or secretarial or information technology skills, for example. When you get that other qualification is really a matter of your own personal choice and circumstances, for example, after a languages degree you could either:

- take a job with a company which would train you for the job they needed you to do; or

- follow up your degree course with an advanced secretarial course; or

- train to become a teacher by taking an approved course of initial teacher training; or

- take a course in teaching English as a foreign language (TEFL) and go to teach abroad perhaps; or

- train for a qualification in speech therapy (particularly if you have done linguistics as a significant part of your degree course); or
- take a postgraduate qualification in translating and/or interpreting (and if you have done a joint degree in a science and a language, or law and a language, you would be particularly well placed to learn to translate specialist texts — there is quite a demand for legal translators, for example).

A significant proportion of modern language graduates go on to further study or training before starting out on their careers, and if you look at the notes on 1996 graduates in the AgCAS statistics, you will see that the further study they undertook was largely related to a specific career, for example, tourism management, translation, bilingual secretarial, bilingual business administration, education, law . . .

If I do a language degree, will I have to allow an extra year for further training?

Not necessarily. You might choose to get the other qualification as part of your degree by combining your language with another specialism — German and business studies, law and Japanese, travel and tourism and Italian, electronic engineering and French, for instance. There is an enormously wide range of joint and combined honours cour-ses which have a language as a greater or lesser part (check carefully just how much!), and the list of subjects which can be studied in combination with a language is very long indeed. Many of these, such as accountancy, banking, business studies, librarianship, law and management are vocational in nature, and successful graduates from these joint/combined courses often find it easier to get jobs than those with a pure language degree. Most courses will give you the opportunity of studying your specialism in the country of your main foreign language, or of undertaking a work placement there.

If you want to combine a language —or two — with another subject, you should consult the relevant chapters in **Section 3**.

Which language should I choose?

There are various important considerations, like:

- which language do you enjoy, or are likely to do well at?
- is it a useful language for the career you have in mind?
- should you choose two languages?
- could you do a language you have not studied at school?
- are you qualified to do the course?

The answers to these questions depend on a variety of factors, all of which are personal to you — your own personal preferences, what career you have in mind, how good you are at languages, how hard you are prepared to study, and so on. In other words, the choice is really up to **you** and is something you should think carefully about — but you should also try to get as much advice as you can from careers publications like this one, as well as from your teachers, careers advisers and others who are in a position to help, like former students of your school or college who are at present at university, or members of a profession you might like to enter who are known to you or your parents.

Ought I to do more than one language?

Two languages — or more! — will definitely improve your chances of getting an interesting job in a field where languages are useful, or if you want to travel. The two languages do not have to be studied to the same level: although you can do a degree course in two main languages, you can also do a course in a major language plus another language as a minor (or subsidiary) subject. Often you can start a new language at university, either as part of your course or as an 'extra' which can even sometimes be accredited as part of your degree.

If you intend to be a teacher of languages, then more than one language is almost essential —

you will be much more useful to a school if you can teach two languages. There have been moves recently to teach a greater variety of modern languages in British schools, but French and German, followed by Spanish, remain the ones most widely taught. Other languages — notably Italian, Russian and, more recently, Japanese — are also taught in schools, so these could be useful 'second' languages for an aspiring teacher to study. If you have studied one language successfully to 'A' level (or an equivalent advanced level), there are many higher education institutions where you can be accepted as a beginner to study Spanish, Italian, Russian or Japanese, as well as some other less commonly-learnt languages, either as a main language or as one of two languages in a joint honours course, or as a subsidiary subject.

Will employers expect degree-level proficiency in my languages?

No; don't assume that you need to be highly qualified in all your languages — employers often welcome any extra linguistic ability. So if you have learnt a language at school or college which you are not planning to continue as part of your HE course, make sure it does not get rusty through lack of use — it could be another valuable asset! There are likely to be opportunities at the university you attend to keep a language going (see **Chapter 16 — Institution-wide language programmes**), or you could try to spend some time in the country where the language is spoken during one of your vacations.

Can I study a 'new' language?

It is often quite a good idea to consider broadening your horizons by studying something you have not had the opportunity to do at school — whether it be a language or any other subject.

Again, you could do this new subject as a single subject degree course, or as a joint or subsidiary subject.

If your 'new' language is to be German, Italian, Russian or Spanish, then there are plenty of places where you may be able to study it from scratch, or at least from a good GCSE (or equivalent).

The range of less commonly learnt languages which can be done as a main degree subject, or in combination with another subject, is quite wide. Such a language may be studied with the more commonly learnt languages, like French or German; or can be put together in related pairs like 'Italian and music', 'Dutch and Indonesian studies' or Japanese and management studies'; or may even be studied with another subject which may appear to have no relation at all.

Arabic, Chinese and Japanese are on offer at some universities, including of course the School of Oriental and African Studies (SOAS) which is part of the University of London and which teaches an amazingly wide range, including Arabic, Hebrew, Turkish, Persian, Chinese, Korean and Japanese. Complete beginners are accepted on most of the courses, but you will need at least two good 'A' levels (or equivalent), and one of these will usually have to be in a language so that the Admissions Tutor has some evidence that you have enough linguistic ability to be able to cope with the course; sometimes an 'AS' in a language is enough.

Is it difficult to study a new language from scratch?

Despite previous experience at learning languages, it is by no means an easy matter to learn a language from scratch to degree level in three or four years — but lots of undergraduates do it! One who did commented:

> Someone intending to study a language from scratch should expect a full timetable and a heavy work load.

Another undergraduate who had chosen to do a joint degree in French and Italian, never having done Italian before, had this to say:

> The Italian course is incredibly intensive. In my first Italian lesson in the first year we had a native speaker who spoke in Italian for virtually the whole lesson.
>
> The first year is spent concentrating mainly on grammar and pronunciation. The grammar can become somewhat tedious as it is so intensive and as most of it has to be learnt parrot-fashion. It takes a lot of dedication to learn everything as you're going along, and not fall behind.
>
> I'm now in my third year, and doing a six-month placement in Trieste working in the headquarters of an international insurance company — without doubt this has been the best part of the course. It has proved to be a valuable experience which has improved my language skills greatly . . .

It is obvious that anyone starting a new language from scratch and intending to get to degree level in the time available will have to work hard in order to cover a tremendous amount of ground.

Languages with a completely different script from our own, like Russian, Chinese, Japanese and Arabic, are not easy for us to learn, and mastery of the script in the case of Chinese is extremely time-consuming. If you choose one of these languages as your degree subject, then you must be prepared for a lot of hard work. In fact, a few students find them more than they can cope with and transfer to another course at the end of their first year. Nevertheless, many students have enjoyed the challenge and have done well.

What qualifications will I need to do a languages degree?

You obviously need to check that you are likely to get the qualifications needed for the courses you want to apply for.

- Are you studying (and are likely to be sufficiently successful in) the right subjects for 'A'/'AS' level, Scottish Higher/Adanced Higher, Advanced GNVQ or GSVQ . . . or other examinations like the International Baccalaureate?
- Do you have the right GCSEs or SCE Standard grades?

There are several books which can help you to assess whether you are studying the 'right' subjects, and whether you are likely to get the necessary grades. They should all be easily found on the shelves of your school/college careers library, your local careers service, or in a public library. Most are published annually, so make sure you consult the up-to-date versions. You will find details in the **Appendix** on pp213–214. The main ones are:

- *The big official UCAS guide to university and college entrance;*
- *Entrance guide to higher education in Scotland;*
- *The complete degree course offers* edited by Brian Heap.

You should also consult the **prospectuses** of individual institutions whose courses interest you, because the tabular format of publications like *The big official UCAS guide to university and college entrance* does not allow the inclusion of complex information about entry requirements, and faculties and departments may also have particular entry requirements in terms of GCSE or SCE Standard grades.

You would be wise to use the information on offers as just a useful guide, rather than as hard and fast rules — particularly since Admissions Tutors often make offers to suit individual circumstances. They have occasionally been known to make a lower offer if they particularly like a candidate at interview but feel that there are special reasons why he or she might not quite meet the standard offer; or to make a high-ish offer to encourage a student to work hard, and then perhaps contact the school or college to say they will still consider the applicant even if he or she does not quite meet the offer — but don't bank on this happening to you!

Which languages can I choose from?

The list of modern languages taught in British universities and colleges of higher education is a very long one, as you can see below. Most institutions offer French and German, and Spanish is quite widely available, but as a general rule, the further away from Europe the language is spoken, the fewer places offer it. Apart from Chinese, Japanese, Arabic and Russian, you will not find Asian, African and Middle Eastern languages widely available, and in some cases the only place you can do them is at one of the two specialist institutions which are part of the University of London — the School of Oriental and African Studies (SOAS) and the School of Slavonic and East European Studies (SSEES.)

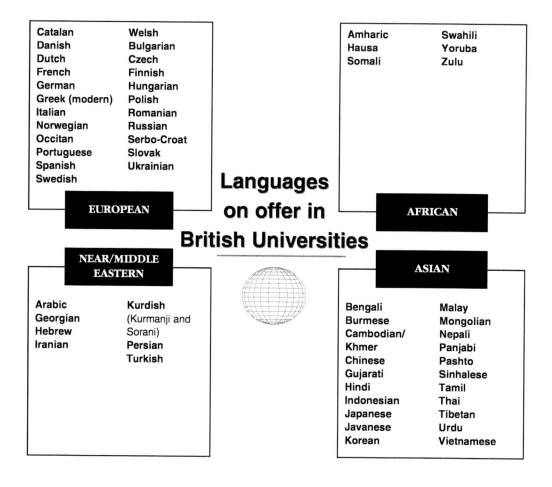

Languages on offer in British Universities

EUROPEAN
Catalan, Danish, Dutch, French, German, Greek (modern), Italian, Norwegian, Occitan, Portuguese, Spanish, Swedish, Welsh, Bulgarian, Czech, Finnish, Hungarian, Polish, Romanian, Russian, Serbo-Croat, Slovak, Ukrainian

AFRICAN
Amharic, Hausa, Somali, Swahili, Yoruba, Zulu

NEAR/MIDDLE EASTERN
Arabic, Georgian, Hebrew, Iranian, Kurdish (Kurmanji and Sorani), Persian, Turkish

ASIAN
Bengali, Burmese, Cambodian/Khmer, Chinese, Gujarati, Hindi, Indonesian, Japanese, Javanese, Korean, Malay, Mongolian, Nepali, Panjabi, Pashto, Sinhalese, Tamil, Thai, Tibetan, Urdu, Vietnamese

NB: many of these languages are available at only one or two institutions.

Degree courses in languages
Checklist

1 Most modern language degree courses take four years and include a year abroad, usually on an approved course of study or on a work placement.

2 Opportunities to combine a language with a career-oriented subject have increased over recent years.

3 The subject of your degree is not always particularly important to employers — they are often just as concerned with your personal qualities and other skills when recruiting.

4 It is often a mistake to think too narrowly about a set career. Choose a degree subject you are likely to enjoy and your chances of doing well are maximised.

5 Numbers of vacancies for graduates have increased recently and the employment outlook for modern language graduates is quite bright at present.

6 There are relatively few employment opportunities directly related to languages alone — you need some other area of expertise to complement your language skills.

7 Consider perhaps learning a new language — either as your main degree subject, or in combination with another language or another subject.

8 A less common European language, an Oriental or African language, or Arabic, can be studied from scratch as a main subject, a subsidiary subject or a minor option.

9 If you study a language from scratch or post GCSE, one of your 'A' levels will normally have to be in a language to show evidence of your linguistic ability.

Languages of the European Union

DEGREE COURSES

In addition to English, the official languages of the European Union are:

Danish, Dutch, Finnish, French, German, Greek, Italian, Portuguese, Spanish and Swedish.

You will be likely to have studied one of these at school, and there are opportunities to study one or more of them to degree level at universities or in colleges of higher education in the UK.

I would like to carry on with the language I am learning now

French and German are widely studied in British schools and if you want to do a degree course in one of these, you should have no difficulty in finding a course to suit you. These languages are offered in most UK universities and colleges of higher education which teach languages, both as single honours subjects, or as part of joint or combined honours, or in modular courses.

Spanish (or Hispanic Studies, which may include other languages of the Iberian peninsula: Portuguese, or Catalan, or even perhaps Galician) is on offer in more than 50 institutions. So, if you are one of the many who have learned Spanish at school, you should find plenty of courses to choose from. And even if you have not studied it to 'A' level (or equivalent), there are many institutions where you can start a degree course in Spanish as a complete beginner, or with little previous knowledge — perhaps just a GCSE qualification in it.

Can I do a degree in a language I have not learnt at school?

Yes, there are many places where you can start a new language. You might perhaps have had an opportunity to do Italian or one of the other EU languages at school but, as with Spanish (and German occasionally), there are several places where you can study one of them from scratch to degree level in the four years that it usually takes to do a language degree course, or you could combine one of these languages with another language (or another subject altogether). Although there might be people on the course who have already reached a high level of proficiency in the language, it would be most unlikely that you would be the only beginner — and, in any case, beginners are usually taught separately for the first year at least.

Studying a language from scratch to the high standard required for a degree doesn't mean, of course, that you can be a complete novice as far as languages are concerned. You would need to have had a language-learning background, and the university or college where you are hoping to study will be looking for some evidence amongst your qualifications that you can cope successfully with language learning. This will usually be a good 'A' level/'AS' grade (or equivalent) in a foreign language.

Although Dutch, Greek and the Scandinavian languages are not widely on offer, some institutions have tended to specialise in a particular language, or group of languages — like East Anglia or Edinburgh in the case of Danish, Norwegian and Swedish; Hull or University College, London, in the case of Dutch; or King's College, London, or Birmingham for modern Greek.

The universities of Oxford and Cambridge offer courses in these languages, as well as in the languages which are more widely studied at school. If you are in line for the high grades required by these universities and you want to do two languages (which is the requirement at both institutions), then you might like to consider 'Oxbridge'. At Cambridge any modern language, apart from French, may be taken from scratch; at Oxford, you can start Italian, modern Greek, or Portuguese as a complete beginner.

Check in the **Signposts** section to find out where you can do these languages. You will not find Finnish listed amongst the EU languages, however, since it is related to Hungarian, and is only on offer at the School of Slavonic and Eastern European Studies (SSEES) in London. You will therefore find it in the table of Russian and Eastern European languages.

Can I do more than one language?

There are possibilities of studying one, two or even three languages. The third will usually be studied from scratch and will probably be one of a range of optional modules.

If you do two languages, they may both be studied to the same level, or one of them may be studied to subsidiary or minor level. Some universities will give you all these options — at the University of Durham, for instance, you can study one language as your main subject, together with a subsidiary subject (perhaps another language, but not necessarily so); or you can do two languages at equal level; or three languages in equal proportions (one or two of them may be taken from scratch).

How much do courses differ from institution to institution?

You would be wrong to assume that one degree course in French (for instance) is very much like another. The structure of language degree courses differs widely from place to place. All language courses include language and communication skills — listening comprehension, speaking, reading and writing the foreign language — with varying amounts of grammar work and translation. But the methods used to teach these linguistic skills will vary from place to place, as will the compulsory topics and options which go to make up the rest of the course.

There is no longer the clear division which there used to be between those departments which offer degree courses consisting largely of language and literary studies, and those which teach little or no literature, but which concentrate instead on sociological, economic and political aspects of the country concerned. Course content and teaching methods have undergone much revision over recent years, and most courses now combine varying proportions of literary and cultural topics with aspects of society, economics and politics. They also offer a wide range of options, often with a practical or vocational bias, and sometimes chosen from other subject areas outside the modern languages department.

Let's suppose that you want to read for a degree in French. You have literally hundreds of courses to choose from, each with its own particularities, and so you will have to do your research very thoroughly in order to be able to make sensible choices. Here is just a small selection of different French degree courses so that you can see what you are up against in your research!

For example, the single honours French language and literature course at the **University of Sheffield** introduces you to French literature and thought from the mediaeval period to the present day, together with modern French culture and film studies, and a study of the history and development of the French language. There is also a wide choice of optional modules, including the opportunity to do a 'new' language, or to take courses from other subject areas. The whole of year 3 is spent in France, either as a foreign language assistant in a school, or on a study course at a university in France, Quebec, the island of Reunion or possibly Martinique, or at a school of interpreting and business studies in Brussels.

At **University College, London,** in your first term you are introduced to the structure and origins of French society and to the study of French literature. After that you are able to put together a programme to suit your own interests, chosen from course modules which include aspects of French society, different authors or periods of literature, film studies, or the literature of other French-speaking countries (in the Caribbean, or Africa, for instance), as well as up to two course-units from outside the department, chosen from humanities, other languages, or even scientific subjects like computer science. The third year is spent in a French-speaking country as a foreign language assistant in a school, or studying at a French university or at the British Institute in Paris.

At the **University of Essex** you can combine a language with the study of linguistics, thus enabling you not only to learn French but also to learn more about 'language' as a more general phenomenon. The emphasis throughout is on contemporary language, with many of the linguistic examples taken from contemporary fiction and journalism. You can also do a 'new' language, like Portuguese or Japanese, as an optional extra. The year abroad is spent as a foreign language assistant in a school, or studying at a French university.

The French degree course at **Aston University** also concentrates on the study of contemporary language and society, using resources like government reports, daily satellite news from France, newspapers and journals. An extensive range of options includes specialised translation in French; contemporary social, economic or political issues; linguistics; the application of computers to language study; as well as modules on the French media, modern French writers, French and international trade, or France and Europe. For the year abroad you have a choice of three options — either a course at a French university, or a job as a teaching assistant in a school, or a job placement with a French company.

The **University of the West of England** in Bristol is one institution which requires you to do two languages — but arrangements are made for those who have thus far had the opportunity to do only one foreign language by providing courses in German or Spanish from beginners' level (as well as post-'A' level), so if you have done only French to 'A' level (or equivalent), you can do French and *ab initio* German, or French and *ab initio* Spanish. The emphasis of the course is on applied languages, including translation and interpreting, computer applications and linguistics. You can also choose from a range of options in contemporary studies, history, politics, economics, or film studies. In the third year undergraduates spend a minimum of eighteen weeks in each of the two countries on industrial placements. There are also opportunities, for those who wish, to do their placement as a school language assistant, or on a university course. If you do really well on this degree course, you can qualify for the 'European route' which involves a year's study at a partner institution in France, Germany or Spain in addition to the normal placement year (two years abroad, therefore) with the opportunity of obtaining two qualifications at the end of the course — a British degree, and a French, German or Spanish qualification.

These five courses are not the only ones of their kind — they are just broad examples of the types of different programmes you will find.

So you will see from all this diversity that whether you want to do French, or German, or Spanish, or Italian, or one of the other languages of the European Union, and whether you want to do a language post 'A' level or from scratch, it is only sensible that you take the time to study prospectuses carefully to find out exactly the content of the courses you are interested in. Only then can you assess whether the course really suits you, your interests and your career aspirations. It is too late once you have started the course to find out that it is not really what you wanted after all!

Often the prospectus is not able to include all the detail necessary, so when you have narrowed your choice down to about a dozen modern language departments, you should also consider writing to them individually for detailed course descriptions. See the

Signposts section to find out which institutions offer which languages.

How important is the experience offered by the placement abroad?

Apart from the actual content of the course it is also worth finding out what sort of experience the period of time spent abroad offers. Most courses expect you to spend varying amounts of time in a country where the language you are studying is spoken. You might be studying at a foreign university or equivalent institution, or you might be working either in business or industry, or as a teaching assistant in a school.

A work placement abroad can provide useful experience which may be taken into account by prospective employers when you apply for a job at the end of your degree course, and many undergraduates who have had a particularly successful work placement have been taken on by the firm once they have graduated.

You also have the advantage of being paid while on a work placement, or while you are a foreign language assistant, which can be a very important consideration if you are trying to make ends meet on a grant.

Some courses offer you the possibility during your time abroad of studying for a degree or diploma at the foreign institution. Many higher education institutions within the EU have negotiated agreements with each other to allow their students to gain qualifications at each other's institutions, and in this way you may be able to obtain not just a British degree, but a foreign qualification as well, which could be very useful to you in career terms.

Can I study languages abroad?

Yes you can. Students from the UK enjoy the same rights as students from other EU countries, in that they have access to higher education right across the Union, provided of course that they satisfy the entry requirements for the course they want to do. Many, but not all, first degree qualifications gained in other member states have equal status with those gained in the UK. If you want to know more about the equivalence of qualifications, you should consult *The international guide to qualifications in education* which is compiled by NARIC (the National Academic Recognition Information Centre).

If you are a student of French, you might like to know that the British Institute in Paris is (the only) part of the British university system situated in continental Europe. Here you can read for a University of London degree in French Studies entirely in Paris! Modern language degree courses usually last four years, including a year spent abroad — but this one only takes three years because you live in France throughout.

But unfortunately there are snags. Even though this course is a London University course (and yes, we are all part of the EU now!), it is not eligible for fee support from Local Education Authorities, because it is held outside the UK. The same situation would apply if you chose to study the whole of your course in another EU country. You could apply to your LEA for a **discretionary** award, however — all LEAs have their own policy on matters such as this. You will probably get a small maintenance grant . . . and they might just pay some of your tuition fees. You may of course qualify for a student loan.

You might possibly qualify for a grant from the EU Socrates/Erasmus programme (see pp4–5) — which was set up to encourage student mobility — towards the extra expenses incurred by studying abroad. This would not affect your eligibility to any UK grant or student loan. If you want more information about the Erasmus (Higher Education) strand of the Socrates programme, you should contact:

UK Socrates/Erasmus Council
R&D Building
The University
Canterbury
Kent CT2 7PD
Tel: 01227 762 712 or Fax: 01227 762 711
email: erasmus@ukc.ac.uk

Does a course in one of the EU languages prepare me for a career?

Language graduates find employment in a wide range of occupations, not necessarily connected with their degree subjects. After postgraduate training, a fair number go into teaching of one sort or another (including teaching English abroad as a foreign language), and a small proportion become professional linguists, using their languages as translators or interpreters.

Others make a conscious effort to use their languages by choosing to work abroad, or by seeking employment with a company which does business abroad, or in an occupational area which involves travel, or communications with other countries — international banking, perhaps, or work in the tourist trade or in the European media, for instance.

Europe is a growing market for job opportunities. Graduates who are fluent in a European language go into areas like the civil service, public relations, European Union institutions, European multinational companies, the armed services, customs and excise, and research bodies within and outside the European university sector.

Speakers of EU languages other than French, German and Spanish are useful in many fields, because they have something of a rarity value. French and German, from surveys of job advertisements, seem to be the languages most in demand by UK employers, yet speakers of Danish, Dutch, Greek, Italian, Portuguese and Swedish are all in demand, particularly in the institutions of the EU, where employees need to speak more than a couple of the EU languages.

You might do well to improve your potential for employment in some fields by studying one of the less commonly learned EU languages — perhaps as a second language to a language you have learnt at school . . . you could do German and Dutch, perhaps; Spanish and Portuguese; French and Swedish . . . Remember you can start one of these languages as a complete beginner.

The vast majority of language graduates, however, go into careers, many of which at first sight have very little to do with languages. For many of these posts a language qualification, although not essential, can prove a bonus, especially for subsequent promotion.

And there is an increasing number of posts for which a language qualification is more than just a bonus. Many employers nowadays expect to recruit people who have practical skills in understanding and in speaking and writing foreign languages, and an ability in more than one foreign language is often especially valuable, particularly when one considers that for many of your contemporaries in other EU member states, two or three foreign languages is often the norm. In the Netherlands, for example, pupils are introduced to English, French and German from the age of five; in the early years of secondary education all pupils must do two foreign languages; and all school leavers who hold an 18+ certificate of education may be expected to be proficient in three foreign languages.

But graduates in modern languages are sought after by employers not merely for their linguistic skills, but for the intellectual training which their course has provided. Linguists are trained to think structurally; they write essays which give them good practice in thinking clearly and in presenting focused arguments; many language courses involve working co-operatively in groups and making formal presentations to an audience — just the sort of teamwork and presentational skills which employers tell us they are looking for.

Many graduates of modern languages go into industry or business where they are trained in the relevant professional skills. For these graduates their language skills are often the extra factor which counts in their favour when they are appointed to their first job. Languages may not be particularly relevant to their first appointment, but they may be useful, and attractive to employers at a later date, as they move up the career structure in their chosen area of employment.

How do I get an EU job?

The activities and legislation of the EU institutions are likely to have an important influence on your education and your future career, whether you wish ultimately to work for one of the EU bodies in Brussels, Luxembourg or Strasbourg, or not.

When you come to choose a higher education course, you will find that many of them involve study or work experience in another member state. The EU Erasmus/ Socrates programmes now support over 40,000 EU students annually, a very large proportion of these coming from the UK. And young people who have taken part in these programmes have found them to be very helpful in obtaining a first job, particularly if it is a job where international experience is appreciated. A survey done at the beginning of the 1990s found that nearly a fifth of students surveyed two-and-a-half years after their period abroad were actually working abroad.

If you wish to work in one of the European Union institutions, there are a number of opportunities. The main centre of administration is the European Commission itself: this is where the Commissioners, appointed by the member governments, have responsibility for different aspects of EU policy. Most officials are based in Brussels, but there are some in Luxembourg, and a few in delegations and offices in other cities across the world.

Posts in EU institutions are classified A, LA, B, C or D:

Grade A

administrative and advisory staff, including scientists (educated to graduate level).

Grade LA

translators and interpreters (educated to graduate level).

Grade B

executives and junior management staff (usually educated to 'A' level standard).

Grade C

officials engaged in secretarial and clerical duties (GCSE standard, plus relevant professional training and experience).

Grade D

officials engaged in manual and support service duties, such as transport, printing, stock control, messenger work.

Each grade is further sub-divided according to the importance and seniority of the post. For example, a new recruit to an administrative post would probably be classified as A8, whereas a top administrator would be A1.

The EU has traditionally tended to employ people with a background in economics or law in administrative posts. A degree in either of these subjects, particularly if it includes a European studies element, could be a good first step on the road to a 'grade A' post. However, EU institutions, unlike their UK counterparts, tend not to employ newly qualified graduates. One way round this potential problem is to apply for selection for the European Fast Stream (EFS) of the UK Civil Service first. This is by no means a soft option, though. Under the scheme, a maximum of 30 good (1st or 2nd class honours) graduates a year are chosen and are offered a programme of training (including language training) and relevant work experience in one of the UK government departments. The EFS programme effectively prepares you for competitions for a post in the EU, but if you were unsuccessful in obtaining such a post, you would still be able to continue with a career in the Home Civil Service.

Entry to posts with one of the EU institutions is via 'open competition'. Advertisements for the jobs are listed in the official journal of the EU (available from EU information offices and the HMSO) and in national newspapers as well. Posts at grades A, LA and B level are usually to be found in *The Times, Guardian* and *Independent;* those for grades C and D in the *Daily Mail* and *Daily Mirror* respectively. Apart from the necessary qualifications for the job, you will also need to be suitably proficient in at least one EU official language, apart from your mother tongue — for some jobs this may mean just good GCSE level. For LA posts you would need two EU languages apart from your own language. If your application were to be successful in the first round, you would be given a written test (for most posts), and if you did well enough in this, you would be invited for interview. This initial process can take anything up to two years, so you would need to have a job, or some means of support, whilst you were applying. Eventual success at interview would not mean that you had got the job, though: you would then be put on a reserve list and might have to wait a further twelve months before being offered an actual post.

While on the reserve list, you should not just wait patiently! It is at this point that a system of canvassing, or lobbying, comes into play, at least for top grade posts. It is expected that you would do all you could to raise your profile by, for example, approaching you MEP, or in fact anyone else you knew who was suitably influential, for support in your application. This might seem to you like trying to gain an unfair advantage, but it is something that those who work for EU institutions come to regard as perfectly normal — it is in fact accepted procedure for top jobs in many other member states.

It is possible, once you have a degree, for you to do a *stage* (a short training scheme) with the EU, which can not only give you up to five months' experience of working in EU institutions in an administrative or linguistic capacity, it can also be of some small help in the competitive recruitment procedure described above. Trainees on this scheme are known as *stagiaires*, and there are openings available at the Commission, the Parliament, the Economic and Social Committee, and occasionally at the Council. A *stagiaire*-ship would give you a first-hand opportunity of seeing how an EU institution operates from the inside, and at the end of your training period you would be assessed and receive a certificate. Each institution makes its own arrangements for recruiting *stagiaires*, and the process is likely to be quite competitive, with the necessity to use your contacts all you can.

Again, your MEP can be of help here, and it is usually considered necessary to go to Brussels and talk to officials in the department for which you are applying. Since these officials are likely to be the ones choosing successful applicants from a very long list of similarly qualified candidates, it is obviously beneficial to get your name known to them!

The Commission employs large numbers of graduates in modern languages as interpreters and translators, and there is a particular demand for those who are proficient in EU languages other than French, German, Italian and Spanish.

It is not at all easy to get an interpreting job with the Commission: you need to be completely fluent in at least two official EU languages in addition to your mother tongue; on average, only 2% of applicants for interpreting posts are accepted; and the training course offered is extremely rigorous. A good preparation — but not an automatic entry route — for an interpreting job with the Commission could be one of their six-month *stages* for trainee interpreters. Again, you would need to have a degree (in any subject) and be proficient in at least three EU languages, including your own.

There is also a demand for interpreters/ translators who are not only proficient in EU languages, but are also graduates in other disciplines, such as law, economics, a scientific subject, or technology. One of the many joint degree programmes in, for example, law and languages, or engineering or a science and a language, could be a suitable preparation for this.

Another possible route into a career with the Commission, once you have a degree, might be via the College of Europe in Bruges which offers postgraduate diploma courses in advanced European Studies in one of three specialised fields of study — economics, law or administration. There are 30 bursaries a year provided by the UK government for British graduates who wish to do one of these College of Europe diplomas. Since the tuition is largely in French, you would need to have a good working knowledge of this language.

The EU itself offers Robert Schumann Scholarships (named after one of the founding fathers of the EU) available to postgraduate students who wish to assist in research projects for a period of about two or three months with the Directorate General for Research, based at the Luxembourg Parliament.

In spite of the very competitive nature of recruitment to the EU institutions, there is a wide range of possibilities for those with a knowledge of EU languages, and there are possibilities of entry to the highest grade administrative and advisory posts for those who are also well qualified in the other relevant disciplines mentioned above. Developments in Eastern Europe are bringing about further expansion in EU activities, including openings for speakers of Eastern European languages.

Languages of the European Union
Checklist
DEGREE COURSES

1	Degree courses in French or German are on offer in most higher education institutions which teach languages; Spanish is on offer in more than 50 institutions.
2	The other EU languages can all be studied for a degree either on their own, in combination with another language, or with another subject.
3	You can study from scratch to degree level in one of the languages less commonly learnt at school, provided that you can satisfy the selectors that you have the ability to learn languages — a good 'A' level in another foreign language perhaps.
4	Language courses differ widely from institution to institution, so you must research the courses you are applying for very thoroughly — it is really too late to find out that the course isn't what you wanted once you have been accepted.
5	Find out what sort of experience is offered during the period spent abroad — it can offer valuable work experience and perhaps extra qualifications.
6	You can go to another EU country to do the whole of your higher education, but you would probably have to pay more of your own money for it than if you went to a university or college of higher education in the UK.
7	Language graduates are employable, not just for their language proficiency, but for the intellectual training which their course has given them.

8	Some go into jobs where they can make use of their languages, but the vast majority go into careers which at first sight do not appear to have much to do with languages, but where their linguistic proficiency is often attractive to employers, and of increasing value to themselves as their career progresses.
9	The recruitment process for jobs with EU institutions is lengthy and competitive. You should be prepared to lobby your MEP and any other important contacts you may have; it often helps to have been a *stagiaire* on an EU short training programme beforehand.
10	For interpreting and translating posts with the EU you would need a high level of proficiency in at least two official EU languages apart from your mother tongue

> See the **Signposts** section to find out which institutions offer which languages.

Scandinavian languages

DEGREE COURSES

The mainland Scandinavian languages are Danish, Norwegian and Swedish. Closely related are the languages of Iceland and the Faroe Isles — Icelandic and Faroese — but these are not available for study as main subjects in any British university. They can, however, be done as options in Scandinavian Studies courses at University College, London.

Although Finland is a near neighbour, Finnish is in fact unrelated to these Scandinavian languages and is distantly related to Hungarian. We therefore deal with Finnish in the section on Eastern European languages. Nevertheless, some Scandinavian Studies courses contain modules or options in Finnish.

The vast majority of students start Scandinavian languages from scratch. In common with all *ab initio* courses, you would need to show evidence of an ability to learn languages — a good pass at 'A' level or 'AS' (or equivalent) in another modern foreign language should do the trick!

Scandinavian languages are related to English and German, and are less inflected than German and rather more regular than English. So, they are perhaps not as hard work to learn as other languages you might take from scratch to degree level.

What degree courses are on offer in Scandinavian languages ?

There are very few institutions where you can specialise in Scandinavian studies — just four in the whole of the UK. These institutions offer courses in Scandinavian languages and the history, culture and contemporary situation in mainland Scandinavia, either as a main specialism or in combination with another subject.

You can combine Scandinavian studies with another language at the University of Hull (with French or German), and at University College, London (with Dutch or German). University College also offers Scandinavian studies with linguistics.

If you want a business-related degree course, you can do Danish with Business Studies at the University of East Anglia; Scandinavian Studies with Business Studies at the University of Hull; and Scandinavian Studies with Management at University College, London.

At the University of East Anglia you can study Danish, Norwegian or Swedish together with European History; at the University of Edinburgh you can combine Scandinavian Studies with Celtic, or Scottish Ethnology (the study of the Scottish people and their traditional culture and folklore) or English Language; and at Lampeter there is a wide range of subjects you can put with Swedish — like anthropology, archaeology, geography, informatics, religious studies, Latin . . .

I should like to specialise in just one Scandinavian language

If you consult the **Signposts** section, you will see that relatively few institutions appear to offer specialist courses in just one of the three languages, but in fact a Scandinavian Studies course will usually allow you to specialise in one of the three languages and acquire a basic knowledge of the other two. In this way you gain a fluent active command of spoken and written Danish or Norwegian or Swedish, together with the ability to read and understand one or both of the other two languages.

How relevant would these languages be in my career?

Graduates in Scandinavian languages have the same range of career opportunities as other Arts graduates — and they go on to a variety of occupational areas, like journalism and the media, industrial and commercial management, tourism, transport planning, the Civil Service, teaching, publishing, the law, librarianship, banking and accountancy.

Many graduates go on to use their Scandinavian languages in their careers — either in such specialisms as interpreting, translating or teaching, or they find their specialist knowledge of languages and cultures of great value to companies and other organisations which have dealings with Scandinavian countries. Both Sweden and Denmark are members of the EU, and speakers of their languages are employed at the European Parliament and the European Commisssion.

The most widely used of the Scandinavian languages is Swedish, with over eight-and-a-half million native speakers in Sweden and Finland — and it is understood by some twenty million people throughout Scandinavia. Sweden is a wealthy, dynamic country, important in commerce and contemporary world affairs, and actively involved in the Third World — there are many fields where a knowledge of Swedish and of Scandinavia could be of benefit to you in your future career.

Scandinavian languages
Checklist
DEGREE COURSES

1 There are only six universities in the UK where you can specialise in Scandinavian studies.

2 At a few of them you can specialise in one of the Scandinavian languages; or if you do a Scandinavian Studies course this will usually allow you to specialise in one of Danish, Norwegian or Swedish, gaining an active command of the spoken and written language, as well as an ability to read and understand one or both of the other two.

3 The vast majority of students start Scandinavian languages from scratch.

4 Graduates in Scandinavian languages often pursue careers where they make use of their language skills and/or their cultural knowledge.

5 Others are employed by companies and organisations who value the general skills, experience and breadth of understanding they have acquired as part of their higher education.

6 Swedish is the most widely spoken of the three languages, and therefore probably the one most widely in demand by employers.

See the **Signposts** section to find out which institutions offer which languages.

Russian and Eastern European languages

DEGREE COURSES

If you have had the opportunity to learn Russian at school, even if only to good GCSE (or equivalent) standard, you may well wish to carry on studying it as a major or minor part of a degree course. It may even have whetted your appetite for learning other languages spoken in Eastern Europe. And if you have not yet become acquainted with the languages of Eastern Europe, you can still entertain the idea of studying one or more of them at university.

Although it is not studied in schools as widely as French or German, Russian is an important world language: a knowledge of Russian will get you round the whole of the former Soviet Union and much of Eastern Europe — an enormous geographical area!

Russia has experienced a series of dramatic changes during the twentieth century, and it is now, once again, undergoing a period of transition. Despite the fragmentation of the former Soviet Union, however, Russian language and culture retain their importance in international political, scientific, industrial and commercial spheres.

Russian is the most widely spoken Slavonic language. The Slavonic group of languages is the third major linguistic group after the Germanic group (German, Dutch, English, Scandinavian languages . . .) and the Romance group (languages derived from Latin, like French, Italian and Spanish). Besides Russian, the Slavonic group also includes Bulgarian, Czech, Slovak, Polish and Serbo-Croat.

Romanian, as its name suggests, is not a Slavonic, but a Romance language, although it contains many borrowings from neighbouring Slavonic languages, as well as words of Turkish origin, and more recent borrowings from French.

Hungarian is not a Slavonic language, either. In fact, it is very different in structure from the other major languages of Europe and is distantly related to Finnish — a language which in its turn is unrelated to the languages of Finland's Scandinavian and Slavonic neighbours.

For the purposes of this publication, however, we are grouping all these languages together, since they are all spoken in Eastern Europe.

What sort of a Russian course could I do?

If you want to study Russian for all or part of your degree, there are hundreds of courses from which to make your choice.

To make up your mind between the range of different courses available, you will not only have to take the relatively simple decision about whether you want to study Russian on its own, or with another language, or with another subject altogether — history, economics, politics, philosophy, psychology, mathematics, theatre studies . . . (there are a lot to choose from!); if you want to do a single honours course in Russian, you will also have to decide what aspects of the Russian language and its history and culture you want to concentrate on in your studies. This is where you must read the university prospectuses very carefully, so you can sort out what topics are on offer, and which of them are compulsory and which optional. You could even send to individual universities for more detailed descriptions of courses which particularly interest you.

As well as the core study of the Russian language, you will find that most Russian degree courses include the study of Russian literature of the nineteenth and twentieth centuries; a few include the literature of Old Russia, from the eleventh to the seventeenth centuries.

You would also expect to study aspects of Russian history and society, as well as the economic, political, social and philosophical aspects of the Soviet Union. Russian departments at some universities place special emphasis on the study of Soviet society, politics and thought.

Have a look at the options offered — does anything particularly appeal to you at one institution which is not offered at another? Individual departments offer special options like, for example, the history of Russian art, Russian women writers, the development of the Russian language from earliest records to the present day, the comparative historical development of Siberia and Canada, Russian folklore, Soviet foreign policy, a second Slavonic language (Czech or Polish, perhaps) . . . Don't bank on all the options listed being available in any one year, but a careful reading of the prospectuses will give you a good idea of the character and content of individual degree courses.

Take a look at the experience provided by the period of study spent abroad. Would you go abroad for a whole year, or just a few weeks or months? If you went for a shorter period, would it be for a three- or four-week vacation course? Could you spend part of your time in Russia and part in another Eastern European country (if you were studying its language)? If you went for a whole year, would you be based in a culturally rich city, like St Petersburg, for example, or somewhere perhaps less attractive?

Can I do a degree in Russian if I haven't studied it before?

If you have not had the chance to learn Russian, it is possible at many institutions to study for a degree in Russian as a main subject, or as part of a joint or combined honours course, with no prior knowledge. You will need to convince admissions tutors that you have a proven track record of learning languages before they will offer you a place, but your GCSE language record, as well as any languages you have done at 'A' level (or equivalent), will all be taken into account.

They will also try to assess your motivation. This is especially important where you would be studying a subject intensively, from scratch. In this respect, what you write in your personal statement, and the way you present yourself at interview, can be particularly revealing.

Learning any language from scratch to degree level in three or four years is hard work, but not necessarily particularly difficult if you are already a successful language learner. And if you enjoy learning languages, learning something exotic can be great fun and very stimulating.

Many universities provide for two language groups running throughout the first two years of the course, so that beginners and non-beginners can be taught separately. The first two years of the beginners' course are very intensive, so that by the final year the two groups are fully integrated.

At other universities the degree course is organised specifically for *ab initio* learners, and those who have done an 'A' level (or equivalent) in Russian are accepted directly into the second year of the course.

I would like to do Russian as part of my degree course, but not as the main part

If you look through the prospectuses carefully, you will find that there are several institutions where you can choose to study Russian as a subsidiary subject, or as an optional third language in a languages degree course. This will usually be an *ab initio* course, but there are occasionally minor courses which cater for those who have some prior knowledge.

There are some institutions where you can do a minor course in Russian as part of a more vocationally oriented degree, or as a component of a modular degree.

Most universities have a 'Languages for All' policy which gives students an opportunity to study at least one language, regardless of their course or year of study, in the university Language Teaching Centre. Russian is usually available in this way, and occasionally other Eastern European languages as well.

Can I study other Eastern European languages from scratch?

Yes — although opportunities to do so are not very widely available. You would usually study another Eastern European language (Czech or Polish most commonly) together with Russian or another language.

The School of Slavonic and East European Studies (SSEES), which is part of the University of London, is unique in that it offers courses in all the main languages and cultures of Eastern Europe. Here, as well as Russian, you can do Bulgarian, Polish, Czech with Slovak or Slovak with Czech, Hungarian, Finnish, Romanian or Serbo-Croat. There is a significant amount of flexibility in course structure since, in common with other London University colleges, degrees are gained by accumulating course units, with the added opportunity of taking extra units offered by other London colleges. Thus at SSEES you can study the language and literature of one culture, or you can combine two languages, or you can combine a language with history or the social sciences.

You can do these less commonly learnt languages from scratch, of course, because few students will have had the opportunity of learning them at school. It is unlikely that you would have the opportunity of doing two languages from scratch — and in any case it would hardly be a good idea!

See the **Signposts** section to find out which institutions offer which languages.

Are Eastern European languages useful for a career?

In common with other arts degrees, a languages degree (in any language) can be regarded as being part of a general education from which students move on to careers in a wide variety of fields, including accountancy, banking, industry, teaching, publishing, tourism, journalism and the media, local government, the Civil Service (including the Foreign Office and the British Council), or the armed services.

Some graduates go on to use their specific linguistic expertise directly in any of these fields; others use their languages by, for example, translating books and journals, researching for art or antique dealers, acting as an interpreter, or by working for an airline company or a travel agency.

Some graduates go on to postgraduate studies in preparation for a career in the law, teaching or interpreting. Others undertake further training which will take them into marketing, personnel management, business administration, banking, accountancy or librarianship, for instance.

Since the collapse of the former Soviet Union, links with Russia and other Eastern European countries are increasing quite rapidly. Demand for graduates with specialist knowledge of the appropriate languages and cultures is increasing too. With a degree in one of these languages, you would belong to a relatively small minority of people with expert knowledge of the language, way of life, problems and strengths of a former Eastern bloc country, which could give you an important advantage in the jobs market.

Russian and Eastern European languages
Checklist

DEGREE COURSES

1. Russian is an important world language, spoken and understood in much of Eastern Europe.

2. There are plenty of courses to choose from if you want to study Russian, either as your main degree subject, or as a part of your degree course.

3. Because the choice of degree courses with Russian is so wide, you should read university prospectuses and course descriptions carefully in order to choose one which will suit you.

4. You can start a course in Russian or another Eastern European language as a complete beginner, although you will need to show evidence that you have the ability to learn a language.

5. Beginners and non-beginners are usually taught separately in the first couple of years.

6. Graduates in Russian and Eastern European languages often pursue careers where they make use of their language skills and/or their cultural knowledge.

7. Others are employed by companies and organisations who value the general skills, experience and breadth of understanding they have acquired as part of their higher education.

8. Since the collapse of the former Soviet Union, links with Eastern Europe have increased, and so has demand for graduates with specialist knowledge of the appropriate languages and cultures.

See the **Signposts** section to find out which institutions offer which languages.

European Studies

DEGREE COURSES

European Studies provides an education in subjects in more than one area of study. It allows you to develop a broad overview and understanding of contemporary Europe, and to obtain qualifications which combine language studies with social science subjects such as politics and economics.

Is it just another name for a degree in languages?

Language study forms an important part of most European Studies courses, yet this is not a languages degree in the ordinary sense. The core of such a programme is the study of contemporary Europe — its geography, history, culture, politics and economics — together with the study of one, and very often two European languages. Many courses introduce you to European literature; others have options in other subjects which might be useful in career terms, such as law, the European media, or information technology.

The number of languages you can do, and the proportion of the programme devoted to language study, varies from course to course. The languages on offer are most frequently French, German and Spanish, but some courses give you opportunities to study other European languages, as the examples given below will show. On very many of them you can start a new language from scratch.

You can expect a period of time during the course to be spent abroad, usually at a university in the country of your main European language, studying the social studies subject you have chosen to specialise in. Some courses allow you to do a work placement abroad, or to work as a foreign language assistant in a school.

Do European Studies courses vary?

European Studies courses differ quite widely from institution to institution: in the number of languages offered, the amount of language study, the experience provided by the year abroad, the way in which the social studies component is organised, the amount of choice you have in planning your own programme, and the scope of the programme — whether it deals mainly with Western Europe, or whether it deals with aspects of the 'new Europe' by including Scandinavia, Eastern Europe and the countries of the former Soviet Union.

In some courses the social science component is planned around a tightly structured, integrated programme throughout the course; in others, after introductory common core courses in the first year, you would be able to specialise in particular subjects or topics, in preference to others you are not so interested in.

We have chosen a few examples of European Studies courses — just a random selection — to illustrate the differences which exist between courses with the name of European Studies. You will see that it would be very unwise to pick out the courses for your UCAS form by name alone!

At **Loughborough University** you can do French, German or Spanish, or two of these languages; you study contemporary France and/or Germany (depending upon the languages you have chosen); and you have a choice of specialism between European politics and European economics. A year abroad is spent working as an English language assistant in a French or German school, or attending a study course at one of a selection of French or German universities with which the university has exchange agreements.

The course at **Leicester University** is planned along modular lines so that you can select your own areas of specialism within a broad framework of life in modern Europe. You study contemporary European politics and one main language (French, German, Italian or Spanish — post 'A' level, although German, Italian and Spanish are available as a second language without any previous knowledge). You can then add further modules, choosing from a wide range of courses on social, historical or cultural aspects of the country whose language you are studying; a second European language; further courses in European politics; and, for example, international relations, law, history, history of art, economics, geography or sociology. This degree programme is an example of one which includes aspects of Central and Eastern Europe too. In the third year students go abroad, either to the country of their main language, or divide the year between universities in two countries, one of which may be in Central or Eastern Europe.

The Contemporary Europe course at **Southampton University** allows you to do two languages — French, German or Spanish as a major language, plus another of those three, or Portuguese as a second language. And any of them, except French, may be done from scratch. In addition, in the first two years you follow five common core courses which underpin the whole of the course. These deal with the historical and political background of European integration; how the European Union and its institutions work; and main themes of economics, society, ideology and culture in Europe today. From the second year onwards you can begin to choose options and special subjects according to your own particular interests. These might be in economics, geography, history, law, politics or languages. The third year is spent abroad in the country of your major language, on a university course appropriate to these interests. There is also a new European Cultural Studies programme which allows you to study Europe-wide movements in ideas and writing, as well as aspects of the main national cultures.

You cannot assume that every course called 'European Studies' will have a language component. If you look at the European Studies course in the **University of Durham** prospectus you will find that it is in fact a three-year geo-graphy programme, with the second year spent abroad studying geography at a mainland European university — but there is no formal language component in the course. However, the university does in fact award a degree for the more usual type of European Studies programme which has a modern language as an important part: elsewhere in the prospectus you will find that **University College, Stockton,** which is a campus of the University of Durham, offers a three-year European Studies course with French, German or Spanish (the last two from scratch if you want to), and you may spend a term studying in an exchange institution in Germany, France, Spain, Belgium, Italy, Sweden, Ireland, Denmark, Romania or the Netherlands. On the four-year programme you spend a year in France, Germany or Spain.

There are two European Studies programmes on offer at the **University of Hull** — European Studies, and Transnational Integrated European Studies (TIES). Both courses deal not just with Western Europe, but Scandinavia, Eastern Europe and the countries of the former Soviet Union, as well as Europe's relations with America and the Third World. The languages available — of which you can do one or two — are French and German (post 'A' level), and Dutch, Italian, Spanish and Swedish, any of which may be studied from scratch. TIES students have to do two, chosen from Dutch, French and German. Besides languages, you can do a number of different specialisms in the areas of economics, politics, history, geography, literature, the media and information technology. All students go abroad to study at a university in mainland Europe, and what makes the TIES course different is that in the fourth year you do a university course in either Amsterdam, Angers or Osnabrück, and are able to gain a Dutch, French or German qualification in addition to the BA from Hull.

This is just a small selection of the 60 or more different European Studies courses from which you may choose. The **Signposts** table will show you all the universities in the UK which offer European Studies courses. It is really a question of searching carefully through all the relevant prospectuses to select your short-list of courses to fit your own needs and interests.

Does a degree in European Studies prepare me for a career?

European Studies graduates enter a wide variety of careers which, as is the case with other arts graduates, are not always related to their field of study. They can be found in posts in industry, marketing, administration, government, international organisations, the European public sector, teaching (both in the UK and abroad), banking, journalism and law.

Their detailed knowledge of contemporary Europe, coupled with a high level of expertise in one or more languages, make European Studies graduates very attractive to companies which have dealings with other companies and clients in continental Europe.

European Studies Checklist

DEGREE COURSES

1	European Studies combines the study of one or more European languages with the study of contemporary Europe.
2	European Studies courses differ quite widely in their content from institution to institution.
3	The languages on offer are most frequently French, German and Spanish, but some institutions provide opportunities to do other European languages.
4	There are 60 or more European Studies courses which all have their differences. You must therefore read course descriptions carefully to find the course for you.
5	Like other arts graduates, European Studies graduates enter a wide variety of careers, not necessarily related to their field of study.
6	Their knowledge of contemporary Europe, and their proficiency in European languages, make them attractive to companies which have dealings in continental Europe.

See the **Signposts** section to find out which institutions offer European Studies courses.

Asian languages

DEGREE COURSES

If you are studying a modern language at school or college, it is more than likely that it is French, German or Spanish — or possibly Italian or Russian. There are some British schools where Asian languages are taught, usually Japanese or one of the Indian languages, but these are still the exception.

If you are enjoying your language studies so much that you want to go on to a languages degree course, you will probably wish to continue with the same language. But did you know that your 'A' level (or equivalent qualification) in a European language can be a qualification to do an Asian language?

The Asian languages taught in UK universities include Chinese, Japanese, Korean, Malay, Bengali, Hindu and Urdu.

It is quite possible at a number of universities to study Asian languages without any prior knowledge, and you can study one of them either:

- as a single honours subject (i.e. on its own); or
- on a joint honours course with another language or another subject; or
- as part of a combined honours or modular programme; or
- as a minor option in another programme.

Complete beginners are accepted on the majority of these courses. However, you will need a least two good 'A' levels (or equivalent) if you want to do one of these languages as a major or joint subject, and one of these 'A' levels will usually have to be in a language, so that an Admissions Tutor has some evidence that you have enough linguistic ability to cope with the course. Sometimes an 'AS' offers sufficient evidence.

You might find, however, if you started an *ab initio* course, that although most members of your year group would start the course from scratch, there might very well be some who have some prior knowledge, and even some who have a lot of prior knowledge. To cater for this, some universities provide a differentiated first year, putting on classes for beginners and classes for those who already have some knowledge of the language — so complete beginners are not at a disadvantage.

I'd like to do an Asian language as my main degree subject

If you want to do a single honours degree course in an Asian language, then Chinese or Japanese are fairly widely available. Korean is on offer at two institutions — the University of Sheffield and the School of Oriental and African Studies (SOAS), London; and Malay is offered by the University of Hull as part of a South-East Asian Studies course.

One of the places where you can do a single honours degree in Chinese is the **University of Durham,** and their course is fairly typical of ones you might find at other institutions.

This is a four-year course, and during the first year you have to get to grips with the Chinese language and commit to memory many Chinese characters. You also study the historical and cultural background of modern China.

In your second year you continue your Chinese studies at a university in China, and have the opportunity of travelling about the country in the vacations.

In the final two years, spent back in Durham, you work to improve upon your reading, writing and speaking skills in modern Chinese; you continue to explore Chinese historical and cultural traditions; and you are introduced to classical Chinese, which is quite a tough challenge.

Japanese courses are similar, usually involving the study of spoken and written Japanese (with an intensive introduction to basic Japanese in year one), together with aspects of Japanese culture and society. In subsequent years further topics are introduced, like Japanese literature, or perhaps the Japanese economy and business. Most courses include a period of time in Japan studying at a university.

I'd like to do an Asian language as part of a joint course

If you are interested in doing an Asian language as half of your degree — in other words, as part of a joint course — then this is possible at a number of institutions.

A joint course would allow you either:

- to study two Asian languages together to the same level, for example, Chinese and Korean; or
- to make up a pair with a European language, like French and Japanese, or Dutch and Indonesian; or
- you could choose a non-linguistic subject to put with your Asian language — Law and Urdu, Bengali and Music, Japanese and Management Studies, Chinese and History . . .

I'd like to include Chinese or Japanese as part of a combined honours course

There are a few combined degree schemes and modular programmes which enable you to include Chinese or Japanese as a major or minor option. This sort of scheme is very flexible, allowing you to construct a course to suit your own particular interests or career needs.

At the University of Central Lancashire you can do Chinese in this way; at the Universities of Ulster or Wolverhampton you can do Japanese; at the University of Newcastle you can do Chinese, Japanese or Korean; and at the University of Luton you can do Chinese or Japanese.

A combined or modular course will usually allow you to study a subject as a major, joint or minor subject, and the award you finally get will often reflect the proportion of time you devoted to each of your chosen subjects — you might get a BA (Hons) Humanities, for example, if you studied two or three subjects on a reasonably equal basis; or if you studied two 'joint' options your award might be BA (Hons) French and Japanese.

Japanese at the University of Ulster can be studied as a major, joint, or minor option.

Is it difficult to take such a language from scratch?

Oriental languages like Chinese and Japanese, with their complex scripts, are not easy to learn if you have been brought up exclusively on Western European languages.

The languages of South Asia — the national languages of the Indian sub-continent — are relatively accessible to speakers of European languages, but they too have a different script which has to be mastered.

If you choose one of these languages as a major degree subject, then you must be prepared for a lot of hard work. This is perhaps particularly true in the case of Chinese where mastery of the script is exceptionally time-consuming. In spite of the heavy workload, however, very many students have enjoyed the challenge and have done well — and it can be a rewarding and enjoyable experience, as this former SOAS student found out:

> Chinese is not the easiest language to learn. All four years demand hard work and commitment but the results are great. The second year being spent in China meant we gathered first-hand knowledge of China and the Chinese. We were overwhelmed by the sheer wealth of culture and long history, and we all had fun communicating our thoughts — you suddenly realise you have, potentially speaking, a billion people to talk to, and that you can read a strange-looking series of lines and strokes in a newspaper.

With so much work to do, you will need a genuine interest in your work to carry you through, so whatever you do, don't choose to study one of these languages just because you feel like a change!

It is sometimes quite difficult to track down all the courses which can offer you a chance to learn a language. Because languages are so important in so many walks of life, there are now many degree courses, whether in modern languages or in any other subject, which give you a chance to learn a language as an option. Often this is not evident from the documentation, because it is impossible to list all a course's options in UCAS publications.

See the **Signposts** section to find out which institutions offer which languages.

How relevant could these languages be in my career?

Another look at the statistics on p39 of **Degree courses in languages** will remind you that language graduates go into a wide range of occupations where their language qualification is not always of prime importance, but is an added bonus for an employer. Studying an Asian language, therefore, does not prepare you for any specific job, but it gives you skills, experience and a breadth of understanding which employers find valuable.

There are Asian language courses which place emphasis on modern aspects of culture, and on political or economic topics, and these might be particularly relevant to a career in, for instance, business, management, law, the media, and finance, either in the West or in Asia. Graduates of Japanese and Chinese degree courses of this type at one university are to be found pursuing careers in business, journalism, publishing, diplomacy, teaching, overseas aid work and tourism throughout China, Japan, Hong Kong, Taiwan and Mongolia. They are also found in the UK, continental Europe and the United States, in jobs which are directly related to their knowledge of Asian languages and culture.

The demand for graduates of Japanese has increased dramatically. With growing Japanese investment in the West, Japanese companies, both in Japan and in Europe, employ Japanese language graduates in considerable numbers. UK and European institutions have a major need for trained Japanese specialists. There are also openings in Japan in teaching, and in Japanese banks and other financial institutions.

As China expands her links with the West, there are increasing opportunities for graduates of Chinese. Many multinational and UK companies have agencies and offices in China and employ speakers of Chinese both in Europe and in the Far East.

Opportunities exist, too, in government bodies, especially the Foreign Office, and in international organisations like the United Nations (Chinese is an official UN language).

The study of oriental or Indian history and culture, which forms a part of most of these degree programmes, can provide a relevant grounding for people who want to work in the fine art world, or in museums and specialist libraries.

As the UK is home to large numbers of people with Asian cultural backgrounds, there is a demand for people specialising in the languages and cultures of, in particular, the Indian subcontinent. Graduates of South Asian languages go into translating, and into journalism and broadcasting, especially as the British media have recently begun to respond more positively to cultural pluralism.

An Asian language linked to another specialism, like law for example, can be a real advantage, particularly if you are thinking of working in local government, in the social services, or in the courts, where your ability to communicate with and assist those who might have an imperfect grasp of the English language would be very valuable.

Graduates of Indian languages also go into teaching, where there is a small, but increasing, demand for South Asian languages to be included in the curriculum. Intending teachers might perhaps consider linking an Asian language with a European one — they could be of real use to a school languages department in an area where there is a large Asian community. And Japanese is a language which has recently been introduced into schools, particularly in those areas of the country where Japanese firms have set up factories.

Asian languages
Checklist
DEGREE COURSES

1	You can do a degree in Chinese, Japanese or another Asian language as a complete beginner.
2	Some courses allow you to combine an Asian language with another language, or another subject; or you can do one (usually Japanese) as a minor option.
3	Although you need no prior knowledge of the language to be studied, you would need an 'A' level (or perhaps an 'AS') in any language as a proof of your linguistic ability.
4	Asian languages have complex scripts, and many are not easy to learn — you must be prepared to work hard.
5	Those who have learned Chinese, Japanese and other Asian languages often pursue careers where they make use of their language skills and/or their cultural knowledge.
6	Others are employed by companies and organisations who value the general skills, experience, and breadth of understanding they have acquired as part of their higher education.

See the **Signposts** section to find out which institutions offer which languages.

Arabic, Middle Eastern and African languages

DEGREE COURSES

If you want to do a language you have not done at school — something completely different, perhaps — then you might like to consider doing Arabic, or one of the other languages of the Middle East (Hebrew, Persian or Turkish) or of Africa (Amharic, Hausa, Swahili, Somali, Sotho, Yoruba or Zulu).

As with all languages rarely studied at school, you will be able to begin a course in a Middle Eastern or African language as a complete beginner. At least one of your 'A' levels (or equivalent) will need to be in a foreign language, or you will need some other evidence of linguistic ability, or aptitude for the language you wish to study.

How difficult would it be to do Arabic?

Arabic is not an easy language to learn. It differs considerably from European languages, and it has a completely different script which you would have to master. But it is quite accessible, given reasonable intelligence and lots of hard work. You would not spend all of your time learning the language — in addition to the language, and written texts, you would also study the history and culture of the Middle East.

Where is Arabic spoken?

Arabic is used throughout the contemporary Arab world, in North Africa, Egypt and the Sudan, in Syria, Jordan, Lebanon and Palestine. It exists in two main types — a classical form which is used for literature, formal speeches and broadcasting; and a spoken type of which there are many different dialects from country to country. The classical, or standard educated form acts as a *lingua franca* throughout the Arab-speaking world, and this is the one you would study, although you would have instruction in the spoken language, and would probably be introduced to at least one of the many dialects.

Are there other Middle Eastern languages which I can do, besides Arabic?

Arabic is the most widely available of the Middle Eastern languages. It is on offer, either as a single honours subject, or in combination with other subject(s), at eleven UK universities. Persian can be studied as a main subject at the University of Oxford and at the School of Oriental and African Studies (SOAS); and as a joint honours subject at the universities of Cambridge, Edinburgh and Manchester. Manchester has a Middle Eastern Studies course where you can choose two languages from Arabic, Hebrew, Persian and Turkish, or you can combine one of these with a European language (Arabic can be done with a European language at a few places). You can do a single honours course in Turkish at Oxford or SOAS. Modern Hebrew is usually studied in combination with another language, but it may be done as a main subject at Oxford.

Which African languages can I do?

African languages are only available at SOAS. Here you may do Amharic, Hausa or Swahili to degree level as single subjects, or you may combine them with another subject from a wide range which includes anthropology, history, geography, politics, development studies, law, management, music and history of art. Other important African languages —

Somali, Sotho, Yoruba and Zulu — can each be studied as an option in other courses, or for two successive years as part of the three-year course in African Studies.

See the **Signposts** section to find out which institutions offer which languages. You can also find out at a glance where all these languages are spoken by consulting the table **Who speaks what where?** on p19.

Would I study in the Middle East or Africa?

Although it is not so easy to spend a year studying or working abroad when you are doing a non-European language, many courses will include this opportunity, or you will be encouraged to spend one of your vacations in a country where the language you are learning is spoken.

If you were to do single honours Arabic at the **University of Exeter**, for instance, you would spend the second year of your four-year course in an Arab country, probably Egypt; whereas if you chose to combine Arabic with French or Spanish, you would divide the year between the Arab country and France or Spain.

The **University of Edinburgh** sends its students of Arabic to study in an Arabic-speaking country for six months during the second and third years. Its students following the joint Arabic and Persian course are sent abroad, if possible, during the first term of the third year to study Persian in a Persian-speaking country.

Students of an African language at the **School of Oriental and African Studies**, together with those following the African Language and Culture degree course, spend two terms of their third year in Africa. If Swahili is their chosen language, they go to Zanzibar and to the University of Dar es Salaam in Tanzania; if they choose Hausa they spend the two terms at Bayero University in Kano, Nigeria. Students of other African languages are not sent abroad as a part of their course, but they are encouraged to spend some time in Africa, both to practise and improve their language competence, and to conduct research. Opportunities exist for undergraduates to undertake a ten-month grant-supported placement in a development project abroad, under the auspices of Voluntary Service Overseas (VSO). The countries included in this programme include Africa. Those who are successful in obtaining such a placement take a year off between the penultimate and final years of their course.

> "I'm interested in languages and wanted to do something 'different' and something that would be useful in my career — hence Arabic! I spent my second year in Egypt which was a golden opportunity to experience life and culture in a Middle Eastern country. I travelled to Israel and Jordan and stayed an extra year in Egypt . . .
>
> *Undergraduate reading Arabic Studies, quoted in University of Exeter prospectus 2000*"

What are the career prospects?

As with all language degrees, there are no specific careers to which these courses lead. Many graduates find jobs in which they can make immediate use of their linguistic and cultural training, but the majority are found attractive by employers who recruit from the general pool of arts graduates. Thus, graduates of Middle Eastern languages find themselves in banking, accounting, insurance, industry, business, administration, law, teaching, translating and interpreting, or working for such organisations as the Foreign Office, the Ministry of Defence or Amnesty International.

Arabic is one of the world's most important languages, since for cultural, political and commercial reasons the Arab world has become a major force in world affairs. For this reason quite a wide variety of careers is open to graduates of Arabic, and such opportunities may well increase.

Graduates from SOAS's Africa Department have been successful in finding employment in a variety of fields. Former students have, for example, taken jobs in teaching (abroad, or in the UK where skills of multicultural awareness are often an asset) or with non-governmental organisations at home and overseas, like Oxfam, Amnesty International and Save the Children. They have also found work with the BBC, with newspapers, or with journals which specialise in African matters.

Arabic, Middle Eastern and African languages
Checklist
DEGREE COURSES

1 Arabic differs considerably from European languages and is not an easy language to learn — but it is quite accessible provided you are prepared to work hard.

2 Arabic, other Middle Eastern languages, and major African languages can all be studied from scratch to degree level at UK universities.

3 Study abroad is not an automatic component of the courses as it is with degree courses in European languages, but most courses will allow you, or encourage you, to spend some time in a country where the language is spoken.

4 Graduates in these languages go into the usual range of careers open to graduates in any foreign language, but those with proficiency in Arabic are perhaps particularly attractive given the commercial and strategic importance of the Arab world just now.

> See the **Signposts** section to find out which institutions offer which languages.

Linguistics

DEGREE COURSES

Linguistics is a branch of the human sciences and includes the structure of human languages, theories of grammar and meaning, the ways in which humans acquire languages, how language is used in communication, how and why languages change and develop, the psychology and biology of language use, and the relationships between language, culture and society. It can be a fascinating study, providing a very wide perspective — it includes aspects of psychology, sociology, biology, anthropology and philosophy, and can involve anything from abstractions of linguistic theory to the details of electronic circuitry for speech processing. In fact, computers are often used as a tool for various kinds of language analysis.

This may sound massively academic, so, put another way (and to quote from the prospectuses of Bangor, Essex and York universities), linguistics is concerned with trying to find answers to questions like these:

- Why do people from different backgrounds speak differently . . ?
- Is women's language different from men's? How and why?
- What are the different stages through which children go when learning to talk?
- What kinds of language handicap can affect children or adults, and what causes them?
- How can contemporary linguistics contribute to our understanding of the brain?
- What kind of errors do people make when learning a foreign language, and why?
- What goes on in people's minds when they make speech errors like 'tips of the slongue' rather than 'slips of the tongue'?
- Do we learn a second language in much the same way as our first (native) language, or differently?
- Why is it that Urdu and Hindi are regarded as two different languages, despite speakers of one usually being able to understand the other, but Mandarin and Chinese, where one is hardly comprehensible to speakers of the other, are called 'dialects' of a single language, Chinese?
- What's special about the language of advertising?
- What exactly is 'slang'?
- How do the styles of authors differ?
- How do we join words together to form sentences?
- Do different languages do this in different ways?
- Can we describe 'meaning'?
- What should dictionaries tell us about meaning?
- How can we describe the sounds that people produce when they talk?
- What is a 'voiceprint'?
- How do we learn and remember words?
- How is artificial speech produced?
- How can we use computers in the study of language, or to teach languages?
- How can we get computers to use language to interact with people?

If some, or all, of these questions interest you, then you might perhaps consider doing linguistics. It is on offer in more than 30 UK institutions — they are listed in the **Signposts** section — and about half the courses allow you to combine linguistics with another subject. Courses are not always called 'Linguistics' — other names like Applied Languages, Language Studies and Language and Communication are often used.

What are language technology and computational linguistics?

Broadly speaking, these integrate the study of linguistics with the use of information technology. Most linguistics courses deal in some way with the use of computers in the study of language, but some universities, for example the University of Essex and UMIST, make this an important part of their linguistics teaching. The University of Essex has a BA course in Computational Linguistics, for example, which would introduce you to the use of computational techniques in the study of natural language, and an understanding of the problems involved in communicating with machines using natural language.

Can I combine the study of a foreign language with linguistics?

Linguistics is the study of language in general, but it takes its subject matter from a wide variety of languages. The study of linguistics at UK universities and colleges does not necessarily involve foreign languages, but there are very many institutions where linguistics can be studied in combination with a foreign language — and not just European languages (including Welsh at Bangor and Cardiff), but also Arabic, Chinese and Japanese which are available at some universities and of course the School of Oriental and African Studies offers linguistics in combination with many of the wide range of languages in which this institution specialises.

At the **University of York** modern languages are studied only in combination with linguistics. You can do French or German (post 'A' level, or equivalent) and Chinese or Hindi (from scratch). The university operates a modular course structure which is very flexible, allowing you to enrol for a three- or four-year course, and to do Linguistics or a language as a main subject, as a subsidiary subject, or as an equal component of a joint honours degree. You can take up to three languages.

UMIST offers several different courses which combine language technology or computational linguistics with languages. You could study French and/or German, and you could also do Spanish or Japanese as subsidiary languages. There is a specialist course in French or German and Computational Linguistics, too. This is a four-year course, the third of which is spent in a French-speaking or German-speaking university studying computational linguistics in the foreign language; or students may spend this year working in industry or in a research centre.

You can usually expect that courses which have a significant component of modern language study — the four-year courses — involve a period of time spent in the country of the language you are studying. This may not be a whole year.

Does a degree in linguistics prepare me for a career?

If you look again at the list of questions on p71, you will see that the study of linguistics is of relevance in a number of careers, including language teaching, speech therapy, lexicography (the compilation of dictionaries), advertising, natural language processing by computer, and any career where verbal communication is important.

Many linguistics graduates, especially those who have done a foreign language as well, go on to teach languages, and frequently to teach English as a foreign language, either in the UK or overseas.

A knowledge of linguistics is also indispensable for a career in speech or language therapy, and many graduates enter this field eventually, after specialist postgraduate training.

The language industries — companies engaged in translating and interpreting, in language teaching and training for commercial and government organisations, in dictionary compilation and in multilingual publishing, as well as those which are actively involved in using new technology in, for example, the fields of machine translation and software development — find linguistics graduates employable.

In addition, graduates go into a wide range of careers not necessarily connected with their degree specialism — in all aspects of business, industry and government — often in environments where those who are proficient in languages can make use of their expertise.

> Mary graduated in 1993 with a BA (Hons) in French and Computational Linguistics. During her 3rd year abroad she worked on automatic extraction of information from CVs at LERI (Laboratoire d'études et de recherches informatiques), Reims. Her final year project studied how to computationally represent information on French computing job adverts for better search and retrieval.
>
> She now manages international fairs and exhibitions for a major British publisher.
>
> *from UMIST prospectus 2000*

> I was attracted by the flexibility of the degree structure which enabled me to study a wide range of subjects in my first year, so I could take my time to decide which subjects I enjoyed. This is particularly important with a subject like Linguistics, which is new to most people. I was also able to spend a year abroad at a German university . . . I was able to take courses which are now proving invaluable to me in my current job at William Blair. I use German on a daily basis and the 'Description of German' course is a brilliant reference to check against the German I use today. I have also transferred the analytical skills I gained in linguistics to practical use in the world of finance.
>
> *Graduate in German Language and Linguistics (1996), currently working as Financial Analyst/ Personal Assistant to a Partner of William Blair and Company, a US investment bank in London*
>
> *from University of Exeter prospectus 2000*

Linguistics
Checklist

DEGREE COURSES

1. Linguistics is about language and how it works, and combines aspects of several specialisms, such as anthropology, biology, psychology and sociology.

2. Some courses deal with the use of computer techniques in the study of language, and with the problems involved in communicating with machines using natural language.

3. You can combine the study of modern languages with linguistics — not just European languages, but also Middle Eastern, Oriental and African languages as well.

4. A joint course in linguistics and a modern language will normally include a period of time spent abroad.

5. Linguistics graduates go on to work in teaching, speech therapy, and any career where verbal communication is important.

6. They are also employed by companies involved in translating and interpreting, lexicography, multilingual publishing, and other language industries.

7. Courses which involve a significant amount of computing are of relevance to careers in machine translation and software development.

8. Those who are also proficient in modern languages make use of their expertise in all aspects of business, industry and government.

> See the **Signposts** section to find out which institutions offer linguistics.

Section 3

Studying languages with other subjects

Institution-wide language programmes

Languages and business-related subjects

Law and languages

Tourism, sport and leisure with languages

Engineering and languages

Science and languages

IT and computer science and languages

Food science and technology with languages

Agriculture, horticulture and other land-based subjects with languages

Preparing to become a teacher of languages

Institution-wide language programmes

Since 1992 and the creation of a much more unified Europe, students in UK higher education have increasingly come to realise that they will be competing for jobs with equally well qualified graduates from mainland Europe, many of whom have the added benefit of high level foreign language skills. In Holland, for example, children have to study four languages during the compulsory period of education (ages five to sixteen), Dutch, English, French and German, with English starting in the last two years of primary school . . . By the time they reach our equivalent of 'A' level at 18+, Dutch students are expected to be proficient in three foreign languages.

The situation in the UK is very different. First, there has always been much less emphasis even on our mother tongue, English, once the compulsory period of education of five to sixteen is over. Those who study English at 'A' level are a small minority of the age group, and even then most do not concentrate on applied language skills but instead, in the main, have been prepared for literary and cultural studies at university. This neglect of our mother tongue has been accompanied by a similar neglect of foreign languages. At the time of writing, of those pupils who gain a grade A–C at GCSE, only about 30% go on to do an 'A' level in the language. In other words, 70% do not.

The result of these policies is that while in countries such as Holland students reach university with high level language skills, the majority of students arriving at university in the UK have little more than a rusty GCSE, usually in French.

And it is also interesting to compare the compulsory language requirements (see p106) for French engineering undergraduates at the ENPC — where they have to do at least ten language modules — with the experience of similar UK engineering undergraduates.

To their credit, however, UK students are now beginning to take matters into their own hands and ask to be taught a foreign language as part of their course. This has led to the upsurge of institution-wide language programmes, where a range of languages is available, typically at five different levels and often corresponding to those of the *National Language Standards*, published by the Languages Lead Body (Level 1: Beginners; Level 2: roughly GCSE; Level 3: roughly 'A' level; Level 4: corresponding to the first stage of a degree; Level 5: professional competence). What you would be expected to do in reading, writing, listening and speaking is spelt out in detail for each level in the National Language Standards. This means that if you were to take one of these courses and succeeded in passing, say, Spanish at Level 3 in all four skills, any major employer would be aware of what this meant in terms of how well you could cope with using Spanish in a working situation.

Many students take the opportunity of learning a new language from scratch in this way. If you decide to do this, you would be well advised to take the language for two years, so that you reached at least Level 2 performance. Alternatively, you might consider taking your rusty GCSE up to Level 3 — or even Level 4, by which time you would be really flying!

The advantage of this sytem is that, in a well-organised university, you would have the opportunity of adding value to your CV in foreign language skills, irrespective of what you were studying as a main subject. And employers would be quick to recognise this when you went for interview.

Languages and business-related subjects (including accountancy)

Languages can be an asset if you are looking for a job in the world of business. Some companies will even pay more for employees who are able to speak one or more foreign languages, and who have an appreciation of foreign lifestyles. And it is not just senior managers and those who travel abroad on trade missions who need this expertise: in many companies languages are important for employees who work at every level — for transactions over the telephone, for reading and responding to communications by letter, fax or e-mail, for understanding the way of life of potential customers in order to be able to 'target' a product or an advertising campaign, for travel abroad, and for face-to-face communication with foreign colleagues and clients.

Business needs languages. In recent years there has been a fairly rapid increase in the use of foreign languages by British business and industry, and this trend was given a further boost with the completion of the European single market in 1993. Companies have come to recognise that they have to be able to communicate effectively with their trading partners abroad if they are not to be at a disadvantage — not everyone speaks (or wants to speak) English! And it is fairly widely accepted now that if companies want to sell their goods abroad they need to employ people who are able to speak the language of the customer — and not just in the professional context, but also socially as well, since a lot of important business is conducted in a pleasant social context, over lunch or a drink, or in people's homes.

This means that whether you intend to go to work in a business environment straight from school or college, or plan to get some higher qualification first, you should consider any successful language-learning experience you have had as a valuable part of your CV, and a 'selling-point' for you with any future employer. Although companies wish to recruit people with higher qualifications, often degrees, for management posts, they will not always want degree level qualifications in a language — a good working knowledge is often all they require.

Which are the useful languages?

This will vary from company to company according to the countries with which they do business. English remains the most widely used language commercially. Evidence of the relative importance of English can be seen in the amount of money foreign firms put into English language training — for example, in a fairly recent survey (Hagen S, *Languages in European business,* CILT, 1993) it was reported that the German firm Siemens was estimated to spend the overwhelming proportion (75%) of their language training budget on tuition in English.

The importance of English does not mean, however, that if you are English you do not need other languages — nowadays you only really have a commercial advantage if you can speak two or three languages at least. Remember the Dutch business man (mentioned on p7) who could speak six languages, but did not find any of them more useful than the others — he just used whichever of the six gave him commercial advantage at any particular time!

Within the EU, English, French and German remain the main languages of business, with the demand for German progressively on the increase. Spanish and Italian are also important. But these five are not the only languages needed by UK companies — surveys have shown that for companies operating both within the EU and throughout the rest of the world, other languages are useful, and chief amongst them are Dutch, Japanese, Arabic, Swedish, Portuguese, Chinese and Russian.

How can I combine business qualifications with a modern language?

You could well find that a degree or diploma course in a subject like business studies, management science, marketing, advertising, retail management, economics, finance, industrial relations, company administration or secretarial administration, together with further language study, will open doors to some very interesting careers.

There are some business-related courses in which language tuition forms a particularly important part, and which include a substantial amount of tuition and work experience abroad — such courses will have names like European Business Studies or Bilingual Administration.

Well-qualified graduates and diplomates from business-related courses with modern languages are employed by UK companies who have substantial dealings abroad; by foreign companies who have opened branches in the UK or who need English speakers in their offices outside the UK; and by international and multinational companies.

Although important, your languages are not likely to be the major factor in your landing a job in one of the aspects of business. A business-related course and/or some experience of the business world will provide you with suitable qualifications, but the fact that in addition you can understand and speak a language or two could well be that extra deciding factor between you and someone else for the job you are after.

Can I do languages as part of an HND Business Studies course?

Higher National Diploma courses in business and finance are amongst the most popular of all higher diploma courses. They are offered at some universities, at colleges of higher education, and at some further education colleges (usually as part of a franchised agreement with a higher education institution). In some cases it may be possible to take the part-time alternative, the Higher National Certificate (HNC).

Many HND and HNC students continue their studies, once they have successfully completed their course at a sufficiently high standard, by reading for a degree in business-related studies, or by studying towards professional qualifications. Those who choose this option of further study can usually obtain exemptions from the early stages of the degree course or the professional course based on the HND/HNC studies.

As well as providing access to degree study, or exemptions from some of the examinations of professional bodies, the HND/HNC is of course a commercial qualification in its own right, accepted widely as such by employers. Successful students go on to gain employment across a wide spectrum of business activity, including accountancy, banking and finance, management, human resource management, marketing, retail management and sales.

The business and finance course is designed as an introduction to the business environment, its organisations, systems and people. The programme is made up of compulsory core studies which are considered to be essential to the development of a career in business and finance. Together with these there are a number of optional modules which allow you to specialise in areas appropriate to your intended career — for instance, accounting, business law, business psychology, employee relations, European law, financial services, information systems, international banking, international marketing, marketing media, public sector management, purchasing and supply management, quantitive methods, or social policy. You can undertake the practical study of a language as one of your optional modules, either continuing with one you have already learnt, or beginning a new one. The languages most frequently on offer are French, German and Spanish.

In addition to language tuition, arrangements can often be made for students to undertake their work placement abroad.

The optional modules available vary from institution to institution, often depending upon student demand and the specialisms of members of the teaching staff. And the same basic course at different institutions may be called by widely different titles — Accounting and Finance, Business Administration, European Business, European Languages and Business Administration, Marketing, to give just a few examples — depending upon the emphasis a particular institution wants to give the course through the range of optional modules it offers.

What qualifications will I need for an HND business course?

The 'A' level points' score you will need will be somewhere between 2 and 8. The institutions requiring you to get higher grades will probably demand DD or EEE; others may only require one 'A' level pass, together with at least three GCSE passes at grade C or above.

If you are doing a National Diploma in business studies, you would need to have achieved Level 3 in order to proceed to the HND; and if you are doing the Advanced GNVQ you would need to have got Level 3.

Can I include languages with accountancy training?

Although it is possible to make a career in accountancy and finance without an HND or a degree, those who do have these qualifications tend to progress more rapidly in their careers. The majority of those who train to be chartered accountants are holders of degrees (any subject is accepted, provided that you are good at mathematics) or HNDs in business/finance, who then enter three-year training contracts with accountancy practices or other financial organisations.

Opportunities also exist for good National Diploma, GNVQ Advanced and 'A' level (or equivalent) students who then go on to do the accountancy foundation course or the final examination of the Association of Accounting Technicians. Career openings exist at this stage, but the best jobs are reserved for those with chartered status, which would mean getting good results in these examinations (at least a credit in the AAT examination, for instance) followed by a four-year training contract.

You will need to get at least three Cs at 'A' level (or equivalent) whether you choose to get chartered status via the degree/HND route, or the National Diploma/GNVQ/'A' level route. For a degree course some institutions require you to have an 'A' level (or equivalent) in mathematics.

Training to be a chartered accountant can be tough, and you need determination and commitment to get you through the fairly lengthy period of professional training during which you have to combine accountancy studies with a full-time job.

If you plan to enter accountancy via the degree route, and wish to prepare yourself for an international career, you could do a degree in languages or European/International studies, and then go on to your three-year training contract after that. Or you could do one of the degree courses in accountancy (or other finance-related subject) which includes language study. You can find out which institutions offer such a course, and the languages you can do, in the **Signposts** section. A degree in accountancy will normally give you exemption from certain of the chartered accountancy examinations, provided appropriate options have been chosen during the course.

An HND course can also give you certain exemptions from professional examinations, as well as an opportunities to do language options.

If you wanted to do French or German with accountancy you would be well catered for, and Italian and Spanish are available also at a fair number of institutions. Welsh is offered at Aberystwyth, Russian at Bangor, and

Portuguese at Southampton. You would need to check on the amount and the nature of the language work on individual courses, as well as the language qualification you would need on entry — some require an 'A' level in a foreign language, others make less stringent demands. Some courses offer the possibility of study or a work placement abroad.

A finance-related degree course provides a basis for a variety of careers, not just with accountancy practices, banks and the Inland Revenue, but also in business, industry, government or education. Degrees which combine accountancy or another finance-related subject with a foreign language are excellent preparation for working in international finance and business — and some of those which include study at a university in another European country can provide exemptions from professional accountancy examinations in that country.

Can I include languages with secretarial training?

You will probably find that there are secretarial courses at different levels available locally (usually at FE colleges) on which you could choose optional courses in languages (again, usually French, German or Spanish). You can get on to these courses after doing your GCSEs (or equivalent).

If you see yourself working eventually in a responsible administrative capacity, perhaps as a personal assistant to a middle manager or top manager, then you should continue your studies in the sixth form or at an FE college first and go on to a secretarial course after 'A' levels or NVQs. The more advanced secretarial certificate or diploma course you could then apply for would include a comprehensive grounding in administration and the structure of business, and could well include optional language modules.

For example, the RSA Higher Diploma in Administrative Procedures which is available at a number of FE colleges would develop your competence in business communications, personnel management, office administration, financial procedures and information technology. You would also have an opportunity of taking modules in a range of office skills, like word processing, typewriting and shorthand, as well as in languages (usually French or Spanish, with an emphasis on their use in the world of business) either at beginners' or a more advanced level. A work placement is integral to the course, and those institutions which have developed strong links abroad may be in a position to send their students on work placements in the country whose language they are studying.

You would not be limiting your employment prospects to a secretarial career if you chose such a diploma course in administration. There would be other career openings, such as: conference planner, personnel administrator, marketing assistant, office supervisor, advertising assistant . . . and of course, if you could speak languages, your range of employment options could well increase.

If a language does not form part of the course you choose, there are likely to be opportunities for you to study a language in another department of the college, possibly for Institute of Linguists examinations, the most advanced of which require you to have reached a very high degree of competence in a language.

You can get on to an RSA Higher Diploma course with an 'A' level (or equivalent) or an NVQ Level 3 in Business and Finance, but the course is also chosen by some graduates to make themselves more employable by adding useful administrative skills to their degree qualification.

If you want languages to form a very important part of your secretarial/administrative training, then you could consider a bilingual (or even trilingual) secretarial course. Choosing a suitable course is not straightforward, since quite a few such courses are merely courses in secretarial skills with some language tuition included. You need to read prospectuses and course descriptors carefully — the best courses would enable you to acquire important skills like taking shorthand in a foreign language, and might offer you an opportunity to get a basic working knowledge of not just one foreign language, but two or perhaps even three.

If you want to do secretarial studies with French, then there is a special course you could do at the *Collège de Secrétariat Bilingue* which is part of the French government-funded Institut Français in London. There is a two-year course for post 'A' level (or equivalent) students, and a one-year course for graduates.

Would I qualify for a grant for a secretarial course?

A secretarial course does not automatically qualify you for financial assistance from your local education authority to cover your term-time living expenses, your books and travel, etc. However, HND courses and Dip HE courses do qualify for a mandatory grant. If you want to do a 'non-designated' course (broadly speaking, anything other than a first degree, Dip HE or HND) it is worth checking whether you might qualify for a 'discretionary' award. Each LEA acts differently in respect of awarding grants to students on non-designated courses, and you should therefore contact your LEA to find out what you are eligible for before accepting a place on a course.

If you choose to go to a private institution — a private secretarial college, for instance — you cannot expect to receive a grant at all.

I want to do a degree course

Most companies like to recruit graduates as trainee managers, and they do not often specify any particular degree subject — a degree in itself is sufficient proof that you are of the calibre they require. However, graduates from business-related degree programmes have a wide choice of potential employment, and have a good record of success in securing interesting and worthwhile jobs in widely differing fields.

Such programmes will usually allow you to specialise in a particular area in your final year or two, and this can be a help in qualifying for a career — for instance, you might take specific finance options to prepare you for a future in accountancy, banking or insurance; or marketing, personnel management or production specialisations which could lead to work in those particular areas.

Business degrees which include the study of one or more languages are widely available. If you look in the **Signposts** section you will see that there are more than ninety UK higher education institutions which offer you the possibility of doing a degree course in a business-related subject (with names like Business Studies, Business Administration, Management Studies, Management Science, European Business, International Business) plus the study of one or more languages.

In addition, there are twenty-four institutions offering degree courses in accountancy with a language; and thirty-two offering marketing with a language.

What languages are on offer?

French, German and Spanish are very widely available. Other European languages — Italian, Dutch, Portuguese, Scandinavian languages and Russian — can be studied at some institutions. Aberystwyth offers five European languages, including Welsh; Swansea offers six, including Welsh, Spanish and Catalan; Glasgow offers seven, including Czech and Polish; and Hull offers seven, too, including Danish, Dutch and Swedish. Of the oriental languages, Japanese is the most widely available — at eighteen institutions; but you can also do Chinese at a few places; and at the School of Oriental and African Studies you can combine Management Studies with a whole range of different Oriental and African languages. Arabic is also on offer at four institutions.

You can normally expect to be able to study from scratch languages which are not widely studied in UK schools — broadly speaking anything other than French and German. At a number of institutions there are both *ab initio* and post GCSE or 'A' level courses in Italian or Spanish or Russian, to cater for beginners, as well as those who have had the chance to learn them at school.

Would there be an opportunity to go abroad as part of the course?

Those who are studying a language will normally undertake a work placement or a business course in the country where their language is spoken. At a few institutions there are opportunities for those who are not doing a language to get some experience of a foreign business environment and to go abroad to study in a country where English is widely understood, and where a special course is put on for them in English. Countries where undergraduates can go on this basis are Denmark, the Netherlands, Sweden, Norway, Finland, Hungary, Portugal and the Republic of Ireland.

What sort of courses are there?

All courses have their differences and their special features, so you really must do your own research in prospectuses with great care and attention. Just to give you an idea of how courses can differ, here are one or two examples:

The Business School at **Kingston University** has developed a new modern languages and business studies degree course, designed to meet the growing demand for international and European managers. The course offers tuition in key business disciplines as well as in a foreign language (French, German or Spanish). After basic business modules, together with your chosen language in year one, the second-year programme concentrates on international business and statistical methods to which you would add three elective modules chosen from financial management, marketing management, human resource management, operations management, or law. You would also, of course, continue and enhance your language competence in preparation for the third year of the four-year programme which consists of a study exchange in one of Kingston Business School's partner institutions in mainland Europe — these are universities or business schools in France (Paris, Dunkerque, Lille, Nice and Rouen), in Germany (Wiesbaden and Worms), and in Spain (San Sebastián and Zaragoza). There is also provision for students to undertake an optional work placement abroad. The final year consists of a core module in corporate strategy, a dissertation, two business electives, and advanced modules in your chosen language. This course aims to develop a high level of language proficiency, and for this reason a good 'A' level (or equivalent) in your chosen language is required as an entry qualification, even if you are applying through the GNVQ/GSVQ/NVQ route.

The **University of Leeds** provides extensive opportunities for undergraduates doing management or economics with a language to study at a university abroad — in France (Dijon, Lille or Pau), in Spain (Madrid or Santander), or in Germany (Bayreuth). Students studying Japanese, Chinese or Russian have an opportunity of studying overseas, in Japan (Tokyo, Fukuoka, Konan, or Kansia), China (Beijing), Taiwan (Taipei) or the former Soviet Union (Kiev or St Petersburg). Because of the flexibility of the university's modular degree scheme, even students who do not do a language as a part of their timetabled degree course can find the time to study a language at the university's special Foreign Language Teaching Unit which specialises in preparing students for study abroad. A feature of the large School of Business and Economic Studies at Leeds is its substantial overseas connections, which means that the atmosphere is fairly international, with large numbers of students from most countries in the EU, as well as from the US, Canada, China, Malaysia, Singapore, Taiwan and other parts of the world.

The **University of Wolverhampton** offers a degree course in European Business Administration which is designed to provide insights into the way business operates, not just in Britain, but elsewhere in Europe. Undergraduates spend half of year two and half of year four studying abroad at either the Hogeschool Holland in

Amsterdam or the Mercuria Business School in Helsinki, Finland. Year three is a supervised work experience placement year, and the Wolverhampton Business School says it can offer opportunities to work with a company anywhere in the world. The business course is taught entirely in English - even in Holland and Finland - and you study either French, German or Spanish throughout the programme. It is possible to study the language from scratch. One of the advantages of this course is the opportunities it offers to understand how business operates in other countries, through study, mixing with other nationalities and working in global organisations. In addition to a BA (Hons) degree you are able to obtain an equivalent qualification from the foreign institution at which you study.

Another degree programme which gives you an opportunity of getting two qualifications is the course in European Management Science with French at the **University of Kent.** Management science is broadly speaking the application of scientific method to problems of decision-making in industry and other organisations. This university also offers four-year programmes combining management science, or management science and computing, with French, German, Italian or Spanish. The third year is spent studying management science in the country of your chosen language, but only the French option allows you to gain a second qualification — a *Maîtrise* — in addition to the British degree.

Anglia Polytechnic University offers a European Business programme at its Cambridge site which is planned and taught in co-operation with five partner institutions in the EU, situated in France (Clermont-Ferrand), Germany (Berlin and Landshut), the Netherlands (Sittard) and Spain (Madrid). As with the Wolverhampton course, the aim is to produce business graduates with the ability and confidence to work effectively in different cultures and across national borders, and in particular in a European business environment. Important parts of the course, therefore, are the study of a language, an extended period spent studying in one of the partner institutions, and a year's supervised work experience, normally undertaken abroad. Another positive feature, common to all courses which are taught in conjunction with foreign partner institutions, is that classes are given extra stimulus by the mix of students from other countries. Successful students are awarded a BA(Hons) European Business as well as an equivalent qualification from the European partner institution. For the French programme you would need a GCSE or an 'A' level; for the Spanish or German programmes, an 'A' level in German or Spanish.

The **University of East Anglia** offers a four-year degree course in Language with Management Studies, allowing you to take units within the language programme which focus on specialised business language. The languages on offer are French, German, Danish, Norwegian and Swedish. One of the four years is spent on a work placement abroad. There is also a three-year variant of this course for high fliers (you would need an A grade in your chosen language at 'A' level — or a top grade in an equivalent examination). In place of the year's work placement abroad, you spend the second semester of the second year at a university in a country where your foreign language is spoken, with the academic work done there counting towards your final degree award.

If you want to do business studies and acquire a high level of proficiency in Japanese, one of the few courses to choose from is the one at **Cardiff University.** In recent years this part of South Wales has emerged as an area containing the highest concentration of Japanese manufacturing investment in Europe, and in response the university has set up a well-equipped Japanese Studies Centre which provides the focus for courses in European languages and Japanese, Law and Japanese, and Business Studies with Japanese. In the first two years of the Business Studies with Japanese course you would take business studies modules, but nearly two thirds of the time is spent learning Japanese, in order to reach the necessary level to be able to spend your third year studying in Japan. At the end of this period of study in Japan you would go on to a three-month work placement with a

Japanese company. The fourth and final year is spent back in Cardiff where you continue with your business studies, including the study of Japanese management systems.

🔍 Then there are the courses which allow you to concentrate on one particular business specialism, like operational research, human resource management or marketing. The Modern Languages and Marketing course at the **University of Salford** allows you to do two languages (from French, German, Italian or Spanish) together with marketing. The two aspects of the course — languages and marketing — are closely integrated, and therefore the language work you do is specifically geared to a career in an international business market. This is a four-year course, and as part of it you spend a minimum of six months on a work placement in each of the countries where the language you are studying is spoken, thus getting valuable business experience as well as developing your linguistic skills. You would need an 'A' level in at least one of the languages to be studied, but the other one could be studied from scratch (although some previous knowledge would obviously be helpful). Because this is a special course (it is one of the only marketing degree courses at a British university which integrates the study of two languages) the entrance qualifications are high — a likely conditional offer would be in the region of BBB or BBC.

But if you think these grades are a bit more than you are likely to achieve, there are places which will not set such high conditions. Have a look through the relevant sections of the UCAS publication, *The big guide: university and college entrance,* to find courses which might correspond with the grades you have been predicted. You might like to look at some of the modular programmes — at institutions like, for example, Keele, Luton or Oxford Brookes universities, or Cheltenham & Gloucester College of Higher Education, which allow you to put together a business and languages programme to suit you.

What grades will I need to get on to a business degree course?

As we have just seen, some business-related degree courses set very high conditions but, provided that you are going to pass at least two 'A' levels, there is likely to be a course for which you are qualified in terms of examination performance: the 'A' level grades required for a business-related degree course with languages range from AAB to DD/DE, depending upon the institution you choose.

Business-related courses are extremely popular, so your UCAS application form must look good as well, with a well-written personal statement, and positive things said about you in your school/college reference. Some evidence of genuine interest in business can only help, too: perhaps you have had some relevant work experience, or you have taken part in a Young Enterprise scheme.

You will need to be studying appropriate subjects, of course. Most business studies course tutors attach importance to mathematical ability; you will need at least an A–C in mathematics at GCSE, and often an 'A' level (or equivalent). You will also need to check the level of language qualification you need for individual courses.

Private higher education providers

🔍 There are a few independent higher education institutions awarding fully validated degrees. The **European Business School,** London, is one of these, offering degree courses in European Business Administration, International Business Studies, International Management Studies, and International Business and Management. The academic year at the EBS is arranged in two 12-week semesters, so that courses can start in either September or January. Its degrees are validated by the Open University and are taken as full-time sandwich programmes, with a 48-week work placement as the 'filling' in the sandwich. A period of study abroad also forms an important element in all EBS degrees. A very wide range of options is offered, and all courses include one or two languages chosen from French, German, Spanish, Italian, Japanese, Russian, and Mandarin Chinese. It is possible to do a new language from beginner level, although you do not have the full range to choose from in this case — in 1999/2000, for example, the available *ab initio* languages are German starting in September and Spanish starting in January. This is an international college, with a very wide mix of students from all over the world — over 700 per year from over 70 countries — so the range of languages spoken, in addition to those taught, is very wide.

Because of the private nature of the EBS, tuition fees are charged, although if you are a citizen of the European Union, you are entitled to receive a mandatory grant of £920 (at present) towards these, for which you should apply through your Local Education Authority if you are a British citizen. However, this mandatory award will cover only about 10% of your tuition fees, and you are not entitled to any maintenance grant from the local authority or other UK government source. You would, however, qualify for a loan from the Student Loans Company if you had been resident in the UK for three years or more at the time of application. Some companies may offer sponsorship to students whom they consider to be a good future investment; and a number of charitable organisations might offer financial assistance.

Details of company sponsorships are available in a publication called *Sponsorships for Students*, available from:

Biblios PDS Ltd.
Star Road, Partridge Green
West Sussex RH13 8LD
Tel: 01403 710 971

Details of charitable organisations can be found in the *Directory of Grant Making Trusts*, published by the Charities Aid Foundation, as well as in the *Grants Register,* published by Macmillan Press. These are available in most public libraries.

Rotary International offers a variety of scholarships. All applicants must be citizens of a country in which there is a Rotary club. Application deadlines are set by individual Rotary clubs in accordance with the district deadline. For more information contact your local Rotary Club.

The address of the Student Loans Company is:

100 Bothwell Street
Glasgow G2 7JD
Tel: 0800 405 010

Languages and business-related subjects
Checklist

1 Languages can be an asset to anyone looking for a career in business, and can be important at every level of a company — just as much for people who answer the telephone in an office in the UK as for senior managers and sales personnel who go abroad on business trips.

2 Whether you mean to go straight from school to work in a business environment, or whether you intend to get more qualifications first, you should consider any successful language-learning you have had as a key part of your CV.

| 3 | English, French and German are the main languages used for business within the EU, and Spanish and Italian are also widely used; but other European languages, as well as Japanese, Chinese and Arabic, are often needed by UK companies with dealings abroad. |

| 4 | There is a demand for graduates and diplomates from business-related courses, and an additional language qualification could prove an advantage to you if an employer has to choose between you and another similarly qualified candidate for a post. |

| 5 | HND business courses are very popular and provide you with a qualification which will take you into employment, or on to higher education studies or further professional qualifications. They provide opportunities to do some practical language work, and at some institutions you might be able to go abroad on a work placement. |

| 6 | You can prepare for a career in accountancy without a degree or an HND, but you would be likely to progress more rapidly in a career with these qualifications. The ability to speak a language in addition could open doors to posts in international finance and business. |

| 7 | Secretarial courses, both basic and advanced, can include opportunities to do some language work. The best bilingual secretarial courses teach you important skills like taking shorthand in a foreign language. |

| 8 | Business-related degree programmes which include the study of one or more languages are widely available, with French, German and Spanish most frequently on offer. Other European languages, Japanese, Chinese and Arabic can also be studied at some institutions. |

| 9 | If you study a language as part of a business course you can usually expect to go abroad to undertake a work placement or to study. There are also opportunities at some institutions for those not studying languages to work or study abroad, usually in a country where English is widely understood, like Denmark or the Netherlands. |

| 10 | Business-related courses differ widely from institution to institution: some place more emphasis on languages, others on specific business topics; some allow you to do more than one language; some are part of a reciprocal agreement between a group of European universities thus providing a stimulating mix of different nationalities; some enable you to get two qualifications, a British one and a foreign one. To find a course which really suits you it is particularly important to research your courses carefully before making your choice. |

> See the **Signposts** section to find out which institutions offer which languages with degree courses in business-related subjects, accountancy or marketing.

Law and languages

If you are considering a career in the legal profession you will probably already know that there are two branches, and may even have made a tentative decision between them as to whether you want to be a solicitor, or a barrister (in England, Wales and Northern Ireland)/advocate (in Scotland).

Recent changes in the legal profession mean that distinctions between these two branches are becoming increasingly blurred, but it is broadly true to say that solicitors work in general legal practice, whereas barristers/advocates offer specialist services to the legal profession — a bit like the distinction in the medical profession between GPs and specialists/consultants.

In addition to these two 'private practice' career routes, law graduates also pursue careers in other walks of life — for example, in public administration, local and national government, the civil service, the tax inspectorate, the crown prosecution service, the armed forces, social work, banking, accountancy, insurance, industrial relations, estate agency, management, journalism, and with professional bodies, and in many commercial organisations.

Are languages useful in the legal world?

Languages can be a real advantage in many branches of the legal profession. Lawyers who have qualified in the UK can be found working all over the world, and several law firms based in the UK have offices abroad. Obviously, people who work in these situations need to be able to understand, speak, read and write foreign languages.

With the growing internationalisation of business, lawyers who can speak one or more foreign languages, and who have an understanding of the legal systems of other countries, are increasingly being employed in international law practices, and in the legal departments of international and multinational companies. The changes brought about within the European Union now mean that small and medium sized companies, too, and quite small legal practices, are discovering that they need to have access to such specialists. The value to an organisation of employing international law specialists is not only the linguistic expertise they bring to the firm, but also their knowledge and understanding of foreign legal systems.

What is the difference between British and foreign legal systems?

> Within the EU there are two distinct legal traditions — **the Common Law** system which is used in the UK (and is also the basis of international law) and the system derived from **Roman Law** which is used in the other member states. As we move even closer to European integration it will become increasingly necessary, not just for solicitors and barristers, but also for those who advise a whole range of organisations on legal matters, to have an understanding of both systems.

There is also a demand for legal translators, particularly with the European Commission. Those with a qualification in law, allied to the necessary linguistic skills — a perfect command of the mother tongue, a thorough knowledge of a second EU language and a reasonable (at least) knowledge of a third —

would be in a position to apply for such a post. Knowledge of one of the EU's minority languages — Danish, Greek or Portuguese — or of one of the languages of the EFTA countries or Eastern Europe, could mean that you would have an advantage in the job market over those who can only offer the more widely spoken languages.

The importance of trade with the Far East means that there are likely to be openings for Japanese and Chinese speaking law specialists, too, especially in the fields of business, banking and insurance.

Closer to home, legal experts with a knowledge of one of the UK's community languages — Hindi, Bengali, Panjabi, Urdu or Gujerati, for example — are employed as professional lawyers, not just in law practices, but also in such areas as legal aid and immigration, and as interpreters on legal matters to members of multi-cultural communities.

How would I qualify?

Over the last ten years, particularly with the advent of the Single European Market, opportunities have increased for higher education students to combine the study of law with a language. Degree courses at British universities in law and languages, or in European law, are now into treble figures. Many of them offer the possibility of studying abroad, and obtaining qualifications at the foreign institution in addition to a British qualifying law degree.

Every bit as important as the study of a language, if you want a law career, is the opportunity to learn not only English law, but also the legal system of the country whose language you are studying. This combination of language work and legal training is not offered by all the law and languages degree courses which are available in our higher education institutions, and it is therefore extremely important to check course content before making your choice between various courses with very similar titles.

Several of the law and language degree courses give you the opportunity of obtaining a foreign law qualification — occasionally one of degree level — in addition to the degree from the home institution. You must read the prospectus carefully to check on such details, as well as to find out if the courses give exemption from professional law examinations. In general, a Bachelor of Laws (LLB) degree is a qualifying law degree, a Bachelor of Arts (BA) is not; and of course it also depends upon which options you choose on your course, even on an LLB course. There are seven Foundations of Legal Knowledge which are essential components of a qualifying law degree:

- Contract
- Tort
- Criminal law
- Equity and the law of trusts
- European Union law
- Property law
- Public law

You must have covered all of these before you can go on to professional training as a solicitor or a barrister in England and Wales. In some degree courses, the seven foundations of legal knowledge are not compulsory within the course of study, and should you wish to proceed to the vocational stage of professional training, you should be aware that failure to take all foundation subjects within your degree studies will result in a delay of twelve months, during which you would have to make good the omission.

How much language work would I do?

When choosing between law and languages courses, you should also find out how much language work you would be required to do, how much actual language tuition you would receive, and to what extent the study of law and the study of the language are integrated. Would you, for instance, be doing a course consisting mainly of law with some language work tacked on? Or would you be studying some of your law courses through your chosen language, with lectures and tutorials conducted in that language (even at the UK institution)? It really depends upon which sort of course suits you, and upon your own level of language proficiency. But it must be obvious that if you eventually want to practise abroad as a lawyer, or work in the legal department of a firm which has dealings abroad, you will be far better equipped to do so, and far more at ease in your chosen foreign language, particularly in a legal context, if you have spent four years studying law partly through that language.

Many of the integrated courses — courses where the language is frequently used as the medium of teaching — are extremely demanding. A law degree course, in any case, requires a lot of sheer hard work spent in private study, but the courses which offer the four-year study of English or Scottish law together with the study of the legal system of another country, plus language study, often require you to fit the British Law components of the course into a couple of years, instead of the three years that undergraduates on 'pure' law courses normally have, in order that you can spend your two further years abroad studying the foreign law components. You need to be prepared to work hard!

Getting in

Quite apart from the hard work involved, the whole business of studying law is extremely competitive. It is not unusual for a law department to receive in the region of 2,000 applications for about 150 places. The requirements for entry to a law degree course are likely to be around the ABB/BBB level for 'A' level entrants, AAAB/AAABB in Scottish Highers, and about 29–34 points in the IB. Vocational qualifications like GNVQ/GSVQ have not yet gained wide acceptance in some quarters, and if you are currently preparing for vocational qualifications you should check on their acceptability with the department concerned before sending your UCAS application for a place on a law course.

You should also know that many of the law and languages courses admit much smaller numbers of students than single honours courses. There are at present only 18–25 places available per year on the LLB (Law with French or German) course at the University of Birmingham, for instance, compared with the 134 on their ordinary LLB course. The University of Bristol has 2,500 applicants for its law courses, admitting 135 undergraduates for Law, and 10 undergraduates only shared between Law and French and Law and German. However, if you decide to apply for such competitive courses, it may be some consolation to you to know that in several institutions you are automatically considered for a place on the single honours law course if you are unsuccessful in gaining a place on the joint law and languages one — you do not therefore need to use up valuable choices on your UCAS form by specifying both courses.

With places relatively scarce, it follows that entrance requirements are going to be high — usually higher than for single honours law, and you will probably need to get at least an 'A' level grade B (or equivalent) in the language you intend to study, as well.

How can I prepare myself?

In addition to a strong academic reference from your school or college, and a good personal statement on your UCAS form, your own 'profile' needs to be good too: have you taken an interest in the law by visiting courts? By doing relevant work experience, like working in a solicitor's office? Have you spent some time in the country whose language you are hoping to study? Have you taken an interest in its legal system? What have you read? Books on the law? Court reports in the press? Reports of legal issues in both the British and foreign press?

Prepare yourself well for higher education entrance, refer to such things in your UCAS personal statement, and talk about them if you are called for interview. It is important not to rely on a good academic track record alone, but to try to demonstrate that you are a strong and genuine candidate for a place on your chosen course in other aspects as well, because when competition for places is so stiff, even quite excellent candidates are often turned down.

What courses are on offer?

In this section you will find a few examples of the wide range of law and language degree courses offered by UK universities and colleges of higher education. You will find a complete list in the **Signposts** section.

🔍 The **University of East Anglia** offers two LLB courses — Law with German Law and Language, and Law with French Law and Language — both of which are qualifying law degrees. These courses provide a training in English law as well as giving you the opportunity to develop a specialist knowledge of the legal system of Germany or France, together with linguistic studies in German or French. The third year of the course is spent at a German university (Berlin, Marburg, Trier or Hamburg) or a French one (Strasbourg, Tours, Nancy or Lyon).

🔍 At the **University of the West of England,** in Bristol, you can do a European Languages and Law course which prepares you for either a BA degree or an LLB, depending upon whether or not you choose the core subjects which are the essential components of a qualifying law degree. This is one of only a few law courses in the UK which allow you to study two languages (you can choose from French, German and Spanish). In your second year you decide which of your two languages is going to be your main one, and you spend about 36 weeks abroad in your third year in the country of this language, where you would either be studying in the law department of a university or you would be undertaking a work placement with a law firm or the legal department of a business organisation.

🔍 The **University of Warwick** has a four-year European Law course which provides a number of options for study abroad. It enables students with a good knowledge of French or German (or both), or of Italian, to combine an English law degree with studying foreign languages and European Union law. The third year is spent in France (Lille or Bordeaux), Germany (Giessen) or Italy (Siena), depending upon the language you choose to study. There is also a special Integrated Common Programme, which is for students who choose to do both French and German; they spend their third year abroad studying German law and then French law in a tri-national, tri-lingual group with equal numbers of French and German students. The first half of the third year is spent in Germany, the second half in France. At the end of the course, successful students receive not just the LLB but also a certificate or diploma from the foreign universities.

🔍 The Law School at **King's College,** London, offers two law and languages programmes: LLB English and French Law, and LLB Law with German Law. These are four-year courses in which students spend their first two years in London learning English law as well as French or German law. For those studying Law with German Law, the third year is spent learning German law (in German, of course) at the University of Passau, leading to a diploma in German law. The fourth year is spent back at King's. Students on the English and French Law degree spend the third and fourth years in Paris at the University of Paris I studying French law. At the end of their four years they will have both the LLB degree and the French equivalent, the *Maîtrise*. Students on this course can therefore proceed to professional training in either or both countries. King's also has a special arrangement with Humboldt University, Berlin, whereby King's students who have the Diploma in German Law from Passau may study for a special one-year Masters degree in law which offers important exemptions from the German Bar transfer list.

🔍 Several institutions offer courses which enable you to study law in Europe, but language tuition does form a major part of the course. Examples of such programmes are European Legal Studies at the **University of Kent,** and Law with Legal Studies in Europe at the **University of Reading.** These allow you to spend the third year of a four year programme studying in the law department of another European university. You could choose to study either in a country which teaches foreign law in English — such as Denmark or the Netherlands — or if you are fluent in the relevant language you could study in another country of your choice, such as Portugal, or Greece.

What languages could I do?

The languages you can study on the vast majority of law and languages degree programmes are French and German. A few offer Spanish, still fewer Italian and Russian.

If you want to look beyond Europe, you will find there are one or two institutions offering law with Chinese or Japanese.

> At the **University of Leeds,** for instance, there are LLB courses in Law and Chinese, and in Law and Japanese, in which the second year is spent abroad studying law through the medium of either Chinese or Japanese.

> At **Cardiff University** you can do an LLB honours degree jointly in Law and Japanese. The third year is spent at a Japanese university on a programme devised specifically for the visiting Cardiff undergraduates. You are not expected to have studied Japanese before starting the course, and tuition in Japanese is given throughout the four years of the course.

> Japanese, Chinese, and a whole range of African and Asian languages (22 in all), including Arabic, Hindi, Bengali, Urdu, Swahili and Turkish, can be studied with Law at the **School of Oriental and African Studies,** which is part of the University of London. You can do these languages from scratch, but you would need to show some evidence of your linguistic ability, for example by gaining a good grade in a foreign language at 'A' level.

See the **Signposts** section to find out which institutions offer law and languages, and which languages they offer.

What subjects should I choose as preparation?

There are no specified subjects which you should have studied at school or college to prepare you for a law degree course — most subjects are acceptable, including arts, mathematics, science, and social science subjects. If you are taking practically based subjects, however, such as art, design, technology, music or theatre studies, you should seek the advice of the Admissions Tutors before submitting your application. Most law departments do not consider 'A' level General Studies as a qualifying 'A' level, although they will be more than happy if you have done it as an additional subject.

There is no particular advantage or disadvantage in having studied law to 'A' level. Admissions Tutors tend to regard it in the way they regard any other academic 'A' level subject, and it is not necessarily better than any other subject as preparation for a law degree course.

However, you will normally be required to have a good 'A' level grade, or equivalent qualification, in the language you intend to study.

> The **University of Wales,** Swansea, offers six joint law and languages courses — Law with French, or German, or Welsh, or Spanish, or Italian, or Russian. Only the first three of these require you to have an 'A' level (or equivalent qualification) in the language to be studied; for the other three, an 'A' level in any language is a suitable linguistic entrance qualification. Broadly speaking, the same situation exists elsewhere — you can nearly always expect courses with French and German to have an 'A' level (or equivalent) requirement in the language. You may well be able to start a course with another language with much lower linguistic qualifications. Often you will not be required to have any prior knowledge at all of the language to be studied — especially in the case of Chinese, Japanese and Arabic — although you will need to give the Admissions Tutor some guarantee of your ability to learn languages, and a satisfactory GCSE or 'A' level in any language will usually do the trick.

How do I get into a legal career?

The most direct route into a legal career is via a law degree course. Not only does such a course give you exemption from Part 1 of the professional examinations which are an indispensable part of your training, they also give you an understanding of the workings of the law, and a foundation of legal knowledge upon which to build in the early stages of your chosen career.

A law course also provides you with an opportunity of assessing whether the legal profession is the one in which you would want to spend your working life.

Those with a good law degree (usually a 1st or a 2(i)) are entitled to go on directly to professional training, provided that their law degree course has covered the seven essential core subjects (see p89). The majority of degree courses cover these, but if you are in doubt as to whether the course you are applying for is a qualifying law course, you can check by sending for a list of qualifying law degrees from the Law Society (for intending solicitors)

Are all law and languages courses qualifying law degrees?

There are a few which are not. It is particularly important to check course content if you are considering applying for a joint language and law course, rather than a pure law course, although the course prospectus will usually state whether or not the course gives exemption from Part 1 of the academic stage of the professional law examinations (the CPE), and if this is the case you should not need to check further.

If, however, you want to be a practising solicitor or barrister and find that you have done a course that is not a 'qualifying degree', all is not lost — you would then have to do two, rather than just one year of further professional study and training before you could qualify for legal practice.

Must I do a law degree if I want a legal career?

No, a degree course in law is not the only route into a legal career. You can go on to further legal training after graduating in another subject. Normally the next move after graduation for a non-law graduate would be a year's course at an approved law centre, leading to the Common Professional Examination (CPE). The majority of these courses require you to study on a full-time basis, although there are a few part-time or distance-learning schemes available.

Entry to the CPE is very competitive indeed, however, with only about 20% of applicants being successful in gaining a place. But once you have successfully completed your CPE year, you are then in a position to proceed to the vocational stage of training.

Another means of 'converting' a non-law degree into a suitable qualification for entry to professional legal training would be to do a shortened law degree course lasting only two years, instead of three, after you have graduated in a non-law subject. This is an expensive option, however, because the second degree does not qualify for funding, and you would have to find not only your living expenses, but your tuition fees as well.

Does a law degree lead only to a legal career?

No, about a third of law graduates decide not to undertake further legal training after graduating — or they do not get good enough degrees to permit them to do so.

Often students embark on law courses with no intention of entering the legal profession. They choose to study law because it is an intellectually stimulating subject in itself, and one which can be a useful preparation for all sorts of careers. The critical awareness, creative thinking and technical expertise which a law course develops are all qualities which are highly favoured by employers.

Preparing for legal practice . . .

. . . in England and Wales

After academic training, intending **solicitors** enrol for the Legal Practice Course at one of the institutions approved by the Law Society. The course involves one year's full-time (or two years' part-time) academic study, which at present costs between £5000 and £5500. The purpose of the Legal Practice Course is to ensure that trainee solicitors have the necessary knowledge and skills to be able to undertake the work that will be required of them when they go on to the next stage of their vocational training, which is when they have to secure a two years' training contract with a firm of solicitors, so that they can learn all about the work under the supervision of an experienced solicitor.

Intending **barristers** have to join an Inn of Court after they have graduated, fulfil an obligation to dine in the Inn on the required number of occasions over the period of their training, and complete the Bar Vocational Course which is run by a number of approved institutions, and which lasts a year (or two years if you choose to do it on a part-time basis). The purpose of the course is to train intending barristers in the practical skills which will be needed for their work in chambers. On successful completion of this course you can apply to your Inn to be *Called to the Bar*. The final stage is *pupillage* which is usually unpaid and which, in general terms, is the period spent learning to be a barrister under the supervision of a set of chambers (or sometimes two sets of chambers).

You will no doubt have guessed by now that the length of training required to become a solicitor or a barrister can put a great strain on your financial resources. If this is a career route you wish to take, you must also be prepared to go on learning for several years after your academic training, so your motivation and 'stickability' must be good.

As far as finances are concerned, scholarships, grants and other awards are available — but the issue of competition comes in here, yet again, since it is usually the case that there are more applicants for financial help than sources of funding available. Having said all this, however, the rewards of a career in legal practice — when you eventually get there — can be considerable, in both financial and job-satisfaction terms.

It is also possible for non-graduates to qualify as a solicitor by passing a Common Professional Examination or Post Graduate Diploma in Law, but this initially involves becoming a 'MILEX' (a Member of the Institute of Legal Executives), by studying and taking examinations over a period of time — usually four years.

The Law Society and the Bar Council are important sources of advice and information about qualification and careers as solicitors and barristers respectively.

The Law Society
Ipsley Court, Redditch B98 0TD

The General Council of the Bar
(Education and Training Department)
2 & 3 Cursitor Street, London EC4A 1NE

. . . in Scotland

In Scotland the legal system is significantly different from that in the rest of the UK, and the training procedures are therefore different, but just as lengthy.

If you wish to practise as a **solicitor** in Scotland you will normally have to have a Scottish law degree. The next stage is a seven-month postgraduate course in Aberdeen, Dundee, Edinburgh or Glasgow, leading to the Diploma in Legal Practice. The Diploma course has been designed to teach the practical knowledge and skills necessary for the working life of a solicitor. After successful completion of the Diploma of Legal Practice, all intending solicitors are required to serve a two-year post-Diploma training contract with a practising solicitor in Scotland.

However, the Law Society of Scotland recognises that it is not always possible for all intending lawyers to spend three or four years at university. As an alternative, it is possible to qualify for the solicitor branch of the legal profession in Scotland by a combination of the Law Society's own examinations and the Diploma of Legal Practice. A good examination record is essential, because this is eventually taken into account by the universities when considering applications for the Diploma course. In order to be eligible to sit the Law Society's examinations, intending solicitors have to find full-time employment as a pre-Diploma trainee with a qualified solicitor practising in Scotland. The pre-Diploma contract lasts for three years during which time the trainee must cover the three prescribed areas: conveyancing, court work (litigation), and either trusts and executries or the legal work of a local authority. There are seven examinations to be passed before the trainee may proceed to the Diploma in Legal Practice. After this, the route to qualification merges with that of law graduates outlined above. Many of those who qualify in this way are already working in solicitors' firms in various capacities.

If you intend to practise as an **advocate**, you will need to take the same initial route as does a solicitor, including successful completion of the Diploma of Legal Practice, before taking further (unpaid) training with an established advocate — this is called *devilling*.

The Law Society of Scotland, and the Faculty of Advocates are important sources of advice and information about qualification and careers as solicitors and advocates in Scotland.

> The Law Society of Scotland
> 26 Drumsheugh Gardens
> Edinburgh EH3 7YR

> The Faculty of Advocates
> Advocates' Library, Parliament House
> Edinburgh EH1 1RF

... in Northern Ireland

Professional legal training for graduates who want to practise in Northern Ireland is provided by the Institute of Professional Legal Studies at the Queen's University, Belfast. The length of the vocational course is dependent upon whether you would want to become a solicitor or a barrister, and the academic requirement for entry to the course is an approved law degree (but not necessarily a degree from Northern Ireland). Those who complete the course successfully are awarded the Certificate of Professional Legal Studies. This qualifies you to become a solicitor or a barrister — although you must also complete a period of apprenticeship.

Non-law graduates have to do a preliminary two-year course in Academic Legal Studies at Queen's University before commencing their vocational training.

The Law Society of Northern Ireland, and the General Council of the Bar (Northern Ireland) are important sources of advice and information about qualification and careers as a solicitor or a barrister in Northern Ireland.

> The Law Society of Northern Ireland
> Law Society House, 90–106 Victoria St
> Belfast BT1 3JZ

> General Council of the Bar
> (Northern Ireland)
> Bar Library, Royal Courts of Justice
> Chichester Street, Belfast BT1 3JF

Law and languages
Checklist

1. A law degree plus further training can take you on to a career as a solicitor or a barrister (or an advocate, in Scotland). Law graduates also pursue careers in many other fields.

2. Languages can be an advantage in many branches of the legal profession, both in the UK and abroad.

3. Lawyers who can speak languages and who have a knowledge of foreign legal systems are increasingly in demand in international law practices and in the legal departments of multinational, and smaller companies.

4. Legal experts with a knowledge of one of the UK's community languages are employed not just in law practices, but also in legal aid, immigration, and as interpreters on legal matters to members of multicultural communities.

5. There are plenty of degree courses which combine the study of law with one or more languages, many give you the opportunity to study abroad, and some allow you to obtain a foreign law qualification as well as your UK law degree.

6. Competition for a place on a law degree course is likely to be stiff, and probably more so for one which combines law and languages, since these often accept fewer students than single honours law courses.

7. It follows, therefore, that to do a law degree you would need to get high grades at 'A' level (or equivalent), have a good reference from you school/college, and have shown an interest in the law by doing some relevant reading, and perhaps visited courts or done some work experience in a 'legal setting'.

8. There is no specific subject which you should have studied at school/college to prepare yourself for a law degree.

9. The languages most widely available with law are French and German. A few courses offer Spanish, or Italian, or Russian, and one or two offer Welsh, Japanese, Chinese, Arabic or African or other Asian languages.

10. For a law and languages degree you are likely to need a good 'A' level (or equivalent) in the language you intend to study. European languages other than French or German can often be done from scratch or with a good GCSE: and although Arabic, Japanese, Chinese and other African and Asian languages can be done from scratch, you will usually need a good 'A' level in a foreign language.

See the **Signposts** section to find out which institutions offer which languages.

Tourism, sport and leisure with languages

Leisure and tourism are growth industries not just in Britain but internationally. In fact, tourism is already the world's largest employer, with 130 million people employed worldwide.

Britain annually attracts 1.5 million visitors from all over the world and the number of jobs in the tourism, leisure and hospitality sectors have increased dramatically over the last twenty years, with openings for school leavers as well as those with more advanced qualifications.

With so many foreign visitors coming to the UK every year, it is obvious that those who work in tourist-related industries really ought to have some knowledge of languages. Tourism and leisure are concerned with people, and helping them to enjoy themselves — not just with the facilities and attractions which are available. A good service can only really be delivered to foreign visitors if there are people on hand who can understand what they have to say, and are happy to converse with them in their language, and not just in English.

The sector of the UK leisure and tourist industry which has as its customers the increasing numbers of foreign visitors to the UK is coming to realise that in order to compete with other world tourist destinations it must recruit people who can speak to these tourists in their own languages.

How good would I have to be at languages?

Not everyone who works in tourism and leisure needs to be totally fluent — even a small amount of a foreign language can be enormously helpful. It really depends on the sort of job you want to do.

If, for example, you are working as a hotel receptionist, or a waiter or waitress, your non-English-speaking customers will be delighted with any help you can give them when they check in to the hotel, or when they are trying to make sense of the menu. Nothing more advanced than your school French or German is all that is needed to be welcoming and polite, and conduct a simple conversation in a foreign language. You don't even have to be grammatically perfect as long as your meaning is clear. And if the need arose you might even be able to learn some basic phrases in other languages! In general, people are delighted if you make an effort to speak their language, and overlook all sorts of mistakes you might make.

Clearly though, there are other jobs where a higher level of fluency is required. Tour guides, and management and sales personnel who deal with overseas customers need to be much more proficient in their use of languages, and much more accurate. They may also have to look beyond the languages they have learnt at school, and learn new ones, depending upon the nationalities of their customers.

How can I combine a leisure or tourism qualification with a language?

If you want to do a vocational course after your GCSEs there are a number of GNVQ courses available, all of which can allow you the possibility of doing extra optional language modules. These courses will usually be offered by FE colleges, and the languages you are able to do will depend on what each one can offer. French and Spanish appear to be the languages most widely available.

If you didn't do too well at school but have nevertheless achieved adequate standards in English and mathematics, the GNVQ Intermediate in Leisure and Tourism covers the basics of the leisure and tourism business. It can take you on directly to a leisure- or tourism-related job, but it will also provide progression to a GNVQ Advanced or a National Diploma in Leisure and Tourism. The GNVQ Intermediate is available quite widely in some, but not all, sixth forms and FE Colleges; you will have to check on availability with your local institutions. The standard programme does not include languages, but at many places language study is available as an additional unit.

The next level up, the GNVQ Advanced in Leisure and Tourism, covers essential aspects of the world of business in the context of the leisure and tourism industries. The course introduces you to specialist aspects of these industries and gives you an opportunity of obtaining additional qualifications, including languages. You can also make your GNVQ fit your own personal requirements by choosing specialist options, depending on what options your institution is able to mount. At some places it is possible to do options in Outdoor Pursuits (mountain climbing, canoeing or sailing), Marine Leisure (yachting, power boating), Horse Studies (stable management, learning to teach riding), Sports Studies, or Environmental Conservation. If you want to do a language option you should be able to build on your GCSE modern language(s), but there are usually opportunities to start a new language from scratch, too.

The GNVQ Advanced is a blend of the academic and the vocational, and is regarded as broadly equivalent to two GCE Advanced levels. It can therefore be used as a vehicle for progression into higher education. Qualifications for entry to a GNVQ Advanced are laid down by individual institutions, but, in general, to get on to a course you will need a GNVQ Intermediate, or a First Diploma or Certificate in Leisure and Tourism (or a related area) at a suitable level; or four GCSEs at grade C or above.

Similar qualifications can take you on to a National Diploma or Certificate course in aspects of Leisure and Tourism. The National Diploma is specifically linked to the workplace and important components of the courses are work-based assignments. Courses are widely on offer in post-16 institutions throughout the UK. You can do optional language modules at a variety of levels which are geared in their content to a career in leisure and tourism.

Can I do languages as part of an HND/HNC leisure- or tourism-related course?

Yes. Languages are available as part of Higher National Diploma and Certificate courses at very many colleges and universities throughout the UK. In general, the languages most commonly taught at school are available — French, German and Spanish, for instance — and often Italian as well. Languages other than these are occasionally on offer, and can be done from scratch.

There are HND/HNC courses in Leisure Management — all broadly similar, but with a variety of names, like Leisure Studies, Leisure and Recreation, Leisure Leadership, Promotion and Events Management . . . depending upon individual institutions and the bias they give to the course through the options they can offer. The programme links studies in leisure provision and planning with business management, and includes work- related tasks. There is at least one work placement on which students have paid employment in the UK or overseas in positions ranging from travel couriers to leisure centre instructors. Students are usually encouraged to undertake a language, and at some places opportunities exist to study part of the programme abroad. There are often opportunities to undertake coaching and other technical awards during the course.

If you are good at sport and wish ultimately to work in the world of sports science, leisure, or the health and fitness industry there is a HND/HNC in Sports Studies. This combines the theoretical study of sports performance, coaching and management, with the development of your own personal sporting or athletic skills. Again, it is possible to do a language module as an optional extra.

HND/HNC courses in tourism or travel and tourism also have a strong business core, and are often called 'Business (Tourism)'. In addition to gaining practical business and management skills (such as financial interpretation, marketing and information technology) you would be encouraged to develop the personal skills and qualities demanded by the tourist industry. You would usually be able to do at least one language, and possibly go on overseas visits and residential activities in popular tourist destinations like the Mediterranean and Eastern Europe. The course will also include at least one paid work placement with a tourism organisation in the UK or overseas, in positions which range from working as travel couriers to undertaking market research.

What are the employment possibilities from these diploma courses?

There are good career opportunities for those with a leisure-related HND/HNC. Leisure is a youthful industry where career advancement can be rapid for those with a management qualification. Opportunities exist in sports development and administration, planning, entertainment and the arts, conference and exhibition management, leisure centres, tourist attractions, outdoor pursuits and the public sector. And a qualification in a language can only enhance your career prospects, particularly if you want to work abroad or in a part of the country which attracts foreign tourists.

The business and management perspective which a travel and tourism course gives you is of relevance to any business-related career. More specific career opportunities exist in tour operations, planning, tourism marketing, transport, conference and exhibition management, visitor attractions, and the arts and entertainment. As with leisure, tourism tends to attract young personnel, and therefore opportunities exist for fairly rapid career advancement provided that you have the relevant skills — proficiency in languages amongst them.

Are there jobs for those with degrees?

Yes, there is a growing demand for graduates to join junior management grades in both leisure management and tourism management. Graduates have found that it is easier to get these management jobs if they have had a tourism, sports or recreation element in their degree — although, of course, a general business-related course is very relevant, too.

Those with a sports and recreation bias in their course frequently go on to the management of all sorts of leisure-related businesses, like leisure centres, cinemas, betting shops, stately homes, outdoor pursuits centres or theme parks; or on to posts in the public sector, in a local authority recreation department, for instance.

For those who have specialised in travel and tourism, there are openings with travel agencies and tour operators. Here it may be a question of starting out in a basic post, but there are good opportunities for fairly rapid advancement to management level.

However, whilst the leisure and tourist industries might seem the most obvious potential employers, as with diploma courses, the general business knowledge and managerial skills acquired on leisure and/or tourism degree courses are relevant to many different careers in business, management and administration.

And if, as well as having business expertise, you can also understand and speak a language or two, then not only will you be employable by organisations in the UK who deal with foreign tourists or who want to market their services and facilities abroad, you will also be eligible to look for employment overseas.

What degree courses are there in leisure and recreation with languages?

Many leisure, recreation and sports science degree courses provide opportunities for you to study a language as an option on the course, or as an extra course at the institution's Language Centre. There are several courses, however, where a language forms a more important part of the course, or where the institution's courses are all designed within a modular structure whereby you can put together two subjects, for instance a leisure- or sports-related course with a language.

At the **University of Wolverhampton** you can do a combined degree linking Leisure Management, Exercise Science or Sports Studies with French, German, Russian, Spanish, or Latin American Studies in a major/minor combination — the language can be either the major or the minor subject — or as two joint subjects. It is also possible to do Italian Studies, Japanese Studies, Russian Studies or Spanish Studies, but as a minor subject only. You can even do three joint subjects, chosen from the very long list of possible subjects at this university. The combined degree programmes normally last three years, but if you do French, German, Russian, Spanish or Latin American Studies the course lasts four years because you also spend a year abroad in a country where the language you are learning is spoken.

The University of Birmingham awards a Leisure Management degree which is taught at **Birmingham College of Food, Tourism and Creative Studies**. The course has an international focus, and students have the option of studying French, German, Spanish, Italian or Dutch. Residential visits are incorporated in the three year programme, with an optional outdoor adventure activity in the first year and opportunities to go abroad in years two and three. At the end of the summer term and in part of the summer vacation in your first year you would do a three month industrial placement in the UK or overseas, probably with a travel company or a leisure centre.

What degree courses are there in travel and tourism with languages?

Just about all tourism-related degree courses have language study as an option. There are some institutions — those listed in the **Signposts** section — where language study forms a significant part of the programme.

As an example, at the **University of Central Lancashire** (in Preston) you can study for a degree in Languages with Tourism which places the emphasis on languages. You study two languages (chosen from French, German, Spanish, Italian, Japanese or Chinese) in your first two years, together with modules in Tourism. You spend your third year abroad on a work or study placement, and return to Preston to continue your studies in your fourth year. You study one language as your main language and for this you would need an 'A' level pass. Your second foreign language may be taken post 'A' level, post GCSE or from scratch. You do not need any prior knowledge of tourism.

The **University of the West of England** in Bristol offers a four-year course leading to a degree in European Business Studies with Tourism which provides a business education for those students who want to pursue careers in the tourist industry. One language is studied (from French, German or Spanish) with the emphasis firmly on the sort of language needed for business. The third year of the course is spent at a higher education institution in France, Germany or Spain, with about four months of the year spent getting first hand experience in a foreign business organisation.

At **Buckinghamshire Chilterns University College** there are three-year vocational degree courses in Hospitality Management, Travel and Tourism Management, and Tourism, all of which may be studied with a language (French, German, Italian or Spanish) as a minor part of the course. The courses combine both practical and theoretical elements and the Travel and Tourism Management course allows you to gain work experience in the tourism industry before starting your career and to spend some time studying abroad.

What grades will I need to get on to a degree course in tourism, or sport and leisure with a language?

Conditional offers in terms of GCE 'A' level are in the range BB to DD for travel and tourism with a language, with the majority around CC/CD; and for leisure, sport and recreation with a language at some institutions you could be set as high as BBB/BBC, at others as low as DE, with the majority around the middle of the range at CC/CD.

One of the 'A' levels might have to be in a language, but it really depends on which language you do, and the level at which the language study is pitched. No prior knowledge of tourism or leisure is required, but for the courses with a strong business element, good ability in mathematics can be an advantage; and for a course with a substantial physical education component you would not need to be particularly good at sport (although it would help!) but you would have to be prepared to take a full and active part in practical sessions, and have a genuine interest in sport — as part of the course you would probably be encouraged to take coaching and proficiency awards.

Tourism, sport and leisure with languages
Checklist

1. Leisure and tourism are growth industries and there are career opportunities for school leavers as well as those with more advanced qualifications.

2. Britain is a major tourist destination and there is a need for those who work in tourist-related industries to be able to understand and speak other languages.

3. The level of language proficiency required varies from job to job: in some jobs it helps if you can speak a foreign language just a little, while in other jobs you might need to be much more fluent and accurate.

4. There are post-16 vocational courses in leisure and tourism on offer, mainly in FE Colleges, which would give you the possibility of doing optional modules in foreign languages.

5. French, German and Spanish, and sometimes other languages are available as part of Higher National Diploma or Certificate courses in sport and leisure, or tourism.

6. There are good career opportunities for those with a leisure- or tourism-related HND/HNC, and promotion for young entrants to these careers can be rapid.

7. There is a growing demand for graduates in leisure and tourism management; and those with degrees in these areas of study also use the general business knowledge and skills they have acquired in careers in other aspects of business and management.

8. Optional language study is possible on very many degree courses in these vocational areas, and there are a few degree courses which offer the study of languages as a significant part of the programme.

> See the **Signposts** section to find out which institutions offer degree courses in travel and tourism, education, sports science or leisure studies with a language.

Engineering and languages

Engineering is about putting science to practical use. Engineers would say that their subject is both a science and an art, and that it requires a combination of imaginative, technological, management and business skills. Basically it involves translating ideas into design and then making something from that design. Nowadays engineers also concern themselves with achieving quality at an acceptable cost, and maintaining or improving the environment.

'Engineering' is an umbrella title covering several branches of the profession, which include:

- aeronautical and aerospace engineering;
- chemical engineering;
- civil and structural engineering;
- electrical and electronic engineering;
- materials science and metallurgy;
- mechanical and production engineering;
- mining and minerals engineering.

In addition you may come across engineering courses with titles like Robotics . . . Astronautics . . . Risk Management . . . Microelectronics . . . Information Systems Engineering . . . Mechatronics . . . Textile Technology . . . Automotive Engineering . . . Manufacturing Systems . . . and so on — all of them connected with one of the types of engineering listed above.

You can also combine aspects of several different branches of engineering by doing a general engineering or integrated engineering course. This is useful for some engineering careers because modern industry is demanding a new type of engineer capable of making decisions about systems which cross the old boundaries between engineering disciplines.

What degree would I get?

There are basically three sorts of undergraduate degree awarded by university engineering departments:

- Bachelor of Engineering (BEng);
- Master of Engineering (MEng);
- Bachelor of Science (BSc).

The BEng is a three-year (or four-year sandwich) course; the MEng is a four-year (or five-year sandwich) course — usually the BEng course plus an additional year — and more often than not involving industrial training as an integral part of the course. Occasionally the MEng programme is a five-year full-time course. The MEng programme used to be aimed at potential industrial high-fliers, but now many universities are moving to a four year course as the norm for engineering courses, which means that in the future most engineering undergraduates are likely to spend four years studying for an MEng degree, with the option of leaving after three years with a BEng.

The BSc degree is intended largely for those students who wish to apply their engineering skills in the fields of business and commerce, rather than become professional engineers.

Can I do a diploma course in engineering?

Yes. Many of the new universities offer a range of Higher National Diploma (HND) courses (and Higher National Certificate (HNC) courses) in engineering.

The HND in engineering is a two-year full-time (or three years with a sandwich year at work) programme providing higher education and practical training in the following branches of engineering:

- software;
- electrical;
- electronic;
- aeronautical;
- mechanical;
- motor vehicle;
- communications.

Although there are advantages in doing a degree course because this is the usual route to becoming a professional engineer, and to achieving chartered status, Higher National Diploma (HND) courses provide you with higher education and practical training in one or more of the engineering fields. Diplomates from these courses gain employment in a wide range of posts as, for example, test engineers or design engineers; they engage in research and development as engineering technicians; or they may even start up in business on their own. More than half of them use their diploma as a qualification to enter an honours degree course at second year level, usually at the same institution.

If you do an HND course in engineering you will find that whereas you may be unable to study a language as a major part of your course, you will very likely be able to study a language at your university as part if its policy of offering language-learning opportunities to all their students (see 'Institution-wide language courses', p77). There are a few diploma courses which provide for the optional study of a language — usually French or German, and you may also be able to go on an industrial visit abroad — France and Germany being the most usual destinations.

Do engineers need languages?

Yes, languages are important for engineers. This is because engineering has become international, and if you have decided to enter one of the many branches of engineering it is very possible that you will one day find yourself working for a multinational company or for a firm which has connections abroad. You would need to be able to communicate with employees at all levels, not only in the context of your work as an engineer, but also in a whole range of social situations. It would also help you to have some knowledge of foreign countries and other cultures, so that you could interact more effectively with your colleagues and gain more readily an appreciation of the culture in which you would be working, and the market in which you would be selling your products.

Engineering companies are on the look-out for professional engineers with linguistic skills. In a fairly recent survey conducted by the *Export Times*, Professor Stephen Hagen, who coordinated the survey, comments:

> *Exporters tell me that they don't want specialist linguists, but people with skills such as **engineering** and law who also **have a grasp of languages**.*

We are not talking about brilliant linguists here, but engineers who can communicate effectively in a foreign language and who are able to accept and appreciate lifestyles which may be completely different from their own.

Even engineers who work in the UK find that they get to use their languages. One Design Engineer who graduated from an Engineering degree course which included study in France has found that:

> " I regularly translate articles of interest to my company from French into English, and the technical knowledge gained during the year abroad has been found to be useful. An ability to look at a problem from the French point of view as well as the British is very useful.
>
> . I hope to be 'let loose' on foreign clients as soon as I am chartered! "

Companies in continental Europe are actively seeking engineers with multi-national education. Such engineers are valuable to a company because not only do they have a grasp of languages, they also have an understanding of engineering practices in other countries.

Our European partner countries are well aware of the need for engineers to be able to use languages in their work. One UK student from Southampton University who went to Paris as part of his MEng course to study at the prestigious higher education institution for Civil Engineering, the *Ecole Nationale des Ponts et Chaussées* (ENPC), found this:

> It is impossible not to miss the multi-national make-up of the ENPC. Up to half a dozen languages may be heard being spoken at any given moment in the cafeteria, with French, Spanish, Arabic and English (the Masters degree in International Business for Engineers is conducted entirely in the English language) featuring prominently.
>
> A French student studying for his or her degree at the ENPC has to take at least ten language modules. All languages are taught by native speakers, who constitute the quite substantial language department within the school. As a result of all this support the average student has, not surprisingly, a much better grasp of foreign languages than his or her UK counterpart and is more willing to 'have a go'.
>
> The students' familiarity with foreign languages and culture gives the school a very international flavour, especially since many students intend to seek work abroad . . .

Engineering is in fact one of very few professions to have a qualification which is recognised throughout Europe. The federation of engineering bodies from European countries — the *Fédération Européenne d'Associations Nationales d'Ingénieurs* (Feani) — awards the title of European engineer (Eur Ing) to suitably qualified chartered engineers. These are letters which are used before your name (like Dr) rather than after it like a degree qualification. You can apply for Eur Ing status once you have achieved chartered status (CEng) — your degree plus two or three years practical training and experience will enable you to register as a chartered engineer with the Engineering Council.

It is expected that the majority of professional engineers will have undertaken degree courses.

Further information on chartered status and other qualifications can be obtained by writing to the Engineering Council at the address given in the Address List.

What languages could I do?

If you want to combine a language with engineering, you now have a huge choice of different degree and diploma courses, and a range of different languages — not just French and German (although these are the more common languages on offer with engineering), but Italian, Spanish, Russian and Japanese as well. And even if you choose an engineering course which does not include language tuition, many universities will give you an opportunity to improve upon a language you learnt at school, or to learn a new one, as well as to spend a year abroad as an approved part of your course.

The **University of Nottingham** offers 'with language' versions of its Electrical and Electronic Engineering degree programmes, with a choice of three languages — French, German or Spanish. Students taking the language option usually spend year 3 abroad. There is also a European option where students undertake a project in a selected European country during the second semester of the third year. Nottingham also offers French, German, Japanese, Russian or Spanish as part of its BEng/MEng courses in Manufacturing Engineering and Management, and Mechanical Engineering, as well as the BSc course in Production and Operations Management. At the time of writing this there was the likelihood of their also offering Italian for the year 2000 intake with Manufacturing Engineering and Management, and with Production and Operations Management, but this had yet to be confirmed. The language entry requirement for all these courses is a GCSE in the language to be studied, except in the case of Japanese, which is taken *ab initio*.

In addition, several institutions have courses which are called *European* Engineering, Engineering with *European Studies* or something similar, or have *a Year Abroad* or *Study in Europe* as part of their title. These offer the possibility of spending a period of time abroad, usually a whole year, at a university or industrial establishment in another European country, prepared for by language study as part of your course, or on a voluntary basis in your university language centre.

🔍 For example, at the **University of Manchester** there is a an integrated European degree programme — a four-year course in aerospace, civil, electrical or mechanical engineering which includes a period of study — your third year — at a university abroad undertaking project work, an industrial placement, and language and cultural studies. The countries involved are France, Germany, Italy, Spain and Sweden; and in the case of electrical engineering there are also opportunities to study in Japan, Singapore or the USA. In Sweden, Singapore (and of course the USA!) the tuition is in English, but in the other countries you would be expected to understand and speak the language. Language tuition is given by the University of Manchester, and although a language can be studied on the basis of 'no prior knowledge', a GCSE pass would give you a better basis upon which to proceed — a good reason to keep your GCSE foreign language going!

The range of countries in which you can study on this basis is burgeoning: most higher education institutions in the UK have links with at least one other higher education institution in each of a whole range of other European countries (not just the EU), and many have links with other countries beyond Europe as well.

🔍 For instance, the **University of Bristol** provides opportunities for students to study in continental Europe as an optional component of its engineering courses. As far as possible you take the same classes as you would if you were a member of the host institution. The overseas period is normally the third year, and language classes are available to you in your first two years, if necessary. The majority of undergraduates go to France or Germany to study, but the university has exchange partner institutions in a number of other mainland European countries.

🔍 The **University of Southampton** offers a four-year MEng course with European Studies which combines degree studies in engineering (choose from Aeronautics and Astronautics, Aerospace Systems, Civil, Environmental, Computer Systems, Electrical, Electromechanical, Electronic, Acoustics, Mechanical, Ship Science . . .) with language work and the study of European politics, economics and law together with a working knowledge of European engineering practice and business. The fourth year of the course is spent at a European university — Paris, Strasbourg, Grenoble, Karlsruhe or Stuttgart — preceded by ten weeks' industrial training (normally in the foreign country). The same university also has a five-year MEng degree with Tripartite Diploma in Electronics on which you could spend two years in continental Europe — one in Germany (at the University of Karlsruhe) and another in France (at the *Ecole Supérieure d'Ingénieurs en Electrotechnique et Electronique,* Paris). If you wanted to do one of these courses you would need at least a good GCSE, and more likely an 'AS' or 'A' level in your chosen language, in addition to the required maths/science 'A' level (or equivalent) qualifications.

Many higher education institutions have modularised their courses, making it easier for students to 'pick and mix' from a menu of course modules in order to construct for themselves a diploma or degree programme which will suit their individual needs. This sort of credit transfer arrangement can make it easier to include a language in your programme of study.

🔍 There is also a European Course Credit Transfer Scheme (ECTS) which enables students to accumulate credits towards their degree in different EU countries. The **University of Glasgow** is one institution where the Engineering faculty has developed close ties under this scheme with a number of other European Union partner institutions. Undergraduates in the department of Mechanical Engineering are encouraged to take a planned year of study at one of these partner universities. The MEng degrees offered by the same university's department of Electronic and Electrical Engineering incorporate a six-month period working on a technical project in a European company. This provides a valuable opportunity to gain direct experience of European industry, fluency in a foreign language, and an introduction to industrial management techniques.

🔍 You really do need to do your research for a course properly and consult prospectuses for individual institutions or you might miss something good. There are many engineering courses available which do not advertise the fact that they are 'European' or 'with a language', but which do nevertheless send their undergraduates abroad. There are established relationships existing between higher education institutions right across the EU, and these provide the basis for exchange arrangements and international co-operation. For example, the **University of Brighton**'s exchange arrangements with French and German higher education institutions provided these graduate Engineers with a valuable experience:

> The year studying at IUT [Institut Universitaire de Technologie], Reims in France was demanding, but to spend a year in a different culture was a great experience which I would not have wanted to miss.
>
> . . . Brighton has an exchange scheme with Mainz in Germany and during my time at Brighton I went on visits and helped with the exchange seminars. After graduation I applied to join the staff of the Civil Engineering department in Mainz and now teach computing and geotechnics.
>
> It's fascinating to be working in a different culture . . .
>
> *University of Brighton departmental prospectus for Civil & Environmental Engineering 1995–96*

Getting in

For degree courses, if you are doing 'A' levels, you are likely to have to get 'A' level passes in maths and physics — and probably three 'A' levels (or two 'A' levels and two 'AS') altogether. For language options you will probably need at least a good GCSE in a foreign language, and often an 'A' level in the language you want to study. The grades you will need will vary from institution to institution.

If you are studying for other qualifications, like the European Baccalaureate or the International Baccalaureate, you will need to get a total score of at least 24 points, often more, including higher level passes in maths and physics. Some universities may prefer you to obtain a pass in 'A' level maths as well.

Those with Scottish qualifications will need four Highers including maths and physics/technological studies, and will often need the Certificate of Sixth Year Studies (CSYS) as well.

If you are preparing for vocational qualifications — Advanced GNVQ, GSVQ Level III or a National Diploma in a subject area appropriate to engineering — you are likely to have to get merits and/or distinctions in some or all of your units. Sometimes the university also requires an additional qualification, like an 'A' level or 'AS' pass in maths. If you are doing GNVQ/GSVQ/ND it is advisable to check with the institution you are interested in.

For HND courses the normal **minimum** qualifications for admission are:

- four GCSE passes including one at 'A' level; or
- a Scottish certificate of education with passes in five subjects of which two are at higher grade; or
- a National Certificate or Diploma; or
- an Advanced GNVQ or a GSVQ Level III in an appropriate subject area.

I would like to do engineering with a language, but I haven't done maths and physics

If you are not studying maths and physics for your 'A' levels (or equivalent qualification) but on reading this think you might like to do an engineering degree course, don't despair! Because of the demand for graduate engineers some universities provide opportunities for those who have good grades in maths at GCSE (or equivalent) but with 'A' level or other qualifications in subjects not normally appropriate for engineering, to convert to an engineering course.

For such applicants there are engineering degree schemes which commence with a **Foundation Year** designed to lead on to the first year programme of a BEng, MEng or BSc course. During this Foundation Year you would acquire the essential grounding for further engineering study, covering core mathematics and physics and being introduced to engineering concepts. After this, you would proceed to the first year of a degree course.

Engineering and languages
Checklist

1	Engineers need languages. Engineering is an international field and, for those who go to work abroad, a knowledge of the language as well as an understanding of the country and its culture are important.
2	Engineering companies are on the look-out for engineers who can communicate effectively in a foreign language — not necessarily highly competent linguists.
3	There are plenty of degree and diploma courses for you to choose from if you want to combine a language with the study of engineering.
4	French and German are the most common options available, but you can also find courses with Italian, Spanish, Russian or Japanese.
5	Some degree courses which do not have a language component nevertheless offer the possibility of spending time abroad, either studying or on a work placement. You would need to be reasonably proficient in the language required, but the university language centre would be able to give you the necessary tuition.
6	The usual route to becoming a professional engineer is via a degree course, but an HND course would provide you with a qualification which can take you into a job as a test engineer or a technician, for example, or qualify you to transfer to the second year of a degree course.
7	You will need to have 'A' level passes in maths and physics to get into an engineering degree course, but some universities offer a Foundation Year so that those who have not studied these subjects can 'convert' by studying the essentials before going on to the first year of the degree programme.

> See the **Signposts** section to find out which institutions offer which languages with engineering degree courses.

CiLT

Science and languages

The term 'science' embraces a wide range of subjects, all of them related in some way to one or more of the science subjects you will have had an opportunity of learning at school. So your 'A' level (or equivalent qualification) in biology, chemistry, physics, geology or psychology could take you on to degree or diploma level study in that subject, but it could also open the door to courses in other related sciences.

All of the sciences mentioned above can be combined with a language at a significant number of institutions, and if you look in the **Signposts** section you will see that there are also opportunities to combine language study with study in other scientific fields like astrophysics, environmental science, physical science, biochemistry, microbiology, life sciences, plant science, marine biology, freshwater biology, zoology, anatomical science, genetics, pharmacology, physiology and neuroscience.

You can also combine a language with agricultural science, horticulture, food science or sports science. Courses in these areas are dealt with elsewhere in this publication — see 'Agriculture, horticulture and other land-based subjects with languages', 'Food science and technology with languages', 'Tourism, sport and leisure with languages' and the related **Signposts** sections.

A science background, particularly in mathematics and physics, is a preparation for engineering courses, and most computer sciences courses require a mathematics and/or science background, too. If studying a language with one of these two scientific areas interests you, you should consult 'Engineering and languages' or 'IT and computer science and languages', together with the related **Signposts** sections.

Do scientists need languages?

Yes, scientists do need languages. Many travel and work internationally for multi-national organisations, or for companies which sell goods abroad. International collaboration goes on in scientific research, and such collaboration is openly encouraged amongst EU member states. So the ability to understand another language, and to communicate with other scientists in their own language, can be highly advantageous, whether you plan to work as a pure scientist, or in a commercial capacity. There is a growing demand from employers for well-qualified people, particularly graduates, possessing foreign language skills.

> Many practising scientists work and travel internationally; and so fluency in a second language is often very valuable in terms of career prospects . . .
>
> Having an international dimension to your studies can be very valuable . . . We have found that students who spend part of their programme abroad return with greater confidence, generally obtain a higher class of degree, and find it easier to secure interesting jobs after graduation.
>
> *University of Sussex prospectus 2000*

Sussex is one of many higher education institutions which offer the possibility of combining the study of a science subject with a language for degree level study. Some other institutions which do not offer a significant amount of language study, nevertheless offer the opportunity of spending some time during the degree course studying at a university or working on an industrial placement abroad. In the **Signposts** section you will find that there are two tables dealing with science degree courses, one devoted to combined science and languages courses, the other to 'study abroad' courses.

Can I do languages as part of an HND science course?

As a nationally recognised course, an HND (or HNC, if you want to study part-time) in one of the branches of science is well accepted by industry for the training that it provides for those who want to be professional technicians.

Higher Nationals provide a broad programme which includes the fundamental scientific knowledge required for the area you are interested in, and more specialist studies which are introduced into your programme through a menu of options. One of these options could be a modern language. Because these courses concentrate on the applied and vocational aspects of science there is also an industrial placement included in the programme.

HND courses are quite widely available; HNC courses less so. By no means all the institutions which offer Higher National programmes offer them in the whole range of sciences — some might do a Chemistry one, another Environmental Science, yet another Applied Physics . . . Some will concentrate on a specific subject area through the options they choose to offer on their course, so that at individual institutions you will find specialist science courses with names like Environmental and Geotechnical Studies, Coastal Zone and Marine Environment Studies, Science (Medicinal and Cosmetic Products), Science (Polymer Technology), Science (Dental Technology), Clothing Technology and Manufacture, Observational Astronomy and Instrumentation . . . Because these specialist courses are scattered right across the country the easiest way of finding a course which will suit your own particular interests would be to access the information through one of the computerised database, which you will probably be able to use in your school/college careers centre or your local careers office.

You will find these courses at some universities and colleges, but many of the courses have been franchised out to FE colleges and specialist FE/HE colleges so you might do part of your course at a different institution.

HND/HNC courses have a strong technical and applied emphasis, and can take you straight into a career in, for example, a technical or research-related post in one of the science-based industries, or as a sales representative or sales engineer perhaps. In some cases an HND/HNC can lead on to a science degree, particularly in the institutions where the course is planned in conjunction with a BSc degree in the same subject area, and where much of the syllabus (the first year in particular) is common to both courses — if you did well enough you would therefore be able to transfer to the final stage of the degree course after your two years on the diploma, or even perhaps into the second year of the degree at the end of your first year.

Can I combine a language with a science degree?

With the increased opportunities for science graduates to make careers overseas, particularly within the EU, more and more higher education institutions have been including opportunities for their science undergraduates to study a language and/or to study abroad as a part of their degree course.

However, whereas the ability to speak at least one other language is an important requirement for work within the EU, so also is the level of qualification possessed, since you would be in competiton for jobs with graduates from other member states. Many three-year UK science degrees do not reach the same level as the first degrees in countries such as Germany, Italy, Denmark and the Netherlands, where degrees typically take four or more years.

So, if you want to make a career for yourself in one of the other EU countries, you should not only learn a language, you should also seek out one of the four-year degree programmes (or five, with a year abroad).

You might also consider going on to post-graduate studies (for an MSc or a PhD) after your first degree — and not just with a career abroad in mind: science graduates with postgraduate degrees have a competitive advantage when they are looking for a job, not only overseas, but in the UK as well.

What languages are on offer?

French and German are the most usual languages on offer, but at some places you can do others, such as Italian, Spanish, Russian and Japanese.

Some institutions do not include language study as an integral part of a science degree course, but offer instead the possibility of spending some time studying abroad in a very wide range of countries in the EU and further afield. Tuition would be available so that you could learn enough of the relevant language to be able to take part in lectures, seminars and laboratory practicals, write essays and lab. reports, as well as socialise. However in some European countries — Denmark, Greece and the Netherlands, for instance — courses are run in English for visiting undergraduates. You would still need to learn the language to be able to communicate with people on a daily basis, and to benefit fully from the experience.

What sort of courses are there?

Science is an enormously wide field, and so of course the range of what is on offer in science and languages is enormously wide too. But here are just a few diverse examples to give you an idea of how individual institutions include the study of a language and the experience of a foreign country with degree level studies in one of the sciences.

The **University of Sussex** has offered science courses with European Studies for many years. The major science components of these degree programmes are the same as those for the comparable science programmes — in other words, you would cover the same topics in Biochemistry with European Studies as in 'traditional' Biochemistry. In the minor European Studies element you study a language and aspects of your chosen European country — which could be France, Germany or Spain. The European Studies component covers aspects of the European economy, the role of science in European society, and the political structure of modern Europe. Year 3 is spent abroad, studying your science specialism at a university with which Sussex has an exchange agreement. Courses and project work chosen at the foreign university can often be chosen to suit your individual interests, and many students spend much of this year doing a practical project. Part of the assessment for the year abroad is a dissertation written in the foreign language, and there is also a language examination, which, if you pass it, gives you a Certificate of Language Proficiency in your chosen language. It would not be necessary for you to have studied your foreign language to 'A' level — the minimum requirement is a B at GCSE, or equivalent. In your first two years, you would build on this fairly modest level through a variety of teaching and learning techniques, and you would also attend tutorials in 'science language' in order to learn the technical vocabulary requirements of your science specialism — a useful preparation for your science studies at the foreign university.

The **University of Liverpool** offers degree courses in Chemistry, Physics, Life Science, Geology or Geophysics with a European language. The science part is to full honours standard, or even master's degree standard in Chemistry or Physics; the language element (French, German or Spanish — but French only in the case of Geophysics) is essentially practical, enabling you to develop skills in speaking, reading, writing and analysing effectively. You also learn about the life and culture of the country whose language you are studying. The third year of the four-year course is spent at a French, German or Spanish university, studying your science subject and the foreign language. You would also have the option of continuing to study the language in your final year. A typical 'A' level conditional offer would be BC (in relevant sciences/mathematics) plus a D (or a B at GCSE for the less advanced language option) in your chosen language.

The **University of Manchester** offers a four-year degree combining various branches of the biological sciences with a language (either French, German, Italian, Spanish or Japanese). The range of options is very wide, because you can combine with one of these languages one of the following biological sciences: anatomical sciences, biochemistry, biology, cell biology, environmental biology, genetics, life sciences, microbiology, molecular biology, neuroscience, pharmacology, physiology, plant science and zoology — seventy different degree programmes! In these courses the study of a biological science takes up about 70% of your study time; the remaining 30% is spent on the study of your chosen language, and the culture (including the literature) and the institutions of the country where it is spoken. Your third year is spent abroad studying in a higher education institution where you do a biological research project and take appropriate courses to continue the study of the language. At the end of your time abroad you have to submit two reports on your research project — a major one, written in English, and a short summary of it in the foreign language. A conditional offer for this programme would probably be in the range BCC at 'A' level, with two of the 'A' levels in appropriate science subjects, and one 'A' level (or 'AS') in a foreign language.

Nottingham Trent University's Chemistry in Europe BSc or MChem degree programmes offer language training, plus a whole year's industrial placement in an EU country with important companies like Rhone-Poulenc, Siemens, Hoechst, Wacker and AKZO, or alternatively, six months on project work at a university in France, Germany, Italy, Spain or the Netherlands. You may undertake a second placement abroad in the second half of your fourth and final year. A conditional offer for this course would be 16 points, including a good 'A' level in chemistry. There is a similar scheme for physics, where the points score would be 12.

At the **University of East Anglia** you can do a four-year undergraduate programme in a range of sciences, the third year of which is spent at a university in mainland Europe. There are a very large number of EU higher education institutions which collaborate in this scheme with UEA: for chemistry-related sciences there are universities in Denmark (Aarhus), France (Poitiers, Nantes or Rouen), Germany (Darmstadt), the Netherlands (Leiden), Italy (Naples), or Spain (Madrid); for Geophysical Sciences: Germany (Kiel), France (Bordeaux), and Belgium (Brussels); for Ecology: Germany (Bonn), France (Grenoble, Marseille, Nice), Spain (Madrid and Oviedo), Italy (Viterbo) and Sweden (Lund); for Physics: Germany (Regensburg), France (Lille and Montpellier), and Portugal (Aveiro); and so on . . . The year abroad is supported in the normal way by grants from local education authorities, supplemented to cover additional costs involved. The programme is designed to lead to an honours degree in whichever science you are specialising in, together with a certificate of proficiency in a European language. You do a compulsory modern language unit in your second year which prepares you for your year abroad. A typical 'A' level offer would be BCC in the relevant science subjects, and if you wish to be considered for the 'ordinary' BSc programme (in the same subject) as an alternative to one of these European programmes, you would not have to apply for it separately on your UCAS form.

Can I do a science degree if I've done the 'wrong' 'A' levels?

Yes you can. Many higher education institutions, as well as some FE colleges, run Foundation Year programmes for those who would like to take a degree in science (or engineering), but who do not have the normal entry requirements for the course of their choice — for example, you might have taken arts or social science subjects at 'A' level, and now want to change direction. During the foundation year you would cover the essential mathematics and science which would enable you to go on into the first year of a degree or HND course. Many such programmes are planned in conjunction with specific degree or HND courses at the same institution or a neighbouring one, and you would be guaranteed a place on the course if you successfully completed the foundation year. The qualifications you would need for the foundation programme would normally be two 'A' levels (in any subject), and three GCSEs at grade C or above, including mathematics.

'A' level entry to a degree course is not the only route available, of course. You will have seen above that it is possible to transfer to a degree course from an HND/HNC course. But a National Diploma or Certificate, or a GNVQ Advanced in Science is an alternative to 'A' levels, particularly if you are interested in work-related education of a more practical nature. And of course Scottish qualifications, and the European and International Baccalaureates have universal recognition in higher education, as well.

Science and languages
Checklist

1. Employers are increasingly seeking to recruit well qualified scientists who have foreign language skills.

2. Fluency in a second European language is an advantage if you want to go into scientific research since there is much international collaboration.

3. Many higher education institutions offer science degree courses which include language tuition and/or study or an industrial placement abroad.

4. An HND or HNC in one of the branches of science can be a good preparation for technical and research posts, or for transfer to a degree course. Optional language study may be included in the course.

5. If you want to work as a scientist within the EU, the ability to speak at least one other language is an important requirement.

6. The level of the science qualification is also an important factor, since you would be in competition for jobs with science graduates from other EU countries where the degree course is longer than in the UK. So if you want to work in Europe, make sure you do one of the four year degrees, or get a postgraduate qualification.

7. French and German are the most usual languages available with degree studies in science, but others, such as Italian, Spanish, Russian and Japanese are also available at some institutions.

8. Universities offering science degree courses with study or industrial experience in Europe have exchange agreements with a large number of European countries.

9. If you have taken non-science subjects at 'A' level (or equivalent) it is possible to change direction and do a science degree by taking a one-year foundation course in science and mathematics before going on to the degree course.

> See the **Signposts** section to find out which science subjects you can combine with a language at degree level, and which institutions allow you to have a period of study abroad as part of a science degree course.

Information technology and computer science with a language

Information technology influences all aspects of our lives, from word processors or computer games in the home, to the on-line information system at your local health centre or the mechanical robots which are used on production lines in the manufacturing industry. Computers play an ever increasing role in just about all businesses these days, and world financial markets and banks rely on them to acquire information instantly about such things as changes in the values of world currencies, or the prices of shares and commodities.

The integration of the European Union makes a working knowledge of both languages and computing advantageous for a career in business or finance. The commercial importance of Japan would perhaps make Japanese another useful language to link with computing.

The additional language skills which you would acquire on a course which includes a language (or even two!) would open up the prospects of a multinational career, as well as opportunities in the relatively new developments in language processing.

Can I do languages as part of an HND course in Information Technology?

There are Higher National Certificate and Diploma courses in computer studies or information technology on offer at colleges and universities. These are practical and vocational courses, providing progression to employment, or transfer to a related degree course. You would be unlikely to be offered language study as a part of the course, but you might well have the option of doing a language as an extra, as part of an institution-wide language programme (see p77).

You would probably need to have computer studies as one of your 'A' levels (or equivalent qualification) plus a GCSE in mathematics, to get on to an HND/HNC in Computing. Alternatively, you could have a National Certificate or Diploma, or a GNVQ Advanced or a GSVQ Level III in a relevant subject.

What degree courses are there?

Choosing a course in computing can be confusing. There are many different types of course which emphasise different aspects of this diverse subject area. Some courses are mathematical and theoretical, others less so. It is important that you take the time to read the course descriptions in prospectuses to find out whether they are science- based or arts-based, and therefore which courses are going to be within your capabilities.

As a general rule, courses in **computer science**, as the name implies, are more concerned with the science of computing and its mathematical basis. **Computing systems** courses bring together the hardware and software aspects of integrated systems design. You are likely to need a science/mathematics background to do courses like these.

Courses called **Computing, Computer Studies, Information Technology** and **Information Systems** also have a technical content, of course, but they tend to be more approachable for the non-scientist. These are very often combined with the study of another subject — linguistics and information technology, computing and business, modern languages and information systems, for example — and are therefore often concerned with the application of computing within another specialism.

Artificial intelligence is a specialist field, combining computing with psychology, linguistics and philosophy. It is concerned with the study of intelligence in both people and machines, and with the design of intelligent computer systems. Because of the interdisciplinary nature of the course it would suit you if you had studied a mix of arts and sciences.

There are courses available which link the study of a language (occasionally two) to any of these aspects of computing. Artificial intelligence, since it involves aspects of linguistics, combines well with languages, or in fact, with linguistics.

What languages are on offer?

French, German and Spanish are widely available, with Italian and Russian on offer at a fair number of institutions. Other European languages (Greek, Dutch, Portuguese, Czech and Welsh), and Japanese or Chinese, can be done at the occasional institution.

Because of the affinities between human languages and the formal languages used for computer programming and systems design, linguistics is occasionally on offer with computing or artificial intelligence.

You can find out which language subjects you can combine with computing in the **Signposts** section.

In trying to choose you need to ask yourself whether you are more interested in a course in computing plus a language or whether you are mainly wanting to do languages, with some computing to help you to be more employable? If you are thinking of choosing a course which combines a language with other subjects, you need to decide how important a part you want languages to play. The language element can range from just a minor part of the course, to an equal half, even to the major part.

There are other questions to ask yourself, too. What sort of language course do you want? One which concentrates on the practical aspects of the language, including perhaps its specialised use in the context of computing and business? Or one which is broader, taking in other aspects, such as politics and society, or literature — you would be more likely to be able to study this sort of course at an institution which has arranged its curriculum on a modular basis. One sort of course is not necessarily better than the other, it is just a question of what suits you.

Other questions which you might like to consider are whether you could do a different language from the one you are studying now; whether you could do more than one language; what the level of entry qualification is for the language component — would you need an 'A' level or just a GCSE?; whether you could go abroad on a work- or study placement; and whether you could go abroad even if you were not doing a language as part of your course.

At the **University of Birmingham** you can do computer studies or artificial intelligence with a wide choice of languages — French, German, Italian, Spanish, Portuguese, Russian or modern Greek — as part of their four-year Combined Honours and Modern Languages scheme. The two subjects are studied with equal weighting throughout the course, which means that you have quite a heavy workload. Unless you are studying Russian (where you have a short course in Russia), you spend your third year abroad on a full-time modern language-related course at a foreign university. You don't necessarily need any previous knowledge of computing to do this combined languages and computing programme. There is no specific subject you should have already studied to do the computer science/artificial intelligence element, although some previous study of a science subject could be very helpful. For French or German you would need an 'A' level or AS (or equivalent) in the relevant language, and for the other languages it would be helpful if you could give some evidence that you can learn languages — an 'A' level or AS or even perhaps just a GCSE in any language should do the trick. A typical conditional offer in terms of 'A' levels would be in the range BBB/BBC.

🔍 If you wanted to start learning Japanese alongside your computing course, one of the places you could do this is at the **University of Salford.** Their four-year Information Technology with Studies in Japan course is largely an information technology degree with the opportunity of studying Japanese as a minor part of it — modules in basic Japanese would take up only about one fifth of the taught programme. But a real bonus on this course is that you would spend one of your four years studying at Osaka International University in Japan. For the main part of your programme you would study a mix of business and information technology topics, with the option of taking either more strongly business-oriented or technology-oriented modules. Salford also offers Information Technology with either French or German language training — a three year course without, at the time of writing, a year abroad, although they are exploring this possibility, and they do have a short four-week exchange programme with Clermont-Ferrand. They welcome applications from both arts and science students, and no previous experience of information technology is expected. You would need a GCSE in French or German to qualify for the French or German options, and for the Japanese course a GCSE in any language is required, in order to prove that you have the ability to learn a language. A conditional offer for this course would be in the BCC/CCC range at 'A' level (or equivalent). A National Diploma or a GNVQ/GSVQ is also acceptable, of course, at a suitably high level.

🔍 At the **University of the West of England** there is a Modern Languages and Information Systems degree course which would give you the opportunity of doing one language or two together with integrated business studies, information systems and systems analysis. You can choose the two languages from French, German and Spanish, and you can do both of them post 'A' level; or you can do German or Spanish from beginners' level; or French post GCSE. Both languages are studied for a year and a half, at which point you concentrate on just one. You would spend from March to July in your second year on a work placement in a country where your main language is spoken, working either in a field like translating, interpreting or business administration, or in an information technology context, such as software development or systems analysis. During your placement you would also do a piece of extended research in business and information systems which would be submitted at the beginning of your third year and which would form part of the assessment for your degree. Conditional offers would be in the 'A' level points range 18–22, including a grade C in French, German or Spanish — and you would need to have a C grade in one of these languages at 'A' level in addition if you were offering GNVQ Advanced or a GSVQ Level III. Other equivalent qualifications are accepted too, of course, but you would need to have done a language.

🔍 Courses at some institutions do not include language study, but you are offered the opportunity to spend a period of time working or studying abroad. One such institution is **Imperial College,** London, where there is an MEng course in Computing which would offer you the option of taking part in their European Programme of Study. On this course you would spend your fourth and final year at a higher education institution in mainland Europe, and the study you would do there would be accredited as part of your degree. Imperial College at present has exchange agreements with more than 50 European institutions. A modern language does not form part of the actual course, but some language tuition would be available before you went abroad. A conditional offer for this course would be BBB at 'A' level, including mathematics, plus a GCSE in a foreign language.

What are the career possibilities?

The application of computer methods in industry, commerce and research increases every year, and graduates with a good computer science/information technology degree are well equipped to enter the main career opportunities in computer application. Such opportunities occur in a wide variety of organisations, including computer manufacturers, software agencies, consultancies, the financial sector, and local and central government. Most graduates go into these sorts of jobs, although opportunities also exist in general business administration, marketing, advertising, and teaching. Career prospects for artificial intelligence specialists are also excellent, both at home and abroad, due to the significant growth of interest in knowledge-based computer systems.

Additional competence in a language and an understanding of the contemporary European or international business environment would be of relevance to any career you might be contemplating with an international organisation, or indeed any company which has dealings abroad.

IT and computer science with a language
Checklist

1 The influence which information technology has in all our lives, coupled with the need for a working knowledge of languages in business and finance, make a course combining computing and a language a useful springboard to a career.

2 You can do a Higher National Certificate or Diploma in computer studies or information technology, and although a language may not form a part of it, you could probably learn a language through an institution-wide language programme.

3 For some computer courses you need a science/mathematics background, others would suit someone with a mix of sciences and arts, or just arts on their own.

4 French, German and Spanish are widely available in combination with degree studies in computing; other European languages, Japanese, and linguistics can also be done at the occasional institution.

5 Before you pick a course you need to decide on the importance you want a language to have in your course — it can be a minor or a major part, or an equal half.

6 You also need to decide whether you want a practical language course, or a broader one which includes cultural aspects; a course in a language you are familiar with, or a new one; and whether or not you want to go abroad as part of your course.

7 Graduates with good computer science/information technology degrees go on to careers in a wide range of computer related fields with, for example, computer manufacturers, software agencies, consultancies, banks and financial companies, and local and central government. They also go into other aspects of business and administration, marketing, advertising and education.

8 Being able to speak a language and having an understanding of the international business environment can be useful additional competences which can only enhance your career prospects.

> See the **Signposts** section to find out which institutions offer which languages with degree courses in information technology/computer science.

CiLT

Food science and technology with languages

Food science is concerned with food production and the chemistry, physics and microbiology of food processing techniques, as well as the effect on our bodies of eating different foods. The study of food science, food technology or nutrition might also include such diverse issues as healthy eating, use of additives, eating disorders, and the politics of food and food production. It is also likely to touch on biotechnology, which has become important in recent years as a means of solving problems like, for example, food contamination, the excessive use of agricultural chemicals, and the control of animal health.

On some courses you would also learn about and develop skills in the packaging, storage, distribution, and retailing of foodstuffs, the management of production processes and the principles of product development.

So, however much you enjoy eating and cooking, in order to do a course in food science, food technology or nutrition, you really need to enjoy science, and be good at it.

Can I make use of my languages in a career in the food and catering industries?

The food industry is one of the largest in the European Union, and there are good career opportunities both in the UK and abroad for people with appropriate skills and knowledge. The great majority of people employed in the food industry work in processing units, large and small, local, national, European and worldwide.

There is a vast choice of careers, both in this country and overseas, for those with a food science, food technology or nutrition qualification: with food and drink manufacturing companies, food package designers and manufacturers, food plant and equipment manufacturers, supermarket chains and other food retail distributers, government (local, national and European), the health service, national and local government laboratories, other research establishments, food law enforcement agencies, food science information and publishing agencies, education establishments and consultancies.

You would find your languages useful if you went to work for a food-related organisation abroad, or for a British one which has dealings overseas. These days food is international — a visit to your local supermarket will show you this. Companies which buy and sell food products all over the world need people with the ability to speak other languages and a knowledge and understanding of other lifestyles.

And this internationalisation is not just limited to food distribution and marketing. To give just one example, the prominence given recently to problems arising from BSE in cattle has shown us clearly that other aspects of the food industry — research, quality assurance and control, and legislation — are not just national, but international, and that the EU has a growing influence in this respect.

Can I combine a language with a vocational course in Food Science?

After your GCSEs you could do National Diploma or Certificate courses, or GNVQ Advanced/GSVQ Level III courses in science which can include specialist study in food science and technology. You would need to find out what science courses were on offer at an FE college or school sixth form near you.

Most schools and colleges which run these courses will be able to provide opportunities for you to do extra courses or modules in modern languages at a variety of levels — you could continue to improve on a language you know already, or perhaps start a new one.

Higher National Diploma courses in food science, offered by colleges of higher education and universities, provide higher education and practical training related to a career in one of the aspects of the food industry. You may find such courses listed under Food Science or Food Technology, but more likely under Science or Biotechnology with a brief explanation of the course content given in brackets like, for example, HND Science (Food Development and Production) or HND Bio-technology (Food and Land-Based Industries). Other titles might be Technology of Food, or Applied Food Studies.

An HNC/HND Food Studies course like this would provide you with an understanding of the techniques involved in food production, together with an understanding of scientific principles, business organisation and food processing. You would also have an opportunity to develop communication and information technology skills. You would also do extensive practical work, both in the kitchens and laboratories of the institution at which you were studying, and during an industrial placement (usually at food establishments such as bakeries, dairies, food manufacturing companies). There are often opportunities to undertake placements in other European countries.

To enhance your opportunities for work and study abroad you should seek opportunities to do a language. Most Higher Diploma courses offer a language study component. French, German and Spanish are the languages most widely available, and can usually be taken at beginners' level, or post GCSE, or post 'A' level.

What are the career possibilities for those with an HND/HNC?

There is a ready market for successful HND/HNC Food Science and Technology students in processing, quality assurance, and the other different areas of the food industry. Some go into the industry as technician staff in various aspects of food processing, food analysis and quality assurance — employment opportunities for skilled technicians are good. Others use the training the course will have given them in modern methods of food analysis, microbiology laboratory management and research to seek careers in laboratory based work. Some go into trainee manager posts.

There are opportunities on completion of the HND/HNC for further study towards a degree or further qualifications, thus opening up all the possibilities of graduate employment (see career possibilities for graduates on the following page).

Can I include a language with a degree course in Food Science?

Degree courses in this area usually offer you the possibility of doing optional language study. Sometimes this is through optional language modules; often it is offered as part of an institution-wide programme whereby students can take advantage of special language courses within the institution and have any study they have undertaken formally recognised and accredited as part of their final qualification.

At the **University of Surrey** there are three nutrition degree courses within the School of Biological Sciences — Nutrition, Nutrition/Dietetics, and Nutrition/ Food Science. These, together with the other programmes offered by the School of Biological Sciences, are modular, with a broad range of modules from which to choose, making it possible to tailor your studies to your individual interests and career needs. It also makes it relatively easy to change course if you need to. Modules in languages are available in the first two years of these three or four year courses, in French, German, Spanish, Italian, Japanese or Russian, with the aim of providing you with sufficient fluency to undertake professional training in the appropriate country in your third year.

There are two institutions, however, where languages can form a significant part of the degree programme — Oxford Brookes University and the University of Nottingham.

At **Oxford Brookes University** where a modular curriculum structure is in place, food science and nutrition can be combined with a very wide range of other subjects, amongst them languages, French, German or Japanese. You would thus be doing a joint honours course, with half your programme devoted to food science, and half to the study of French or German, with the third year of your four year course spent on a university course or a work placement in France or Germany. To be accepted on to the course you would need to get at least two 'A' levels in the range CC-DD (or equivalent) with one of the 'A' levels in the language you wanted to study, and one in an appropriate science.

At the **University of Nottingham** there is a special, fully-integrated course in European Studies in Food Science. This is a four-year course, divided into semesters. You would spend your first three semesters following appropriate food and science courses. The next semester would be devoted to studying a European language, together with the political, social, cultural and economic aspects of life in the country of which you were learning the language. You would spend the following semester in a European country at a university attending relevant academic courses (and, of course, developing the necessary language and social skills which would prove useful for a career within the EU). Industrial placements may also be arranged during this period. Nottingham University has links with most major European countries, so you would have a wide choice of countries and languages to choose from. After your period abroad you would return to Nottingham for your final three semesters, when you would complete your science-based course, but if you wished you would also be able to follow an option drawn from another department of the university. You might want to choose something to fit in with your career aspirations — languages perhaps, or contemporary politics . . .

Although not an accredited part of the course, the opportunity also exists for students to spend the whole of year 3 abroad working in industry in order to gain relevant and valuable work experience.

The entrance qualifications to this European Studies in Food Sciences course would be likely to be in the region of BCD at 'A' level, and two of the 'A' levels would have to be in mathematics or a relevant science. You would need at least a grade C GCSE in a modern language — but not necessarily in the language you wanted to study, because there are *ab initio* courses available — but of course it would be an advantage to you if you were continuing with a language you had studied for 'A'/'AS' level (or equivalent).

What are the career possibilities for graduates?

There is a great demand for well qualified people trained in food sciences. Graduates from these courses are competent to undertake jobs as managers in the dynamic and changing European food industry (particularly if they are able to speak a European language or two) where a wide range of opportunities are opening up, from raw material procurement, through manufacture, to marketing, sales and distribution.

Some go into the fields of research and quality control; many of these may undertake a second degree (a doctorate, for example), to give themselves further, more specialised qualifications.

A few acquire qualified teacher status by undertaking initial teacher training, and go on to teach a related subject in schools — environmental science, food and nutrition, biology, chemistry, perhaps.

Food science and technology with languages
Checklist

1. To do a food science course you need to be good at science.

2. The food industry is one of the largest in the EU, and there are good and varied career prospects both in the UK and abroad for well qualified people.

3. Languages are useful because there are international opportunities in all aspects of the food industry, as well as in international legal and political fields.

4. After your GCSEs you could do a vocational course in science/food science, which could include optional language modules.

5. Higher National Diploma courses in food science or food technology provide higher education together with practical training. These courses can include language study, as well as opportunities to work or study abroad.

6. There are plenty of career opportunities in the food industry for those with Higher National qualifications; and some go on to convert their HND/HNC to a degree via further study.

7. Many degree courses in food science and food technology offer the possibility of doing languages as optional modules, or as part of a university/college-wide language programme.

8. If you want languages to constitute a significant part of your degree course you could do a joint language and food science course at Oxford Brookes University via their modular curriculum; or you could do an integrated course in Euro-pean studies and food sciences at the University of Nottingham, which offers a wide range of languages, and study at a European university.

9. Food science/technology graduates go into a wide range of careers in the food industry at management level, or in research.

> See the **Signposts** section to find out which institutions offer which languages with a degree in food science.

Agriculture, horticulture and other land-based subjects with languages

Agriculture is about much more than crops, dairying and meat production. It is also concerned with all aspects of the use of the countryside, with soil science, plant science, animal science, and with food production, food marketing and distribution. It can cover aspects as diverse as ecology, wildlife conservation, animal health and farm business management. It is in fact a blend of science, husbandry and economics.

Horticulture is not just gardening, either. It encompasses the growing of plants to improve the quality of the environment, and of fruit and vegetables for food, as well as aspects of science and technology like plant physiology and biochemistry, plant cell biology, soil and water engineering, and the mechanisation of crop production. It is also concerned with landscape design, the establishment and maintenance of parks, sports grounds, golf courses and other open spaces, and the management of garden centres.

Agriculture and horticulture, together with forestry, ecology and conservation, countryside planning, and landscape management are often referred to as 'land-based' subjects — for reasons which are obvious.

What careers could I go into with a land-based qualification?

Career opportunities for those with qualifications in land-based subjects exist in many areas — in farming, estate management, gamekeeping, animal care, horticulture (parks, nurseries, garden centres, landscape design), forestry, conservation, and countryside and town planning, of course; but also with commercial firms involved in production, servicing or marketing, in aspects of the food industry, in the leisure industry, with Local Authorities, with National Parks, in executive and technical posts, in government advisory posts both nationally and internationally, in development and advisory services, in scientific research, in education . . .

Would languages be useful?

Now that increasingly close links are developing within Europe, and indeed worldwide, there is a need for professionals working in the land-based industries to have an understanding of international issues and concerns, including European agricultural and environmental policies and the management of food resources in the Third World, and to possess the necessary linguistic skills to allow them to communicate with fellow professionals in other countries. After all, the issues which concern the land-based industries are frequently international — the management of natural resources, famine in the Third World, the development of alternative land use, global warming, increasing levels of pollutants, protection of the environment, conservation of habitats, alterations in soil fertility . . . . The discussion of such issues and the search for solutions to them frequently depend upon international understanding and co-operation.

With greater free time and wealth throughout the developed world there is an increasing demand for more and better facilities for leisure and tourism, like golf courses, ski runs, farm trails, public parks and nature reserves. Career opportunities in the leisure and tourist industries exist for well qualified people with a blend of land-based and management skills to develop these amenities, and of course the addition of foreign language skills can only enhance European and international employment opportunities.

Can I do a land-based subject with a language after my GCSEs?

If you chose to do a GNVQ/GSVQ or a National Diploma in one of the land-based group of subjects, you would almost certainly be able to choose modules or an extra course in languages — probably in French, German, Spanish, or perhaps Italian. What is on offer in terms of different languages, and the levels to which you can study them, will depend upon what individual institutions choose to put on, the needs of their students, and possibly the staff they have available.

GNVQ/GSVQ courses in land-based industries at intermediate and advanced levels, or GSVQs at Levels II and III, are on offer in some school sixth forms, sixth form colleges and FE colleges. GNVQs/GSVQs are modular, and blend academic and vocational study, preparing you for broad areas of work or for further and higher education. In general, the intermediate level can provide entry to the advanced GNVQ/GSVQ Level III for those who did not do too well at school; the advanced GNVQ/GSVQ Level III can be a qualification for employment, or for entry into higher education in a related subject. You can make a GNVQ/GSVQ fit your personal requirements by choosing from a selection of different options, and some large colleges which put on a range of different GNVQs/GSVQs can let you mix and match across the different subject-areas. For example, if you are interested in the management of the environment, or the commercial side of sports and leisure facilities, you might find an advanced GNVQ/GSVQ Level III in business studies with options in environmental conservation, or leisure management would suit you.

National Diploma and Certificate courses in the land-based industries are modular courses, allowing you to specialise in agriculture, horticulture, forestry, animal care, rural skills like gamekeeping, or leisure management skills like golf green-keeping. Not all these options are available at all centres, and you would need to check on exactly what the courses offered in your area would allow you to do. On a National Diploma/Certificate course you could expect to do both practical and classroom work, as well as a work placement in your area of special interest.

Entry qualifications for these courses vary from institution to institution, but for a GNVQ Advanced/GSVQ Level III or a National Diploma/Certificate course you would usually need to have GCSE or similar qualifications in English, mathematics and science. Many colleges would prefer you to have had experience of farming or horticulture before you begin a National Diploma/Certificate course.

Can I combine languages with a higher education course in land-based subjects?

There are Higher National Diploma and Certificate courses on offer in agriculture, horticulture or other land-based subjects will almost certainly be three year sandwich courses, with the second year being spent on a work placement. A language can be an option on these courses, and at some institutions you may be able to study abroad or do part of the work placement component abroad. HND/HNC land-based courses are wide-ranging, and apart from agriculture and horticulture, they are called by a variety of names which reflect their content, for instance, Arboriculture, Commercial Horticulture and Garden Design, Crop Production and Protection, Forestry, Golf Course Management, Horse-Studies, Equine Technology and Business, Land Use and the Environment, Landscape Studies, Rural Studies, Rural Resource Management, European Rural Business Management . . .

Career opportunities for the holder of an HND/HNC in these subjects are also many and varied. Depending upon the particular specialism you chose to take, you could find yourself qualified to work in areas such as farming or farm management, the agriculture supply industry, garden centre management, landscape design, tree surgery, pot plant production, beekeeping, sports turf maintenance, mushroom growing, glasshouse crop production, nature conservation, country-side management, woodland management, research and development, as well as in journalism, teaching, the agrochemical and fertiliser industry, consultancy, and contracting work. Some diplomates have even successfully set up their own businesses.

Some students who have done well on an HND course have been able to transfer to the final year of a degree course in a related subject.

If you wanted to go on to a degree course in a land-related subject after your 'A' levels (or equivalent), or a National Diploma or GNVQ/GSVQ you would need to have taken science as part of your course. Many institutions require you to have studied chemistry or perhaps biology, and often require one or two further science subjects, or mathematics, geography or geology.

For agriculture and horticulture courses it is advisable, and compulsory in the case of some of them, to have had an extended period of first hand experience working on a farm or with a garden centre, nursery or parks department; and even if you come from a farming background, you will often be required to get some experience on a different type of farm. Students usually spend a year working before commencing their course.

Many higher education institutions which offer land-based degrees, including the specialist colleges like the Royal Agricultural College, Cirencester, have links throughout the world with higher education institutions and research organisations. Some have developed their degree programmes together with other universities and colleges abroad, which has increased the opportunities for UK students to go abroad on study and work placements, as well as for foreign students to come to the UK.

At the **Royal Agricultural College,** for example, there are currently links with universities and agricultural colleges in Brazil, Austria, the Czech Republic, France, Poland, Portugal, Germany and Spain; and students have undertaken their sandwich placements (perhaps the most notable recently being at the Spanish Riding School in Vienna) and periods of study overseas in mainland European countries, including Italy, Denmark and Hungary. For this type of course, which has an 'international flavour', tuition in a language is usually available within the institution.

There are some institutions which offer land-based courses where languages take on a more significant role. These are listed in the **Signposts** section.

At the **University of Reading,** for instance, there is a range of agriculture/horticulture related degree courses — Agricultural Botany, Crop Protection, Crop Science, Horticulture, and Landscape Management — each of which offers a 'with studies in Europe' option. This option would provide you with a working knowledge of a European language (starting in the first week of the first year), a course on European Integration in the second year, and a valuable European dimension to your studies through the third year of the four-year course being spent in another European country.

In terms of 'A' levels, for these courses at Reading you would need to get grades in the range CCD, preferably from biology (or botany), chemistry, mathematics, physics, geography or geology. A GCSE grade C in a foreign language is usually required, too.

At the **University of Nottingham** there is a range of special, fully-integrated courses in European Studies with agriculture, horticulture, and other related subjects. These are four-year courses, divided into semesters. You would spend your first three semesters following appropriate agriculture or horticulture courses. The next semester would be devoted to studying a European language, together with the political, social, cultural and economic aspects of life in the country of which you were learning the language. You would spend the following semester in a European country at a university attending relevant academic courses (and, of course, developing the necessary language and social skills which would prove useful for a career within the EU). Industrial placements can also be arranged during this period. Nottingham University has links with most major European countries, so you would have a wide choice of countries and languages to choose from. After your period abroad you would return to Nottingham for your final three semesters, when you would complete your agriculture or horticulture course, but if you wished you would also be able to follow an option drawn from another department of the university. You might want to choose something to fit in with your career aspirations — languages perhaps, or contemporary politics . . .

The entrance qualifications to this European Studies and Agriculture/ Horti-culture course at Nottingham would be likely to be in the region of CC/CCD at 'A' level, and two of the 'A' levels would have to be in mathematics or a relevant science. You would need at least a GCSE in a modern language — but not necessarily in the language you wanted to study, because there are *ab initio* courses available — but of course it would be an advantage to you if you were continuing with a language you had studied for A/AS level (or equivalent).

Harper Adams Agricultural College in Shropshire is the largest higher education college in the UK offering land-based courses. The college believes that it is essential that students are aware of developments within Europe and the rest of the world. The international content of their courses has increased and there are plenty of opportunities for students to select international options. French, German and Spanish are available as optional modules and at three different levels on most degree courses (and, incidentally, most HND courses); you can add optional modules, such as International Agricultural Policy or International Marketing; you may take your industrial placement abroad; and you can spend a semester of study in another European country — Harper Adams has links with colleges in the Netherlands, Spain, France, Germany, Greece, Finland, Portugal and Sweden. The more motivated students can opt to undertake a prescribed set of options which would lead to the inclusion of 'International' in the title of their degree. In order to qualify for an 'International' award, you must have studied a second language, undertaken your industrial placement overseas and have spent one semester studying abroad. This international option is currently offered on selected agriculture, business management, agri-food and agricultural engineering courses.

A likely conditional offer, in terms of 'A' level grades, would be in the range CC/DD.

Agriculture, horticulture and other land-based subjects with languages
Checklist

1 Agriculture, horticulture and other land-based subjects cover a very wide range of subjects and career areas which go far beyond farming and gardening.

2 There is a growing need for professionals working in the land-based industries to have an understanding of national issues and concerns, and to be able to communicate with fellow professionals abroad.

3 You can do a language as an optional module on a vocational course in a land-based subject, either post-16, or in further and higher education.

4 Many degree courses in land-based subjects provide opportunities for undergraduates to study a language or to go abroad on work or study placements.

5 A few degree courses include the study of a language as a significant component of the course.

6 Graduates obtain posts in one of the many aspects of their subject, and others go into careers which are not directly associated with the land. Those who have learnt languages find that employers value their language skills.

> See the **Signposts** section to find out which institutions offer the possibility of studying a language with a degree course in one of the land-based subjects.

Preparing to become a teacher of languages

Teaching is a demanding, often challenging and stressful job requiring plenty of resilience and commitment, but it is rewarding, stimulating and full of variety. Teaching modern languages, in particular, requires lots of energy, but it is immensely satisfying to see your pupils master something new, or communicate with you or with each other in the language you are teaching them.

Teachers of modern languages are in demand. Secondary schools now have to teach a language to all pupils up to the age of sixteen, and this has created a need for more language teachers in schools. The government has made money available to encourage more teachers in subjects where there are shortages, payable in the form of extra bursaries to postgraduate students training in these subjects. Modern languages is one of the subjects where there is a need to encourage more teachers into the profession, and where a bursary is payable. The Postgraduate Certificate in Education is also the one postgraduate course for which you would automatically get a grant.

Modern languages are mostly taught in secondary schools, but some state primary schools, middle schools and independent schools teach languages to pupils below the age of eleven. Opportunities for language teachers also arise in sixth form and further education colleges and in adult education. There are also opportunities in universities and colleges of higher education, of course, although the preparation for this does not require you to get Qualified Teacher Status in the same way as for school teachers, but would involve you in further study and probably the acquisition of a further degree.

Many graduates, especially modern linguists, teach English as a foreign language either in this country or abroad. Some teachers — not just modern language teachers — decide to make their careers overseas in the network of British schools across the world.

Which is the most useful language?

First of all, you are almost certainly going to need more than one language. If you want to teach in a secondary school, you would be well advised to make sure you are proficient in two languages when you eventually start your career — secondary teachers usually have to teach more than just one subject, and you would be more useful — and hence more employable — in a modern languages department if you were qualified to teach two languages.

If you have only had the opportunity to study one language up to now, remember that there are many higher education institutions where you can study a second language from scratch, as part of a joint honours course, or as a subsidiary subject.

There have been successive national initiatives to encourage the teaching of a greater variety of modern languages in schools, but as the situation stands now, French is still the most widely taught (although not always as the first foreign language) closely followed by German and Spanish. Italian and Russian are also taught in a significant number of schools, and Japanese is now increasingly taught in schools, particularly in Language Colleges. Languages other than these — other European languages (Dutch or Swedish for example), Chinese and Arabic are taught in a very few sixth forms and FE colleges, as well as in some larger schools in the independent sector.

In areas of the country where there are large numbers of pupils who come from homes where English is not the first language — usually homes where one of the Asian languages is spoken — one or more of these languages may be taught in schools.

There are opportunities to teach Welsh in schools in Wales; as well as to teach through the medium of the Welsh language in Bilingual Schools in Wales. Either of these might appeal to you if you were a Welsh speaker. Of course, what is needed in the Bilingual Schools is teachers who are able to teach subjects other than languages, not in English, but in Welsh. So your teaching qualification would need to be in one of these subjects. Almost every county in Wales has now established at least one Welsh-medium school, and there are both primary and secondary schools in the scheme.

How do I prepare myself for a teaching career?

Teaching is now virtually an all-graduate profession. To teach in a state maintained school you must achieve qualified teacher status (QTS) by following an approved course of initial teacher training (ITT). This is obtained through two main routes — a degree course incorporating professional education studies, the acquisition of teaching skills and the subject(s) you wish to teach; or a degree course in the subject(s) you want to teach followed by postgraduate training. All intending teachers must also have attained at least a GCSE grade C (or equivalent)in both English language and mathematics.

If it is languages you want to teach, you can

- take a degree in one or two modern languages followed by a one-year Postgraduate Certification in Education (PGCE) at a university or a college of higher education. (This is the most usual route for teachers of modern languages in secondary schools.); or
- take a degree in one or two modern languages followed by a two-year postgraduate course provided by a school (this is called school-centred ITT, and leads to 'articled teacher' status); or
- take a degree combining subject study in one or two modern languages with teacher training — either a Bachelor of Education (BEd) or a BA with QTS; or
- (for French only) take a degree in French (plus another language to make you 'marketable') followed by a part-time PGCE (up to two years) available at various institutions, including the Open University.

Can I teach languages with qualifications other than these?

You might want to teach languages with another subject — say physical education and French, or geography and Spanish. This is quite possible, but you are likely to find that schools may not frequently be advertising vacancies in just the combination which you offer. You would clearly be more viable if the two subjects you offered were both languages.

However, if your degree is jointly in languages and another subject you will need to find out from your chosen teacher training institution whether your qualification meets their requirements.

It is possible to go on to a PGCE course without a degree, provided that you have a qualification which is equivalent to a degree. Again you would need to discuss this with the teacher training institution you would like to go to — many will accept an alternative qualification as long as they are satisfied that it is of equivalent status, and that the content is relevant to a teaching career.

In schools in the private sector a PGCE is not strictly necessary, and many independent schools have their own salary scales, and a range of perks (such as free accommodation in boarding schools, in return for weekend and evening duties).

There are other routes into teaching for graduates: as a more mature entrant — perhaps after working in another career for a while — or as a 'licensed teacher'.

The Graduate Teacher Training Registry (GTTR) handles applications for teacher training schemes within England and Wales, and training is funded by the Teacher Training Agency (TTA), which also provides information and advice about teacher training. If you want further information, therefore, you should write to:

> The TTA Communication Centre
> PO Box 3210
> Chelmsford
> Essex CM1 3WA

The TTA's website — www.teach.org.uk — covers a range of careers information on teaching as a profession. It also includes a course search database which lists all postgraduate initial teacher training courses.

Postgraduate teacher training courses in Scotland and Northern Ireland are not recruited through the GTTR. You should write to the appropriate address in Scotland or Northern Ireland:

> Advisory Service on Entry to Teaching
> The General Teaching Council for Scotland
> Clerwood House
> 96 Clermiston Road
> Edinburgh EH12 6UT

> Department of Education for Northern Ireland
> Rathgael House
> Balloo Road
> Bangor
> Co. Down BT19 7PR

Do I need any other qualifications?

Acceptance for teacher training, whether it is via the BEd/BA with QTS route, or the degree plus postgraduate training route, is not dependent on academic qualifications alone. The teacher training institutions you are applying to will be assessing your personal suitability through interview, and many institutions will also look for some evidence of a real interest in young people or some experience with children, such as voluntary work, work experience helping in a school, or other activities. You should consider in advance how you will be able to meet these criteria, so that you can set up some opportunities for yourself.

Once you were qualified and launched on a teaching career, you would find that teaching is a profession in which training opportunities continue, giving you opportunities to acquire new skills, to improve you teaching methodology, even sometimes to acquire further qualifications. It would be important that as a teacher you kept abreast of new developments, and tried to select training opportunities suited to your own professional needs and to fit in with your own long-term career plans.

How do I qualify to teach English as a foreign language?

In the past, teaching English to foreign students has often been looked on as a convenient way of earning some money in the summer vacation, or in a Gap Year. But if you want a more secure career in this aspect of teaching, then you must get properly qualified.

You can do this by taking a TEFL (Teaching English as a Foreign Language) course. You do not need a degree, or in fact any language qualification to do this, although the experience of having gone through the language-learning process oneself can be a great help to any language teacher.

TEFL courses vary in their content and their length. They are also offered by a wide range of providers, including many private firms. If you wanted to build a career in this field you would almost definitely need a degree; you should ensure that your TEFL course leads to internationally accepted qualifications and that you apply for posts through well-established organisations (The British Council, International House, The Bell School, The Centre for

British Teachers (CfBT)), or Voluntary Service Overseas (VSO). The British Council has something in the region of 60 centres abroad, but will only accept well-qualified teachers with at least two years' teaching experience. VSO, as a voluntary organisation, cannot afford to pay the highest rates, but they look after their volunteers well.

Career progression beyond the classroom in TEFL is very competitive — there are not many opportunities to progress into top management since the number of these posts is limited. So before making your career in this field you would need to do some hard thinking about your long-term goals.

A similar career field is teaching English as a foreign language in the UK. There are three branches of this type of teaching: English as a Second Language (ESL), English for Specific Purposes (ESP), and English for Academic Purposes (EAP). No formal qualifications are needed for this type of teaching, although there are organisations which provide training, particularly for teaching ESL. Some experience of learning languages would enable you to appreciate any difficulties your students might be having, and some experience of teaching would also help.

ESL work is generally undertaken with immigrants and other visiting foreigners who need to learn English for day-to-day communication, or in order to work in the UK or in another English speaking country.

ESP work usually requires a level of specialist knowledge, since, as its name implies, it involves teaching a form of English which is specific to a particular field, perhaps science, technology, business, law, for instance... which could be problematical unless you have the specialist knowledge and vocabulary. EAP work deals with teaching English to foreign students who come to do a higher education course in the UK. The aim is to improve on the English they already know so that they will be able to benefit from their studies, communicate in lectures, seminars and tutorials, write essays, and so on.

Preparing to become a teacher of languages
Checklist

1. There is at present a demand for qualified modern language teachers in secondary schools.

2. Secondary school modern language teachers usually need to be able to teach more than one language.

3. French is the most widely taught modern language in secondary schools, closely followed by German and Spanish.

4. There are sometimes opportunities to teach other European languages, and occasionally Japanese, Chinese and Arabic.

5. Asian languages are sometimes taught in schools in areas of the UK where there are large numbers of pupils who come from homes where English is not the first language.

6. Welsh is taught in schools in Wales; and other subjects are taught through the medium of Welsh in Bilingual Schools in some parts of Wales.

7. You need Qualified Teacher Status to teach in a state maintained school; this can be obtained by having a degree which combines professional education studies and the subject you want to teach; or a degree in your teaching subject(s) followed by postgraduate teacher training.

8. A postgraduate qualification is not always required for teaching in an independent school.

9. If you want to make a career teaching English abroad you would be well advised to do a TEFL course prior to obtaining a post through a well-established agency.

10. There are openings for teachers of English as a foreign language in the UK, too. There are three main areas: English as a Second Language (ESL), English for Specific Purposes (ESP), and Emglish for Academic Purposes (EAP).

Section 4

Signposts to degree courses

Studying for a degree in languages — 135

Modern European languages — 135
   Dutch — 136
   Modern Greek — 136
   Italian, Spanish, Portuguese and Catalan — 136
   Scandinavian languages — 138
   Russian and Eastern European languages — 139
European Studies — 140
Asian languages — 141
Arabic and Middle Eastern languages — 142
African languages — 142
Linguistics — 143

Studying for a degree in languages with other subjects — 144

Business and management studies — 144
Accountancy or finance — 147
Law — 148
Tourism — 150
Physical education, sports science or leisure studies — 150
Engineering — 151
Science — 153
Science with a period of study abroad — 156
Information technology/computer science — 160
Food science — 162
Agriculture, horticulture and other land-based subjects — 162
Theatre arts, dance and music — 163
Social policy, social administration, public policy or community studies — 164
Politics or international relations — 165
Marketing — 167
Information studies and librarianship — 168
Art, art history, design, visual communication and media studies (including journalism and publishing) — 169

Explanation

The tables in this section provide a quick 'at-a-glance' reference guide to what languages you can do where, and what subjects you can combine with languages.

In the second part of this section, **Studying for a degree in languages with other subjects,** only vocational and semi-vocational subjects have been included — but other non-vocational subjects can also be combined with languages, particularly in joint honours, combined honours and modular courses. (Remember what we said about such courses in Chapter 8? — it is possible to combine the study of languages with just about any other subject for a degree).

It is not intended to give you the whole picture — we think that would make it all too confusing to be useful. You should use it as an index to your further research.

The majority of the tables are arranged to show you which languages you can study with the various subjects. We felt it was more useful to arrange eight of the tables — European Studies, Linguistics, Agriculture/Horticulture, Art, etc, Physical Education, etc, Science Theatre Arts, etc, and Travel and Tourism — according to individual subjects and the institutions at which you can do them.

NB: this section is devoted to degree courses. Diploma/certificate courses have not been included, since languages do not normally constitute a major part of them. In theory, language modules or other short language courses can be added to any vocational diploma/certificate programme.

KEY

To the most frequently used symbols in the tables

(Other symbols are explained on the relevant tables)

---

c only offered in combined honours or as part of a modular course

j only offered as part of a joint honours programme with another subject (often another language)

m only offered as a minor option

Studying for a degree in languages

Degree courses in modern languages, European studies and linguistics

Modern European languages

French and **German** are offered widely in UK universities and colleges, both as single honours, or as part of joint, combined or modular language courses. For this reason it is not felt appropriate to publish **Signposts** tables for either of these two languages.

You will find **Signposts** tables showing which institutions offer degree courses in each of the following European languages, or groups of languages, on the next five pages

- Dutch

- Greek (modern)

- Italian, Spanish, Portuguese and Catalan

- Scandinavian languages

- Russian and Eastern European languages

- European Studies

Languages of the rest of the world

- Asian languages

- Arabic and Middle Eastern language

- African languages

Linguistics

Degree courses in Dutch

Institution	
Cambridge	To be studied with another language
East Anglia	May be studied as a subsidiary language
Hull	Dutch Studies; or in combination with another subject
Liverpool	As part of a combined course
School of Oriental and African Studies, London (SOAS)	With Indonesian
University College, London	As a main subject; or in combination with another subject

Degree courses in Modern Greek

Institution	
Birmingham	Modern Greek Studies; or in combination with another subject
Bradford	In combination with History or Politics
Cambridge	To be studied with another language
Edinburgh	
King's College, London	Modern Greek Studies; or in combination with another subject
Oxford	To be studied with another language

Degree courses in Italian, Spanish, Portuguese and Catalan

A number of institutions listed below which offer Spanish and Portuguese also offer major or minor courses in Latin American Studies. These are not listed separately here – please consult prospectuses.

Institution	Italian	Spanish	Portuguese	Catalan
Aberdeen		*		
Aberystwyth	*j	*		
Anglia	*j	*c		
Bangor	j			
Bath	*j			
Birmingham	*	*	*j	
Bradford		*		
Bristol	*	*	*m	*m
Bristol UWE		*j		
Buckingham		*j		
Cambridge	*	*	*	*m
Cardiff	*	*	*j	

Institution	Italian	Spanish	Portuguese	Catalan
Central Lancashire	*c	*j		
Coventry	*j	*j		
De Montfort		*j/c		
Derby		*c		
Dundee		*j		
Durham	*c	*j/c		
East London		*j/c		
Edinburgh	*	*	*j	
Essex		*	*j	
Exeter	*	*		*m
Glamorgan	*			
Glasgow	*	*j		*m
Goldsmiths		*j		
Heriot–Watt		*j		
Huddersfield		*j		
Hull	*	*		
Kent	*j	*j		
King's College, London		*	*j	
Kingston		*j		
Lancaster	*j	*j		
Leeds	*j	*	*j	
Leeds, Trinity and All Saints		*j		
Leicester	*j	*j		
Lincolnshire & Humberside		*j		
Liverpool	*j	*	*j	*j
Liverpool John Moores	*j	*j		
London Guildhall		*c		
Loughborough		*j		
Luton	*j	*j		
Manchester	*j	*	*j	*m
Manchester Metropolitan		*j/c		
Middlesex		*c		
Newcastle		*j/c	*j/c	
North London		*c		
Northumbria		*j		
Nottingham		*j	*j	

Degree courses in Italian, Spanish, Portuguese and Catalan (cont'd)

Institution	Italian	Spanish	Portuguese	Catalan
Oxford	*	*j	*	*m
Oxford Brookes		*j		
Plymouth		*j		
Portsmouth	*j	*j	*j	
Queen Mary & Westfield		*j		*m
Queen's Belfast	*	*		
Roehampton		*j		
Reading	*			
Royal Holloway	*	*j		
St Andrews		*		
Salford	*j	*		*m
Sheffield		*	*m	*m
Southampton		*	*c	
Staffordshire		*c		
Stirling		*		
Strathclyde	*c	*c		
Sunderland		*j		
Sussex	*j			
Swansea	*	*		*j
Thames Valley		*c		
Ulster		*c		
UMIST		*j		
University College. London	*	*j	*m	
Warwick	*j			
Westminster	*j	*j		
Wolverhampton	*c	*	*m	*m

Degree courses in Scandinavian languages

Institution	Danish	Norwegian	Swedish	Icelandic	Scandinavian Studies
East Anglia	*	*	*		*
Edinburgh	*j	*j	*j		*
Hull			*		*
University College, London				*	*

Degree courses in Russian and Eastern European languages

Institution	Russian	Other
Airedale and Wharfedale College	*	
Bangor	*	
Bath	*j	
Birmingham	*	
Bradford	*j	
Bristol	*	Czech (m)
Cambridge	*	Czech with Slovak (j) Hungarian (j)
Coventry	*j	
Durham	*	
Edinburgh	*	
Essex	*	
Exeter	*	
Glasgow	*	Czech (j) Polish (j)
Heriot-Watt	*j	
King' College, London	*j	
Leeds	*	
Leicester	*j	
Liverpool	*c	
Liverpool John Moores	*j	
London School of Economics	*j	
Manchester	*	
Nottingham	*	Serbo-Croat (j) Slovene (m)
Oxford	*	Czech with Slovak (j)
Portsmouth	*	Slovak (m)
Queen Mary & Westfield	*	
Queen's Belfast	*	
School of Slavonic and East European Studies, London	*	Bulgarian, Czech with Slovak, Finnish, Hungarian, Polish, Romanian, Serbo-Croat
Sheffield	*	Bulgarian (m), Czech, Polish
St Andrews	*	
Strathclyde	*c	
Surrey	*j	
Sussex	*j	
Swansea	*	
Westminster	*j	

Degree courses in European Studies

European Studies courses differ widely one from another, not least in the amount of language study they offer. On such a course you can expect to gain a broad understanding of Europe's geography, history, literature, philosophies, culture, politics, economics and society.

On most courses you would study one, and perhaps two modern European languages; these are more usually French, German or Spanish, but occasionally there are opportunities to study other European languages like Dutch, Italian or Russian.

The following is a list of the institutions which offer European Studies courses — but you will need to do your research in their prospectuses to find out the precise content of each course, and the languages you can study.

Aberdeen	Manchester
Aberystwyth	Manchester Metropolitan
Aston	North London
Bath	Northumbria
Birmingham	Nottingham
Bradford	Nottingham Trent
Bristol UWE	Plymouth
Cardiff	Portsmouth
Central Lancashire	Queen Mary & Westfield
Coventry	Queen's Belfast
De Montfort	Reading
Derby	Ripon and York St John
Dundee	Royal Holloway
Durham	Salford
East Anglia	Southampton
East London	Southampton Institute
Edge Hill	Southampton New College
Edinburgh	South Bank
Essex	Staffordshire
Evesham College	Stirling
Goldsmiths	Strathclyde
Hertfordshire	Sunderland
Huddersfield	Surrey
Hull	Sussex
Keele	Thames Valley
Kent	Ulster
King's College, London	University College, London
Lancaster	University College Stockton
Leeds	University College, Worcester
Leicester	Wolverhampton
Liverpool John Moores	
Loughborough	
Luton	

Degree courses in Asian languages

Institution	Chinese	Japanese	Other
Cambridge	*	*	Hindi
Cardiff		*j	
Central Lancashire	*c		
Durham	*	*	
Edinburgh	*	*	
European School		*j	
Hull			
Leeds			
Liverpool John Moores			
Luton	*cm	*cm	
Newcastle	*c	*c	Korean (c), Hindi (c)
Nottingham		*jeng	
Oxford	*	*	
Oxford Brookes		*j	
Reading		*j	
Salford		*jit	
School of Oriental and African Studies, London (SOAS)	*	*	Korean; and joint courses in Bengali, Burmese, Gujarati, Hindi, Indonesian, Nepali, Sinhalese, Tamil, Thai, Tibetan, Urdu, Vietnamese
Sheffield	*	*	Korean
Stirling		*	
Sunderland		*jbus	
Ulster		*c	
Westminster	*j		
Wolverhampton		*cm	
York			Hindi (jl)

jeng: offered as part of a joint programme with Mechanical Engineering or Manufacturing Engineering & Management
jit: Information Technology with studies in Japan
jbus: International Business with Japanese
jl: offered as part of a joint programme with Linguistics

Degree courses in Arabic and Middle Eastern languages

Institution	Arabic	Hebrew	Persian	Turkish
Cambridge	*j	*j	*j	
Durham	*j			
Edinburgh	*		*j	
Exeter	*			
Leeds	*			
Manchester	*j	*j	*j	*j
Oxford	*	*	*	*
Salford	*j			
School of Oriental and African Studies, London (SOAS)	*	*j	*	*
St Andrews	*j/c			
Westminster	*j			

Degree courses in African languages

Institution	Amharic	Hausa	Swahili	
School of Oriental and African Studies, London (SOAS)	*	*	*	These three languages can each be studied to degree level as single subjects, or in combination with another subject
	In addition, Somali, Sotho, Yoruba and Zulu can each be studied for two successive years as part of the BA in African studies, or as options in some of SOAS's many other courses			

Degree courses in Linguistics

Institution		
Aberdeen	*jls	
Bangor	*	
Brighton	*j	
Bristol. UWE	*j	
Central Lancashire	*c	
Durham	*j/c	
East Anglia	*	
East London	*	
Edinburgh	*	
Essex	*	
Hertfordshire	*	
Kent	*	
Lancaster	*	
Leeds	*	
Luton	*	
Manchester	*	
Newcastle	*	
Nottingham Trent	*j	
Queen Mary & Westfield	*j	
Reading	*	
Salford	*j	
Sheffield	*c	
School of Oriental and African Studies, London (SOAS)	*	
Southampton	*c	
Sussex	*c	
Ulster	*	
UMIST	*	(Computational Linguistics)
University College London	*	
Westminster	*c	
Wolverhampton	*j	
York	*	

jls: Language and Literature of Scotland

27 Studying for a degree in languages with other subjects

Degree courses in business and management studies with a language

This table shows you which institutions offer you the possibility of doing a degree course in a business-related subject (Business Studies, Business Administration, Management Studies, Management Science, European or International Business, . . .) with a language.

Institution	Fr	Ger	It	Sp	Other
Aberdeen	*	*		*	Celtic
Abertay, Dundee	*	*		*	
Aberystwyth	*	*	*	*	Welsh
Anglia	*	*		*	
Aston	*	*			Two languages possible
Bangor	*	*			Welsh
Bath	*	*			
Bell College	*	*		*	
Birmingham	*	*	*	*	Japanese, Portuguese
Bolton Institute	*	*			
Bournemouth	*	*			
Bradford	*	*		*	
Brighton	*	*			Study in the Netherlands, Sweden or Greece is possible (tuition in English)
Bristol UWE	*	*		*	
Buckingham	*			*	
Buckinghamshire Chilterns	*	*	*	*	
Canterbury Christ Church	*				
Cardiff	*	*	*	*	Japanese
Cardiff, UWI	*	*		*	
Central England	*	*		*	Two languages studied
Central Lancashire	*	*	*	*	Chinese, Japanese
Cheltenham & Gloucester	*				
Coventry	*	*	*	*	Portuguese, Russian
Derby	*	*		*	Two languages studied
Durham					Chinese, Japanese

Institution	Fr	Ger	It	Sp	Other
East Anglia	*	*			Danish Two languages possible
East London	*	*		*	
Edinburgh	*	*	*	*	Arabic, Russian
European Business School	*	*	*	*	Chinese, Japanese, Russian Two languages possible
Glamorgan	*	*	*	*	Third year study placement abroad in France, Germany, Italy or Spain. Those not including a language in their programme may spend the third year studying in Denmark, Ireland, the Netherlands, Norway or Sweden (tuition in English)
Glasgow	*	*	*		Celtic, Czech, Polish, Russian
Glasgow Caledonian	*	*		*	Two languages possible
Greenwich	*	*		*	Polish, Russian
Gyosei International College, Reading	*	*			Japanese
Heriot-Watt	*	*		*	
Hertfordshire	*	*		*	Chinese, Japanese. Two languages possible
Huddersfield	*	*		*	
Hull	*	*	*	*	Danish, Dutch, Swedish
Keele	*	*			Russian. Two languages possible
Kent	*	*	*	*	
King Alfred's Winchester					Japanese
King's College, London	*				
Kingston	*	*		*	
Lancaster	*	*	*	*	
Lampeter	*	*			
Leeds	*	*	*	*	Arabic, Chinese, Japanese, Portuguese, Russian
Leeds Metropolitan	*	*	*	*	Two languages studied
Leeds, Trinity and All Saints	*			*	
Lincolnshire and Humberside	*	*		*	Study or work placement in France, Germany or Spain; or in Finland, Hungary or Sweden for those not studying a language (tuition in English)
Liverpool John Moores	*	*	*	*	Japanese, Russian
London Guildhall	*	*			
Loughborough	*	*			
Luton	*	*	*	*	Japanese
Manchester Metropolitan	*	*	*	*	

Degree courses in business and management studies with a language (cont'd)

Institution	Fr	Ger	It	Sp	Other
Middlesex	*	*		*	
Napier	*	*		*	
Newcastle	*	*		*	Japanese, Korean
North London	*	*		*	
Northumbria	*	*		*	
Nottingham	*	*		*	Portuguese
Nottingham Trent	*	*		*	
Oxford Brookes	*	*	*	*	Japanese. Two languages possible
Plymouth	*	*	*	*	
Portsmouth	*	*	*	*	Portuguese, Russian
Queen Mary & Westfield	*	*		*	Russian
Queen's Belfast	*	*	*	*	
Reading	*	*	*		
Regents Business School		*		*	
Robert Gordon	*	*			
Roehampton	*				
Royal Holloway	*	*	*	*	Japanese
Salford	*	*	*	*	(two languages)
St Andrews	*	*	*	*	Arabic, Russian
School of Oriental and African Studies, London (SOAS)					Arabic, Chinese, Japanese, and many other Oriental and African languages
Sheffield Hallam	*	*	*	*	
Southampton	*	*		*	
Southampton Institute	*	*		*	Study abroad also possible in Finland
South Bank	*	*			
Staffordshire	*	*			
Stirling	*	*		*	Japanese
Strathclyde	*	*	*	*	Russian
Sunderland	*	*		*	Japanese, Russian
Swansea	*	*	*	*	Russian, Welsh
Teesside	*	*		*	Study placement also possible in Denmark, Finland, the Netherlands, Norway or Portugal (tuition in English)
Thames Valley	*	*		*	
Ulster	*	*		*	Japanese (International Business course offers two languages [Fr with Ger or Sp])

Institution	Fr	Ger	It	Sp	Other
UMIST	*	*			
University College, Northampton	*	*	*	*	
Warwick	*	*	*		
Westminster	*	*		*	(International Business course offers placements in countries where French, German, Spanish, Italian or Russian are spoken)
Wolverhampton	*	*		*	Study abroad at a Dutch or Finnish institution

Degree courses in accountancy or finance with a language

This table shows you which institutions offer you the possibility of doing a degree course in accountancy or other finance-related subjects with a language.

Institution	Fr	Ger	It	Sp	Other
Aberdeen	*	*		*	Gaelic
Aberystwyth	*	*	*	*	Welsh
Bangor	*	*			
Birmingham	*	*	*	*	Portuguese
Bolton Institute	*	*			
Bristol	*	*	*	*	
Cardiff	*			*	
Heriot-Watt	*	*		*	
Hertfordshire	*	*	*	*	Russian
Keele	*				
Kent	*	*			
Lancaster	*	*	*	*	
Lincolnshire & Humberside	*	*		*	
London Guildhall	*	*		*	
Luton		*	*	*	
Manchester Metropolitan	*	*		*	
Oxford Brookes	*	*		*	Japanese
Queen's Belfast	*	*		*	
Southampton	*	*		*	
Stirling	*	*		*	
Teeside	*	*			
Thames Valley	*	*			
University College, Northampton		*	*	*	
Wolverhampton	*	*		*	Russian

Degree courses in law and languages

Institution	Fr	Ger	It	Sp	Rus	Jap	Other
Aberdeen [Scots law]	*b	*		*			Belgian law
Aberystwyth	*	*	*	*			
Anglia	*	*	*	*			
Birmingham	*	*					
Bristol	*	*					
Bristol UWE	*	*		*			One or two languages
Brunel	*	*					
Buckingham	*			*			
Buckinghamshire Chilterns	*	*	*	*			
Cambridge	*						
Cardiff	*	*	*	*		*	
Central Lancashire	*	*					
Coventry	*	*	*	*	*		
De Montfort	*	*					
Dundee	*	*		*			
East Anglia	*	*					
Edinburgh	*	*		*			Scandinavian Studies
Essex	*b	*		*			e
Exeter	*	*					
Glasgow [Scots law]	*	*		*			
Greenwich	*	*		*			
Hull	*	*					
Keele	*						
Kent	*	*	*	*			
King's College, London	*	*					
Kingston	*	*		*			
Lancaster	*	*	*	*			
Leeds	*					*	Chinese
Leicester	*						
Liverpool	*	*					
London Guildhall	*	*		*			
London School of Economics	*						
Luton	*					*	Chinese
Manchester	*						

Institution	Fr	Ger	It	Sp	Rus	Jap	Other
Manchester Metropolitan	*						
Newcastle	*						
Northumbria	*						
Nottingham	*	*					
Nottingham Trent	*	*					
Oxford	*	*					
Oxford Brookes	*	*					
Plymouth	*	*	*	*			
Queen Mary & Westfield		*					e
Queens' Belfast	*			*			e
Reading	*						e
School of Oriental and African Studies, London (SOAS)						*	A range of Oriental and African languages
Sheffield	*	*		*			e
Sheffield Hallam	*	*					e
South Bank	*	*					
Staffordshire	*						
Strathclyde	*	*		*			
Surrey	*	*			*		
Sussex	*	*	*	*	*		
Swansea	*	*	*	*	*		Welsh
Thames Valley	*	*		*			
University College, London	*	*	*				
University College, Northampton	*	*	*				
Warwick	*	*	*				
Westminster	*			*			
Wolverhampton	*	*	*	*	*	*	

b study in Belgium instead of France possible

e study possible in another European country if you are able to speak the language, or if they teach European lawin English (as e.g. in Denmark, the Netherlands, Sweden)

Degree courses in tourism with a language

It is obvious that languages are of importance in the tourist industry, and for this reason the majority of courses have language study as an option. There are travel and tourism degree courses on offer in more than 50 higher education institutions in the UK, many of them providing a range of subject combinations. French, German and Spanish are the most usual languages on offer, but at some places others are available — you will need to check prospectuses to find out for sure which languages you can do.

The institutions below offer you the possibility of continuing the study of one (or more) language(s) as a **significant** part of a degree course in travel and tourism.

Institution		Languages
Bangor Bolton Institute Bournemouth Bristol UWE Buckinghamshire Chilterns Central Lancashire Cheltenham & Gloucester Derby Greenwich	Liverpool John Moores Luton Napier Oxford Brookes South Bank Swansea Thames Valley Wolverhampton	French, German and Spanish are the languages most commonly on offer. Check which languages are offered before you apply, and whether you go abroad to study or to undertake a work placement as part of the course.

Degree courses in physical education, sports science or leisure studies with a language

This table shows you which institutions offer you the possibility of continuing the study of a language while you do a degree course in a sport- or leisure-related subject. French and German are the most usual languages on offer, but at some places you can do others, like Italian, Spanish, Russian or Japanese. You will need to check prospectuses to find out for sure which languages you can do.

Institution	PE/Sports Science	Leisure Studies/Management
Birmingham College of Food, Tourism & Creative Studies		*
Bolton Institute		*
Canterbury Christ Church	*	*
Cheltenham & Gloucester	*	*
Chester	*	
De Montfort	*	*
Edge Hill	*	
Glamorgan	*	*
Liverpool John Moores		*
Luton	*	*
Oxford Brookes	*	*
Roehampton	*	*
Thames Valley		*
Teesside	*	
University College, Northampton	*	
Wolverhampton	*	*

Degree courses in engineering and languages

This table lists only the engineering courses which make provision for language study; it does not therefore take account of courses which just offer the possibility of study abroad, of which there is quite a number.

j indicates that the course is offered as part of a joint honours programme with another subject – often business studies.

Institution	Fr	Ger	Sp	Other
Aeronautical/Aerospace Engineering				
Bath	*	*		
Imperial College, London	*	*		
Southampton	*	*		
UMIST	*			
Chemical Engineering				
Aston	*	*		
Bath	*	*		
Birmingham	*	*	*	Japanese, Russian
Bradford	*	*		
Imperial College, London	*	*	*	Italian, Japanese
Sheffield	*	*	*	Italian, Japanese
Surrey	*	*	*	
UMIST	*	*	*	
Civil Engineering				
Aston	*	*		
Birmingham	*	*	*	Japanese, Russian
Bolton Institute	*	*		
Cardiff	*	*	*	
Coventry	*	*	*	Italian, Russian
Greenwich	*	*	*	Italian
Imperial College, London	*	*	*	Italian
Manchester	*	*	*	Italian, Japanese
Nottingham	*	*	*	
Sheffield	*	*	*	Italian
Southampton	*	*		
Surrey	*	*	*	
Swansea	*	*	*	Italian
Electrical and/or Electronic Engineering				
Abertay, Dundee	*	*	*	

Degree courses in engineering and languages (cont'd)

Institution	Fr	Ger	Sp	Other
Anglia	*	*	*	Italian
Aston	*	*		
Bath	*	*		
Birmingham	*	*	*	Japanese, Russian
Central England	*	*		
Coventry	*	*	*	Italian, Russian
Imperial College, London	*	*	*	Italian
King's College, London	*	*		Italian, Japanese
Leicester	*	*		Italian, Portuguese
Manchester	*	*	*	Italian, Japanese
Manchester Metropolitan	*	*	*	Italian
Nottingham	*	*	*	
Sheffield	*	*	*	
Southampton	*	*		
Sunderland	*	*		
Surrey	*	*	*	
Sussex	*	*		Japanese
Teesside	*	*		
UMIST	*			
General Engineering/Technology				
Brighton		*		
Brunel	*	*		
Cardiff	*	*	*	
Coventry	*	*	*	
Glasgow Caledonian	*	*	*	
Liverpool	*	*	*	
Queen Mary & Westfield	*	*	*	
Surrey	*	*	*	
Materials Science and Technologies				
Birmingham	*	*	*	Japanese, Russian
Brunel	*	*		
Liverpool	*	*	*	
Sheffield	*	*	*	Italian
Surrey	*	*	*	

Institution	Fr	Ger	Sp	Other
Mechanical and Manufacturing/Production Engineering				
Abertay, Dundee	*	*	*	
Aston	*	*		
Bath	*	*		
Birmingham	*	*	*	Japanese, Russian
Brunel	*	*		
Cardiff	*	*	*	
Central England	*	*		
Hertfordshire	*	*		
Leicester	*	*		Italian, Portuguese
Manchester	*	*	*	Italian
Newcastle	*	*	*	
Nottingham	*	*	*	Japanese, Russian
Sheffield	*	*	*	Italian
Southampton	*	*		
Sunderland	*	*		
Surrey	*	*		
Sussex	*	*		Japanese
Swansea	*	*	*	Italian
UMIST	*	*		

Degree courses in science and languages

This table shows you which institutions offer you the possibility of continuing the study of a language while you do a science degree course. French and German are the most usual languages on offer, but at some places you can do others, like Italian, Spanish, Russian or Japanese. You will need to check prospectuses to find out for sure which languages you can do.

On many of these courses you would be able to go abroad to study, too.

Institution	Biochemistry	Biology	Chemistry	Environmental science/studies	Geology/Earth science	Physics/Physical Science	Psychology	Other
Aberdeen			*			*	*	
Anglia		*	*				*	Ecology
Aston		*	*				*	
Birmingham			*					

Degree courses in science and languages (cont'd)

Institution	Biochemistry	Biology	Chemistry	Environmental science/studies	Geology/Earth science	Physics/Physical Science	Psychology	Other
Bolton Institute		*		*			*	
Buckingham							*	
Canterbury Christ Church				*			*	Natural Science
Central Lancashire	*					*	*	Applied Microbiology, Pharmacology
Cheltenham & Gloucester					*			
Chester College		*					*	
De Montfort							*	
Derby					*		*	
Dundee						*	*	
East London		*		*			*	
Glamorgan		*	*	*	*		*	
Glasgow							*	
Goldsmiths							*	
Greenwich		*	*					Human Physiology, Pharmaceutical Science
Heriot Watt			*					
Hull			*					
Keele	*	*	*	*	*	*	*	Astrophysics, Medicinal and Biological Chemistry
King's College, London						*		
Kingston		*	*		*		*	
Lancaster			*		.		*	
Leeds			*			*		
Liverpool			*		*	*	*	Geophysics, Life Sciences
London Guildhall							*	
Loughborough			*					
Luton	*	*		*	*		*	Ecology, Pharmacology, Physiology
Manchester	*	*						Anatomical Science, Genetics, Life Sciences, Microbiology, Molecular Biology, Neuroscience, Pharmacology, Physiology, Plant Science

Institution	Biochemistry	Biology	Chemistry	Environmental science/studies	Geology/Earth science	Physics/Physical Science	Psychology	Other
Manchester Metropolitan			*	*			*	
Napier		*	*			*		
Nottingham				*		*		Food Microbiology
Oxford Brookes		*	*	*	*		*	Ecology
Paisley		*	*			*		
Plymouth			*		*		*	
Queen Mary & Westfield			*					
Roehampton		*		*			*	Human and Social Biology
St Andrews		*	*				*	
Salford						*		
Staffordshire				*				
Stirling							*	
Strathclyde							*	
Sunderland	*		*		*		*	Ecology, Microbiology, Physiology
Surrey			*					
Sussex	*	*	*	*		*		Chemical Physics, Medicinal Chemistry
Swansea		*					*	
Teesside							*	
UMIST	*							Paper Science
University College, London			*					
University College, Northampton					*		*	Ecology
Environmental Chemistry								
University College, Worcester		*						
Wolverhampton	*	*	*	*			*	Biomedical Science Biotechnology Environmental Chemistry Human Physiology Microbiology Pharmacology

Degree courses in science with a period of study abroad

The following institutions offer the possibility of spending some time studying abroad while you are following a science degree course.

Language tuition is provided, usually in the institution's language centre, although universities in some European countries — Denmark, Greece and the Netherlands, for example — conduct science courses in English for visiting UK undergraduates in English.

Institution	Biochemistry	Biology	Chemistry	Environmental science/studies	Geology/Earth science	Physics/Physical Science	Psychology	Other
Aberdeen		*	*				*	Zoology
Abertaye Dundee		*		*				
Aberystwyth	*	*			*	*		Genetics, Microbiology, Zoology
Anglia		*	*					
Aston		*					*	Pharmacy
Bangor	*	*	*	*			*	Botany, Zoology
Bath		*				*		Pharmacy
Birmingham	*	*	*	*		*	*	Biotechnology, Botany, Genetics, Microbiology
Bradford	*		*					Pharmacy
Bristol		*	*			*		
Bristol UWE		*						
Brunel	*	*			*		*	
Cardiff	*	*	*		*	*	*	
Central Lancashire	*	*	*			*		
Cheltenham & Gloucester					*		*	
Chester		*		*				
City			*				*	
Colchester				*				
Coventry	*	*	*	*				
Cranfield/Silsoe				*				
De Montfort		*				*		Pharmacy
Derby		*	*	*				
Dundee		*	*	*		*		Botany, Pharmacology
Durham		*					*	
East Anglia	*	*	*	*				Ecology, Geophysical Sciences, Meteorology and Oceanography

Institution	Biochemistry	Biology	Chemistry	Environmental science/studies	Geology/Earth science	Physics/Physical Science	Psychology	Other
East London		*						Pharmacology
Edinburgh			*				*	Environmental Chemistry
Essex						*		
Exeter			*			*	*	
Glamorgan						*		Biotechnology
Glasgow	*					*		
Greenwich	*	*	*	*	*	*		Analytical Chemistry, Human Physiology, Medicinal Chemistry, Pharmaceutical Sciences
Heriot Watt			*			*		Microbiology
Hertfordshire		*	*	*	*	*		Astronomy, Astrophysics, Biological Chemistry, Biotechnology, Ecology and Agricultural Biology, Environmental Pollution Sciences, Human Physiology, Microbiology, Molecular Biology, Pharmaceutical Sciences
Huddersfield			*	*				
Hull		*	*			*		
Imperial College, London	*	*	*			*		Biotechnology
Kent	*	*	*			*	*	Biological Chemistry, Chemistry and Physics, Chemistry with Management Science, Molecular and Cellular Biology, Microbiology, Pharmaceutical Chemistry, Physics with Space Science, Physics with Astrophysics, Theoretical Physics
King's College, London		*	*			*		Chemistry with Management
Kingston	*	*	*	*		*		Pharmacology
Lancaster	*	*	*	*		*	*	
Leeds	*	*	*			*	*	Biotechnology, Genetics, Microbiology, Pharmacology, Zoology
Leeds Metropolitan				*				
Leicester	*	*	*			*		Botany, Genetics, Microbiology, Pharmacology, Physiology, Zoology

Degree courses in science with a period of study abroad (cont'd)

Institution	Biochemistry	Biology	Chemistry	Environmental science/studies	Geology/Earth science	Physics/Physical Science	Psychology	Other
Lincolnshire & Humberside				*				
Liverpool Hope		*		*				
London School of Pharmacy								Pharmacology, Pharmacy
Loughborough						*		
Luton				*				
Manchester	*	*	*			*	*	Genetics, Microbiology, Pharmacology, Physiology, Zoology
Manchester Metropolitan		*	*	*			*	
Middlesex		*		*				
Napier		*	*	*		*		Microbiology
Nescot	*	*						
Newcastle	*	*	*			*	*	
North East Wales IHE				*				
North London		*						
Northumbria			*			*		
Nottingham	*	*		*			*	Biotechnology, Botany, Microbiology
Nottingham Trent		*	*			*		
Oxford	*					*		Physiology
Oxford Brookes		*	*	*			*	
Plymouth		*	*				*	
Portsmouth		*				*	*	Pharmacy
Queen Mary & Westfield		*	*			*		Zoology
Queen's Belfast	*		*			*		
Reading	*	*	*			*	*	Biotechnology, Physiology, Zoology
Robert Gordon		*	*			*		
Roehampton		*					*	
Royal Holloway						*		
St Andrews	*	*	*			*		Microbiology
Salford	*	*	*	*		*		Physiology

Institution	Biochemistry	Biology	Chemistry	Environmental science/studies	Geology/Earth science	Physics/Physical Science	Psychology	Other
Sheffield	*	*	*		*	*	*	Botany, Microbiology, Zoology
Sheffield Hallam		*	*					
Southampton			*		*			
Staffordshire	*	*	*	*	*			Microbiology
Stirling		*					*	
Strathclyde			*	*		*		
Sunderland							*	Pharmacy
Surrey	*		*	*	*	*	*	Microbiology
Sussex		*	*			*	*	
Swansea	*	*	*			*		Biomolecular and Biomedical Chemistry, Chemistry with Analytical Science, Chemistry with Business Management, Chemistry with Computer Science, Chemistry with Environmental Chemistry, Chemistry with Law, Genetics, Microbiology, Zoology
Teesside	*		*					Biotechnology
Ulster		*		*			*	
UMIST	*		*	*		*		
University College, London			*				*	
University College, Worcester		*		*			*	
Warwick						*	*	
Wolverhampton		*		*				
Wye College		*		*				Botany
York	*	*	*			*	*	Chemistry Life Systems and Pharmaceuticals, Chemistry Management and Industry, Chemistry Resources and the Environment, Physics with Astrophysics, Physics with Business Management, Physics with Computer Simulation, Theoretical Physics

Degree courses in information technology/computer science with a language

The following table shows you which institutions offer the possibility of combining the study of information technology, computer science or artificial intelligence with a language.

The table also indicates where linguistics can be combined with IT/computing — there are affinities between human languages and the formal languages used for computer programming and systems design, and the study of linguistics can provide insights into these links.

Institution	Fr	Ger	It	Sp	Rus	Other
Aberdeen	*	*		*		
Aberystwyth	*	*	*	*		
Anglia	*	*	*	*		
Aston	*					
Bangor	*	*				
Birmingham	*	*	*	*	*	Modern Greek, Portuguese
Bolton Institute	*	*				
Bristol UWE	*	*		*		English as a foreign language Two languages studied
Buckingham	*			*		
Canterbury Christ Church	*					
Central Lancashire		*	*	*		Chinese
Cheltenham & Gloucester	*					
Chester	*	*		*		
Coventry	*	*		*		
De Montfort	*	*		*		
Derby	*	*		*	*	
East London	*	*	*	*		
Edinburgh						Linguistics (Artificial Intelligence)
Essex	*	*		*	*	
Glamorgan	*	*				Welsh
Glasgow	*			*	*	Celtic, Czech
Greenwich	*	*	*	*		
Heriot-Watt	*	*		*		
Hertfordshire	*	*				Japanese
Huddersfield	*	*				
Imperial College, London						MEng course in Computing with European Programme of Study offers language study and work/study abroad in a choice of countries in mainland Europe

Institution	Fr	Ger	It	Sp	Rus	Other
Keele		*			*	
Kent	*	*	*	*		European Studies
King's College, London	*	*		*		Modern Greek, Portuguese
Lampeter	*					Welsh
Lancaster	*	*	*	*		
Leeds	*	*				
Leicester	*	*		*		BSc course in Maths and Computer Science (Europe) provides language study and a year at a university in Denmark, France, Germany or Spain
Lincolnshire & Humberside	*	*		*		
Liverpool	*	*	*	*		
Liverpool Hope	*					European Studies
London Guildhall	*	*		*		European Studies
Luton	*			*		Chinese, Japanese, Linguistics
Nottingham Trent	*					
Oxford Brookes	*	*		*		Japanese
Paisley	*	*		*		
Plymouth	*	*	*	*		
Reading		*				
Roehampton	*			*		
Royal Holloway	*					
St Andrews	*	*				
Salford	*	*				Japanese (with a year at a university in Japan)
Sheffield	*	*		*	*	
Stirling	*	*		*		
Sunderland	*	*		*		
Surrey		*				
Sussex	*	*	*	*	*	
Swansea	*	*	*	*	*	Welsh
University College, Northampton	*		*	*		
Wolverhampton	*	*	*	*	*	Japanese, Latin American Studies BA Languages for Business course involves the study of two languages, IT and business studies

Degree courses in food science with a language

This table shows you which institutions offer you the possibility of combining degree studies in Food Science or Food Technology with a language.

In addition to the courses listed below where a language forms a significant part of the programme, many courses in this field at other institutions allow you to study a language as an optional extra.

Institution	Fr	Ger	Sp	Other
Nottingham	*	*	*	
Oxford Brookes	*	*		Japanese
Surrey	*	*	*	Italian, Russian, Japanese
Thames Valley	*	*	*	

Degree courses in agriculture, horticulture and other land-based subjects with a language

This table shows you which institutions offer you the possibility of continuing the study of a language while you do a degree course in a land-based subject.

French and German are the most usual languages on offer, but at some places you can do others, like Italian or Spanish. You will need to check prospectuses to find out for sure which languages you can do.

On many of these courses you would be able to go abroad to study, too.

Institution	Agriculture	Ecology, Conservation, Environmental Management	Horticulture	Landscape Management	Other
Anglia		*			
Cheltenham & Gloucester		*			
Harper Adams	*				
Nottingham	*		*		
Reading			*	*	Agricultural Botany, Crop Protection
Royal Agricultural College	*				

Degree courses in theatre arts, dance and music with a language

This table shows you which institutions offer you the possibility of combining the study of performing arts or music with a language.

French, German. Italian and Spanish are widely on offer, but at some places you can do other languages such as Czech, Modern Greek, Polish, Portuguese, Russian, Irish, Welsh, or Japanese; and the School of Oriental and African Studies offers Music with a wide range of Oriental and African languages. You will need to check prospectuses to find out for sure which languages you can do.

You will also need to check in the prospectuses to find out how much language study you would do as part of your course. Some of the courses listed below are joint honours courses, others are combinations which you would put together yourself as part of a combined honours, or a modular programme.

Institution	Drama/ Theatre Studies	Dance	Music	Other
Aberdeen			*	
Aberystwyth	*			
Anglia			*	
Birmingham	*	*	*	
Bolton	*			
Bristol	*		*	
Bristol UWE	*			
Canterbury Christ Church			*	
Cardiff			*	
Chester	*	*		
De Montfort	*			Music Technology
Derby	*	*		Popular Music
Durham			*	
Exeter			*	
Glamorgan	*			
Glasgow	*		*	
Hertfordshire				Electronic Music
Huddersfield			*	
Hull	*		*	
Keele			*	Electronic Music
Kent	*			
King's College, London			*	
Lancaster	*		*	
Leeds			*	

Degree courses in theatre arts, dance and music with a language (cont'd)

Institution	Drama/ Theatre Studies	Dance	Music	Other
Liverpool Hope			*	
Luton	*			
Nottingham			*	
Oxford Brookes			*	
Plymouth	*			
Queen Mary & Westfield	*			
Queen's Belfast			*	
Reading			*	Film and Drama
Roehampton	*	*	*	
Royal Holloway	*		*	
School of Oriental and African Studies, London (SOAS)			*	
Sheffield			*	
Southampton			*	
South Bank			*	
Sunderland			*	
Warwick	*			
Wolverhampton	*		*	

Degree courses in social policy, social administration, public policy or community studies with a language

This table shows you which institutions offer you the possibility of continuing the study of a language as a significant part of a degree course in social/public policy, or community studies.

You will need to check in the prospectuses to find out how much language study you would do as part of your course. Some of the courses listed below are joint honours courses, others are combinations which you would put together yourself as part of a combined honours, or a modular programme.

Institution	Fr	Ger	Sp	Other
Anglia	*	*	*	
Aston		*		
Bangor				Welsh
Bolton	*	*		
Central Lancashire	*	*	*	Chinese, Italian Business French, German or Spanish

Institution	Fr	Ger	Sp	Other
East London	*	*	*	Italian
Edinburgh				Scandinavian Studies (Danish, Norwegian or Swedish)
Glamorgan	*	*		Welsh
Glasgow			*	Celtic, Czech, Polish, Russian
Hertfordshire	*	*		
Keele		*		Russian
London Guildhall	*	*	*	
Luton	*	*	*	Chinese, Italian, Japanese
Paisley	*	*	*	
Plymouth	*	*	*	Italian
Roehampton	*		*	
Royal Holloway	*	*		Italian, Japanese, English as a foreign language
South Bank	*	*	*	
Staffordshire	*			
Teesside	*	*		
Wolverhampton	*	*	*	Italian, Japanese, Russian, Latin American Studies

Degree courses in politics or international relations with a language

This table shows you which institutions offer you the possibility of doing a degree course in politics, international politics, political science, international relations or government with a language.

You will need to check in the prospectuses to find out how much language study you would do as part of your course. Some of the courses listed below are joint honours courses, others are combinations which you would put together yourself as part of a combined honours, or a modular programme.

In addition to the courses listed below, some courses in this field offer the possibility of language study as an optional extra, or the opportunity to undertake a work- or study-placement abroad.

Institution	Fr	Ger	It	Sp	Other
Aberdeen	*	*		*	
Aberystwyth	*	*		*	Welsh
Anglia	*	*	*	*	
Bath		*			Russian
Bradford	*	*	*	*	Modern Greek
Bristol	*	*	*	*	Russian
Buckingham	*			*	
Cardiff	*	*	*	*	Portuguese, Welsh

Degree courses in politics or international relations with a language (cont'd)

Institution	Fr	Ger	It	Sp	Other
Central Lancashire	*	*	*	*m	Chinese, Japanese, Business French, Business German, Business Spanish (m)
Cheltenham & Gloucester	*				
De Montfort	*	*		*	
Derby	*m	*		*	Russian
Dundee	*	*		*	
Durham					Arabic, Chinese, Japanese, Persian, Turkish
East Anglia	*	*			Danish, Swedish, Norwegian
East London	*	*	*	*	
Edinburgh	*	*		*	Arabic, Persian, Scandinavian Studies
Essex	*	*	*	*	Modern Greek, Russian, Portuguese
Exeter			*		
Glamorgan	*	*			Welsh
Glasgow	*	*	*		Czech, Celtic, Polish
Hull	*				
Keele	*	*			Russian (two languages possible)
Kent	*	*	*		Study in Finland possible too
Kingston	*	*		*	
Lancaster	*	*		*	
Leeds	*			*	Arabic, Chinese, Russian
Leicester	*				
Liverpool	*	*		*	Catalan, Portuguese
Liverpool John Moores	*	*		*	
London Guildhall	*	*		*	
Loughborough	*	*		*	
Luton	*			*	Chinese, Japanese
Manchester Metropolitan	*	*	*	*	
Newcastle	*	*		*	Chinese, Japanese, Korean Also Government and European Studies (with a year abroad)
Northumbria	*	*		*	
Nottingham	*	*			
Nottingham Trent	*	*	*	*	
Paisley	*	*		*	
Plymouth	*	*	*	*	
Portsmouth	*	*		*	Russian

Institution	Fr	Ger	It	Sp	Other
Queen Mary & Westfield	*	*		*	Russian
Queen's Belfast	*	*		*	Celtic, Russian
Reading	*	*	*		
Royal Holloway	*	*	*	*	
St Andrews	*	*	*	*	Arabic, Russian
Salford	*	*	*	*	(Two languages possible)
School of Oriental and African Studies, London (SOAS)					Arabic, Japanese, Chinese and many other Oriental and African languages
Sheffield	*	*		*	Japanese, Korean, Russian
Southampton	*	*		*	Portuguese
Staffordshire	*	*		*	
Stirling	*	*		*	Japanese
Strathclyde	*	*		*	
Sunderland	*	*		*	
Sussex	*	*	*	*	Russian
Swansea	*	*	*	*	Russian, Welsh
Teesside	*	*			
University College, Northampton	*		*	*	
Warwick	*	*	*		
Wolverhampton	*	*	*	*	Japanese, Russian, Latin American Studies

Degree courses in marketing with a language

This table shows you which institutions offer you the possibility of doing a degree course in Marketing with a language.

You will need to check in the prospectuses to find out how much language study you would do as part of your course. Some of the courses listed below are joint honours courses, others are combinations which you would put together yourself as part of a combined honours, or a modular programme.

Institution	Fr	Ger	It	Sp	Other
Abertay Dundee	*	*		*	
Aberystwyth	*	*	*	*	Welsh
Bolton	*	*			
Bristol UWE	*	*		*	
Buckingham	*			*	
Buckinghamshire Chilterns	*	*	*	*	

Degree courses in marketing with a language (cont'd)

Institution	Fr	Ger	It	Sp	Other
Canterbury Christ Church	*				
Central England	*	*		*	
Central Lancashire	*m	*	*	*	Chinese, German or Spanish for Business; French for Business (m)
Cheltenham & Gloucester	*				
De Montfort	*	*		*	
Derby	*	*		*	
Dundee	*	*		*	
Glamorgan	*	*			Welsh
Greenwich	*	*		*	
Hertfordshire	*	*	*	*	Japanese, Russian
Huddersfield	*	*		*	
Keele		*			Russian
Lancaster	*	*	*	*	
London Guildhall	*	*		*	
Luton	*	*	*	*	Japanese
Napier	*	*		*	
North London	*			*	
Oxford Brookes	*	*		*	Japanese
Paisley	*	*		*	
Regents Business School		*		*	
Roehampton	*			*	
Salford	*	*	*	*	Two of these languages studied
Stirling	*	*		*	Japanese
Sunderland	*	*			
University College, Northampton	*				
Wolverhampton	*	*	*	*	Japanese, Russian, Latin American Studies

Degree courses in information studies and librarianship with a language

This table shows you which institutions offer you the possibility of combining the study of Information Studies/Science or Librarianship with a language.

In addition to the courses listed below where a language forms a significant part of the programme, many courses in this field at other institutions allow you to study a language as an optional extra.

Institution	Fr	Ger	Sp	Other
Aberystwyth	*	*	*	Welsh, Irish
Loughborough	*	*	*	
Northumbria	*	*	*	Russian

Degree courses in art, art history, design, visual communication and media studies (including journalism and publishing) with a language

This table shows you which institutions offer you the possibility of combining the study of art, history of art or media studies with a language. (Courses which have Visual Arts in their title usually combine aspects of fine art and media studies.)

French, German, Italian and Spanish are widely on offer, but at some places you can do other languages such as Dutch, modern Greek, Russian, Polish, Czech, Welsh, Irish, Gaelic, Arabic or Japanese. You will need to check prospectuses to find out for sure which languages you can do.

You will also need to check the prospectuses to find out how much language study you would do as part of your course. Some of the courses listed below are joint honours courses, others are combinations which you would put together yourself as part of a combined honours, or a modular programme.

Institution	Art	Art History	Media Studies/Media and Cultural Studies	Communication Studies	Visual Arts	Design	Other
Aberdeen		*					
Aberystwyth	*	*					Film and Television Studies
Anglia	*	*		*		*	Film Studies, Printmaking
Birmingham		*	*				
Bolton		*			*	*	
Bristol		*					
Buckingham		*					
Canterbury Christ Church	*		*				Radio, Film and Television Studies
Central Lancashire					*	*	Audio Visual Media Studies, Film and Media Studies, Journalism
Cheltenham & Gloucester			*		*		Film Studies
Chester	*						
De Montfort	*		*				History of Art and Design
Derby							History and Theory of Art and Photography, Film and Television, Architectural Design, Product Design

Degree courses in art, art history, design, visual communication and media studies (including journalism and publishing) with a language (cont'd)

Institution	Art	Art History	Media Studies/Media and Cultural Studies	Communication Studies	Visual Arts	Design	Other
East Anglia			*				
East London		*	*	*			History of Art Design and Film
Edge Hill							Communication and Media
Edinburgh		*					
Essex		*					
Exeter	*					*	
Glamorgan		*	*		*	*	Image Processing
Glasgow		*					Film and Television Studies
Huddersfield			*				
Keele					*		
Kent		*					Film Studies
Kent Institute of Art and Design							European Fashion
Kingston							History of Art Architecture and Design
Leeds		*					
Leeds, Trinity and All Saints			*				
Leicester					*		
Lincolnshire & Humberside	*						Animation, Graphic Design, Illustration, Media Technology, Museum and Exhibition Design
Liverpool		*					History of Art and Architecture
Liverpool Hope		*					
Liverpool John Moores			*				
London Guildhall	*			*		*	Textile Furnishing Design, 3D/Spatial Design
Luton			*				And a range of other Media-related courses
Manchester		*					
Middlesex							Product Design

Institution	Art	Art History	Media Studies/Media and Cultural Studies	Communication Studies	Visual Arts	Design	Other
Napier				*			Film and Photography Studies, Journalism, Graphic Communications Management, Industrial Design, Interior Design
Newcastle							Film Studies
Nottingham		*					
Nottingham Trent				*			
Oxford							Arabic or Persian or Turkish with Islamic Art and Archaeology
Oxford Brookes	*	*					Publishing
Plymouth		*	*		*		
Queen Margaret University College, Edinburgh			*				
Reading		*					
Robert Gordon				*			
Roehampton							Art for Community, Film and Television Studies
St Andrews		*					
School of Oriental and African Studies, London (SOAS)							History of Art and Architecture (with an Asian or African language)
Southampton							Fashion Studies, Film Studies, History of Art and Design
Southampton Institute							Antiques (History and Collecting)
South Bank			*				
Staffordshire		*	*				European Media Culture and Politics, Journalism
Stirling							Film and Media Studies
Sunderland		*	*				
Sussex		*	*				
Thames Valley			*				Art and Design History, Digital Arts, Journalism
UMIST							Textile Design and Design Management
University College, London		*					

Degree courses in art, art history, design, visual communication and media studies (including journalism and publishing) with a language (cont'd)

Institution	Art	Art History	Media Studies/Media and Cultural Studies	Communication Studies	Visual Arts	Design	Other
University College, Northampton	*						Architectural Studies, Media and Popular Culture
University College, Worcester							Art and Design
Wolverhampton			*	*		*	Animation, Film Studies, Fine Art as Social Practice, Graphic Communication, Illustration, Painting, Printmaking, Sculpture, and a range of courses related to Interior Design and Product Design in various media

Section 5

Studying and working abroad

Studying in Europe

Work placements in Europe

Taking time out: the gap year

Studying in Europe

The creation of the European Union has stimulated considerable interest among students in spending part of their undergraduate programme abroad. Indeed it is not unusual now for UK universities to receive applications from students in mainland Europe who would like to spend the **whole** of their undergraduate programme in the UK. This is because higher education in the UK has the reputation of being less of a mass education system than those of some of our neighbours, where first year classes in particular may be large, where there is little personal contact between tutor and students, and failure rates may be as high as 70%. Many thousands of UK students cross the Channel in the opposite direction to spend part of their degree abroad, though it is unusual for this to be more than an academic year.

Are courses abroad the same as in the UK?

The first thing to realise is that there is no single model of higher education in Europe. A degree in the UK usually takes three years to complete (four for linguists spending a year abroad). In most countries in Europe, four years is the norm and five is not unusual. In Germany, it is not uncommon for students to take seven years to complete their degree (the *Diplom*). In this sense, Scotland (where the degree takes four years) has a more 'European' system than the rest of the UK. A UK student deciding to take the whole of a degree in an EU country is almost certainly going to spend more than three years getting it. This has important financial implications now that student grants are being phased out, and many students have to pay tuition fees.

Secondly, there may be less diversity available in some disciplines than one finds in this country. Universities in the UK have, at least in some subjects, considerable freedom to design their own curriculum. In other countries the Ministry of Education may keep a much tighter control over what may and may not be taught, and the curriculum remains more traditional. A joint degree in humanities and science, for example, would appear strange to many of our continental neighbours, but you could certainly follow such a programme in a modular scheme in the UK.

If you were intending to spend the whole of an undergraduate programme abroad, you would be well advised to take professional advice before proceeding, starting with the embassy of the country concerned.

Can I go abroad as part of a course in the UK?

Yes. 'Approved residence abroad' as part of a degree based in a UK university is a very common method of studying in another country. The advantage of doing it this way is that in all probability the study placement will be tried and tested and tutors will have personal contacts in the partner university who could offer you advice and encouragement when needed. Normally, the period spent abroad is an intrinsic part of the programme of study so you won't have to 'catch up' by doing extra work when you come back, or extend your degree beyond its normal duration. To be on the safe side you should check these details before you accept a place on the course.

Do I need to speak the language?

If you do not have a good working knowledge of the language of the country you are visiting, it is important to make sure that by the time you leave you have the necessary skills to benefit from a study placement abroad. Although the European Commission is keen to see more students studying in another member State, they have been critical at times of the linguistic preparation given to some students, who then can't benefit as they should from their classes. Your higher education is too important, and too short, to lose part of it in this way. By contrast, if you are linguistically prepared, it can be an enriching experience both socially and academically.

If you have not lived abroad for any length of time, it is worth taking a long look at yourself before taking a decision. Studying abroad will have a totally different feel from the experience you may have had on holiday or as a traveller through the country. In particular, it will need a different set of skills of adaptation. Adaptability is a key quality in studying abroad for any length of time. This involves an opening of the mind to let in new perspectives of the world, a sympathetic approach to everything that is different rather than letting prejudices dominate from the outset. If this willingness to keep an open mind is not the starting point, travel will narrow the mind rather than broaden it. Better stay at home!

Fortunately, many eighteen- to twenty-year-olds are open to new ideas and cultural values, so that in practice the 'value added' by the study period abroad is usually very evident in their level of maturity and independence when they return. This is particularly the case when they have lived with a family or shared accommodation with native students rather than their own compatriots. You are strongly recommended to resist the temptation of seeking friends among the English-speaking fraternity. This is a very natural tendency, but understanding the social and cultural values of the country means working hard from day one to meet the people of the country concerned.

Studying in Europe
Checklist

1	Many thousands of UK students currently spend part of their degree course abroad — usually a maximum of one academic year.
2	You would need to think carefully, and take advice, before deciding to study abroad for the whole of your degree course — there is no single model of higher education in Europe, and the fact that degree courses on the continent usually take longer than British ones could have important financial implications for you.
3	Universities in the rest of Europe generally have less freedom to design their own courses than British universities, and you might find you had less choice of degree course if you went to study abroad.
4	If you go abroad as a planned part of your UK course, you are likely to get all the advice, help and encouragement you need, and you will not have to 'catch up' on your studies when you get back, or extend the length of your course.
5	To take full advantage of any time spent abroad, you should ensure that you are sufficiently competent in the relevant language, and that you go with a mind sufficiently open to new experiences and perspectives.
6	Most students return from their period of residence abroad with greater maturity and independence, particularly if they have made an effort from the outset to mix with the people of the country concerned, and resisted any temptation to spend their time with English-speaking friends.

Work placements in Europe

Could I do a work placement as part of my course?

Yes. Many UK students now opt for a job placement in mainland Europe as part of their undergraduate experience. Some University departments offer this as part of the degree package and offer to provide — or more usually help to provide — a job, usually for between three and nine months. It is important to establish at the outset whether this is a compulsory or optional part of the course. In a degree in which the year abroad is compulsory, you should check how many of their current students in approved residence abroad are actually in employment. Employment may be 'gainful' (that is, paid), or 'non-gainful' (unpaid). Under current grant regulations students in compulsory residence abroad as part of their course, and in an **unpaid** work placement, are still entitled to a grant. Students in receipt of a salary in a **paid** placement forfeit their right to a grant for that period, for obvious reasons. (Grants are gradually being replaced by loans in any case, so placements may not be differentiated in this way for very much longer.)

Could I take a year out even if it's not part of the course?

In practice, there is nothing preventing a student on a three-year degree requesting a year out to work abroad even when this is not part of the course. The teaching department has to agree to this, but many departments will do so provided the student concerned applies to intermit in good time and provides a solid justification for taking this course of action. There is a down side of which you should be aware: by taking a year out when all your classmates are continuing their degree uninterrupted you will find yourself among a different cohort of students when you return. However, if you are the gregarious sort you won't have any difficulty making new friends, and the final year tends to be the one in which you buckle down and work hardest, so by that time your social life may not be so hectic anyway . . .

Why would I want to take a year out to work abroad?

Good question. Before you decide to start looking for a work placement abroad, do sit down and ask yourself some basic questions:

- Why do I want to do this?
- Will it improve my knowledge of my subject?
- Will it improve my chance of getting a better degree?
- Would it be better to wait until I have graduated, then look for a work placement abroad?
- Am I doing this for negative reasons rather than positive ones? Is it simply to escape something at home or at university that I'll have to cope with in the long run anyway?
- Have I discussed it with my tutors, and are they supportive?
- Do I have the necessary language skills to cope?

This may all sound a bit negative, but it helps if you have a 'game plan' and know broadly where you are going in career terms before deciding on a course of action.

Now, let's assume that you have thought through these issues and still think it is a good idea.

How do I go about it?

Many university departments will have a database of addresses of current and past employers of their students, and will help you construct a *curriculum vitae* and letter of introduction in the foreign language. It is very important to present yourself as professionally as possible. The employer you are writing to will probably receive dozens of letters in the post every morning, including lots of unsolicited mail like yours. Unless there is something in the letter of application to make the employer at least stop and think, it will very quickly end up in the waste paper bin!

There are four basic ways in which you can find a work placement, with or without the help of the department.

- You can write directly from this country to the employer.

- You can advertise in a *Situations wanted* section of a foreign newspaper — preferably a regional or local one.

- You can contact employment agencies or other organisations that have a list of vacancies and may contact the employer on your behalf.

- Or you can use the opportunity while you are in the country concerned to make contact with an employer and ask if you may visit to discuss the possibility of a work placement.

In all cases, have ready a *curriculum vitae* and written statement in the foreign language. This will save a lot of time and explanation even in the case of face-to-face meetings.

If you are writing from this country, it helps to enclose a pre-addressed envelope so that the employer feels under some obligation, at least to acknowledge your letter! Any good careers library or even a public library will have sources of addresses such as the *Europa Yearbook*, which lists banks, universities, radio and TV stations, and newspapers. If you are thinking of working in an hotel, restaurant, theatre, museum or art gallery, try one of the tourist guides such as *Fodors, Michelin* or *Blue*. Your local Chamber of Commerce may also be willing to help.

But don't assume that the job for which you are searching is always a vacancy waiting to be filled by external advertisement. It is just as likely that you can persuade someone to create a job for you, particularly since it is not going to be either permanent or very costly to the company concerned. Many companies see advantages in having a native English speaker available, particularly when that person also speaks the foreign language to a reasonable level. For this reason, you should exploit potentially useful networks as well as follow the application processes described above.

Such networks might be:

- parents and friends;

- tutors and teachers, past and present;

- members of social groups or clubs to which you may belong;

- family advisers (bank manager, solicitor, etc);

- your MP and EuroMP.

The main characteristic of networking is that one contact will lead to another. There will inevitably be disappointments, dead-ends and blind alleys, but there is a good chance of success since a large number of people will eventually know that you are looking for work abroad and sooner or later an opportunity will present itself. If you can actually carry out some of this networking abroad among your friends and contacts in the country concerned, this is an even faster way of making progress.

The learning contract and credit for residence abroad

If you decide to choose a course which requires residence abroad, you may be offered a choice of three ways in which to do this:

- study in a university department;

- employment (paid or unpaid) in a commercial or industrial setting;

- employment as a foreign language teaching assistant.

Students are three times more likely to be offered a study placement than a post in a company or a school, and well paid jobs are particularly rare for students who at this stage in their career may not have any highly developed skills to offer employers.

Would the time abroad count towards my degree/diploma?

Many universities now operate credit schemes for their undergraduate programmes, so that typically a year's study would attract 120 credits. To obtain an honours degree in such an institution you would have to clock up 360 credits (i.e. a minimum of three years' study). Most degrees that we would call 'languages degrees' involve an extra year, spent abroad, so in these cases you would need 480 credits before the degree could be awarded. The year abroad would attract the same number of credits as any other year, so you would have to show that they had been earned.

Learning contracts

The need to be able to demonstrate the value of residence abroad has led to the notion and practice of the 'learning contract'. It is not difficult to show that learning has taken place if you set coursework or exams in the home university, but it is not so straightforward when students are hundreds of miles away and scattered over several different countries.

The publication *The year abroad: preparation, monitoring, evaluation*, edited by G Parker and A Rouxeville (CILT, 1995) in-cludes a number of interesting examples of how universities resolve this dilemma. A project run by the University of Leeds tries to get students to think about what they expect to get out of the year abroad by spending time before they go setting out a list of learning objectives.

For example, by means of a process known as the 'card sort,' you would identify the things you might learn while you are abroad and try to put them in an order of importance for you personally.

There is a total of 87 cards ranging from: 'Improve your oral language skills to cope with a work environment' and 'Be positive' to 'Improve your organisation, planning, project and time management skills' and 'Take a greater responsibility for your own learning and development.' Some cards aim at opening up new horizons for students: 'Develop a network of useful contacts.' Others are reminders that they still have a course to complete back in the UK: 'Create and maintain links with your home institution.'

Once you had thought through the relevance to your own case of these objectives and set them in some order of priority, you would be in a position to draw up a personal action plan using forms that may look something like the ones opposite.

You would then be asked to keep a record of your experience and reflect on what it was you were learning, personally, professionally and academically. When you returned, the initial aims and objectives would be compared with the actual achievements.

The above process is by no means universal nor as detailed as is described here, but the principle behind approved residence abroad is to acquire this range of skills and knowledge, including self-knowledge. It is simply that departments have all sorts of different ways of achieving these aims, and a *learning contract* is a structured way of doing so.

Examples of cards used for personal action planning

Record of objectives   **Ranking:** 1= most important, 2= important, 3= less important

OBJECTIVES	Ranking
1. ACADEMIC/LINGUISTIC SKILLS ■ ■	
2. ACADEMIC/CULTURAL ■ ■	
3. PERSONAL SKILLS ■ ■	
4. PROFESSIONAL SKILLS ■ ■	
5. OTHER SKILLS ■ ■	

Personal action plan — learning contract

AREAS	DECISIONS	ACTION
1. CONCERNS	1. 2. 3.	
2. OBJECTIVES	1. 2. 3.	
3. STRATEGIES	1. 2. 3.	
4. SKILLS	1. 2. 3.	
5. OTHERS	1. 2. 3.	

C*i*LT

Work placements in Europe
Checklist

1. Many undergraduates now opt for a job placement in mainland Europe as part of their course, either as a compulsory or as an optional part of their degree course.

2. Under current grant regulations, if your job placement offered paid employment, you would forfeit your right to a grant while you were employed; if you were unpaid, you would still be entitled to your grant.

3. Even if your course does not offer work experience abroad, you can choose to take a year off from your studies to get employment abroad, with the agreement of your university teaching department. Of course, on your return you would find yourself studying with a different group of students!

4. You would be well advised to think seriously about your reasons for wanting to take a year out to work abroad. Are your reasons positive ones?

5. There are four basic ways to find a work placement; you can write directly to a foreign employer from the UK; you can advertise in a foreign newspaper; you can go through an organisation such as an appropriate employment agency; or you can use an opportunity when you are in the foreign country to make contact with a potential employer.

6. To save time, you should make sure you have your CV and a written statement already prepared in the foreign language for when you start the process of job seeking. And enclose a pre-addressed envelope with each application, so the employer feels under some obligation to reply!

7. Why not persuade an employer to create a temporary job for you, rather than wait for a vacancy to occur? Many employers can see advantages in having a native English speaker available.

8. To set up such a 'customised' post, it is worth exploiting useful networks, like family, friends, acquaintances, teachers and influential people such as your MP or MEP.

9. There are three ways of spending time abroad as part of your course — study in a foreign university, a work placement, or a post as a foreign language teaching assistant. The first of these is the most commonly available option.

10. In order to measure the way in which the year abroad can count towards your degree, some HE institutions have introduced *learning contracts* and encouraged students to identify what they intend to get out of the experience abroad, so that actual achievement can be measured against this.

Taking time out: the gap year

It is not essential to go straight on to another course or into a job. Some students feel in need of a break after leaving school or college, in order to broaden their experience before starting work, or three or four more years of studying. You may be one of them! On average, about 15% of 'A' level students take some time off from their studies before going on to higher education; statistics for those on NVQ courses are much lower — possibly because the vocational nature of NVQ courses means that students following them have clear ideas about their futures and it makes sense to proceed directly to what they see as the next stage in a definite career progression.

Should I take a year out?

There are advantages and disadvantages in taking time out, and the relative importance of these will depend upon your own personal circumstances. The key question to ask yourself is what you expect to gain from the experience.

This is because you need to be clear why you want a year out, so that you make some positive plans and do not waste your time footling about. It is all too easy to put off making decisions, and get to the end of the year with not very much to show for it. The more effort you put into the planning of your gap year, the more successful, rewarding and enjoyable it is likely to be.

You may feel that you have done enough studying for a while, or you want to gain some new experiences, or to go abroad to get really fluent in a language, or perhaps you need the time and space to earn some money. As well as giving you an opportunity to acquire new skills, taking a year off from academic work can give you a very useful opportunity to get your life in perspective, and to discover whether the plans you have made for your future career are really what you want. And at the end of your 'year out', although you may find it a little difficult at first to get back into the habit of study, you are likely to be more independent and resilient, and able to cope more readily with the new experiences which student life brings.

A good reason for taking time out is to try to gain some experience related to your proposed course. This is of particular importance if you want to study languages. Think what an advantage you would have when you started your course if you were already at ease speaking the language! And you would also have valuable first-hand experience of the life and culture of the country.

Students who have gained some other experience before starting on a higher education programme often get more out of their course. Statistics have shown that as the age of the student increases, so does his or her chance of successfully completing the course.

Some students find that the experience causes them to reassess what they want out of higher education, and even end up choosing a different course to the one they originally picked out. During a year out you have time to make up your own mind about what *you* really want to do. If you found out that you had made a wrong choice after you had started the course it might perhaps be possible to change, but you could have to waste a year while you applied for something different, and it could also cause you financial problems with your grant.

An increasing number of students want to take a job not just to get useful work experience, but also to get some money in the bank in order to avoid or to ease the debt problems which can beset so many students these days. You should make a list of the advantages and disadvantages as you think they might affect you. To start you off, here are a few suggested pros and cons:

> **PROS**
>
> - I'll get some useful work experience
> - I'll be able to earn some money
> - I can travel and see a bit of the world
> - I'll learn to stand on my own two feet
> - I can really improve my languages
> - I will broaden my outlook on life
>
> **CONS**
>
> - It will be yet one more year before I can start earning
> - I'll get out of the habit of studying
> - Am I just putting off preparing for a career?

What you might do will depend largely on your personal circumstances and your preferences.

You could simply take the year off to earn some money, possibly locally, possibly further afield, and give yourself time to do some serious reading before your course.

Or you could consider some of the many paid or unpaid options which offer work-related experience or travel.

Not all of the possibilities available to you will take a whole year. Some of the schemes mentioned here last for only a few weeks — some even less. Many young people plan to undertake several different activities during a year out, and short-term schemes are therefore useful to know about.

Should I apply for a university place before or during my gap year?

If you intend to do a higher education course after your year out, you can apply for *deferred entry*, going through the standard UCAS application procedure before taking your 'A' levels (or whatever qualifying exams you are doing). To indicate to your chosen institutions that you want a deferred place you simply put a D in the appropriate box against each choice for which you wish to defer entry. Provided that your results are satisfactory, and you get a place on a course, you would then have a completely clear year to do with as you pleased.

Alternatively you might decide to wait until you had your results before submitting an application. In this way you would already know your results when you applied, and if they were good enough, and you had made a realistic choice of institution and course, you would stand a reasonable chance of getting an 'unconditional offer' of a place for the following year. This option would probably mean that you would need to stay around for the process of submitting the application, lining up a reference and being on hand for possible interviews/open days — which means that if you wanted to go abroad you would not be able to go until about Christmas time, although you would have a good eight or nine months available after that.

What is the universities' view?

Universities are generally in favour of a gap year, but it is advisable for you to get their advice first. You should consult the prospectuses of the institutions you are interested in to see if they mention their policy on deferred entry (most do), and when you have narrowed down your choice to the six courses you want to put on your UCAS form, then you could well contact individual admissions tutors to discuss options.

Most universities will want to know your plans in advance — you should explain what your plans are in the *Personal Statement* section of the UCAS form, avoiding vague descriptions like 'I shall spend the year travelling' or 'I hope to broaden my experience'. Remember that institutions are not under any obligation to allow you to defer, and some departments are only sympathetic if they feel that your plans are sufficiently 'serious'. The following are extracts from some recent prospectuses, just to give you an idea of what a range of institutions feel about deferred entry:

> "The University in general is prepared to consider an application from you if you wish to broaden your experience further by taking a year away from formal education . . . it is essential to go into some detail about your plans in the Personal Statement section of your application form . . . "

> "The University welcomes applications from students who do not come straight from school or college. About one in seven of our undergraduates have travelled or had work experience before coming to university."

> "Most faculties are willing to hold open, for one year, any offer of a place which has been accepted, provided reasonable notice is given."

> "If you are considering applying for deferred entry you are strongly advised to consult the faculty in which you wish to study. Due to pressure on places some faculties are able to offer deferred entry to only a small proportion of applicants."

> "It may be necessary to restrict the number of deferred entry offers made to ensure fairness to candidates applying in the following year."

> "Applications can normally be accepted more than twelve months before the date of admission if there are good reasons — for example, if you will be gaining relevant work experience, spending time abroad to improve your modern languages . . . "

In fact, applicants for deferred entry can cause quite a few headaches for Admissions Tutors. They have the very difficult task of reducing hundreds of applicants to the relative handful they are reasonably sure will achieve the conditional offers they are making. At the same time they have to bear in mind the number of places they have promised to the deferring applicants from the previous year. And they cannot commit large numbers of deferred places — it would not be fair to other applicants in that year. For this reason they usually have a set quota of deferred places in any one year.

What can really throw all their calculations out is if one or more of the applicants to whom they had given conditional offers decided at the last minute — just as the results were published — that they wanted to defer.

So, if you want to take a year out before starting your higher education course, you have two courses of action to choose from:

- apply in your final year at school/college, declare your plans on the UCAS form, and if possible discuss options with the admissions tutor(s);
- apply during your year out, making sure that you are not out of the country when you need to be available for interview.

I want to get some experience in industry

A potential engineer, or a science, computer science, business studies or banking student could find a firm to offer a sponsorship. A number of industrial companies and professional and government organisations, including the armed services, sponsor promising students at selected universities and offer them a year in valuable pre-course employment, as well as periods of work during vacations and good prospects of a job when they graduate. There is a limited number of sponsorships available, and you therefore have to apply fairly early — some companies require you to apply well before Christmas in your final year at school/college. Obtaining sponsorship is a highly competitive process, and employers are looking for high fliers in line for good 'A' level (or equivalent) results. *Students' Money Matters*, published by Trotman, and *Engineering Courses*, published by UCAS/Trotman, give details of firms which regularly offer sponsorships. There may be some opportunities open to you with local firms. The best way to find out is to consult your school/college careers department or your local careers office.

Some companies have special schemes for pre-university students which offer them a year's work experience — usually office work. If this interests you, you can find out more about which companies do this by consulting *Opportunities in the gap year* which is published by ISCO.

There are a few organisations which help place gap year students in work experience. One of these is the Shell Technology Enterprise Programme (STEP). This is a national programme run through a network of agencies around the UK, and sponsored by Shell UK and the Department of Trade and Industry. The projects run over eight weeks during the summer months — usually in July and August, although dates vary to suit local circumstances. Increasingly, however, opportunities are for second-year or penultimate-year undergraduates. To find out more, visit the STEP website:

- www.shell-step.org.uk

Another organisation through which you would be able to find an industrial placement is 'Year in Industry'. You would have to be prepared to spend about eleven months of your year off on the scheme, starting in September, be aged eighteen or over, and already have the offer of a university place. The scheme is for young people who are genuinely interested in finding out more about a career in industry, and not only provides work experience (for which you would earn a minimum salary of £130 per week) but also a pre-placement induction course and further short courses during your placement. A very wide range of industries participates in the scheme, and the type of project work is wide-ranging and varied. You might be able to go abroad for part of the year, if you get a placement with an organisation which conducts some of its business abroad. You would be sure to find the work challenging, and it would give you opportunities to exercise responsibility, and to manage yourself

and your time effectively. It is also likely to enhance your career prospects. Find out more by visiting the Year in Industry website:

- www.yini.org.uk

or you can write to

- Year in Industry National Office
  University of Manchester
  Simon Building, Oxford Road
  Manchester M13 9PL

- or e-mail them on yini@fs3.eng.man.ac.uk

If you are planning a career in accountancy, finance or business, you might be interested in the four-year scholarships offered to young people over the age of seventeen by Arthur Andersen, a major chartered accountancy firm. These provide a package of paid training and work experience in the fields of accountancy, finance and business, support during a degree course, and paid summer work during university vacations. Such a programme could well lead to the offer of a job with the firm on your graduation. You should be in line for As and/or Bs at 'A' level (or equivalent), and ability in maths is important — you should have a GCSE grade A (or equivalent) in maths, and preferably should be doing an 'A' level in the subject. If you want to find out more, you should contact:

- The National Scholarship Programme Manager
  Arthur Andersen Chartered Accountants
  1 Surrey Street, London WC2R 2PS

I would like to do some voluntary work

Many young people want to get some experience of helping others, especially if they want to enter one of the caring professions eventually, or if they perhaps want 'to put something back' into society.

If you would like to do this near your own home then get in touch with appropriate organisations in your area, your local Council Offices, or local branches of charities like Oxfam, to see if any help is required in old people's homes, in hospitals, in centres for the disabled, in play groups, or in charity shops.

An organisation called:

> Community Service Volunteers
> 237 Pentonville Road, London N1 3NJ
> Freephone 0800 374 991
> or www.csv.org.uk

can help you to get placements for four- to twelve-month periods in community or residential care in various parts of the UK. You would be paid your basic expenses, would be fed and housed in or near your place of work, and would receive a small weekly allowance. You could find yourself working with the physically handicapped (either children or adults), with old people, with those who have just been discharged from hospital, with young people in care or in trouble, with those recovering from mental illness, or with the homeless. This may sound a little daunting, but your work would be reviewed after a month, and you (or those running the project you are on) would have the opportunity of saying whether you should continue or not. There would also be someone on the project who would be responsible for supervising you, and on whom you could call for support and guidance.

Gap Activity Projects organises voluntary work in more than 30 countries worldwide. If you chose France, Germany or Latin America, you would need to be able to speak the relevant language — and of course this could provide you with some excellent language practice if you were planning to start a language course on your return to the UK! The range of activities includes assisting with general activities in schools, teaching English as a foreign language, caring work, conservation work and hospital work. Placement lengths vary, but most last for five or six months, and additional travel before or at the end of the placement is actively encouraged. A new list of opportunities is published every August, and applications are accepted throughout the year. GAP has produced a video *Passport to the Future* which is probably in your school or college library, or you can visit their website — www.gap.org.uk — or write to them at

> Gap Activity Projects Ltd.
> Gap House, 44 Queen's Road
> Reading, Berks RG1 4BB

Youth for Britain runs a computerised worldwide volunteering database enabling you to match your wishes against the requirements of more than 800 organisations in the UK and in over 200 countries worlwide. In effect, this allows you to build an on-screen profile of your ideal placement from a total of about 250,000 volunteer projects. For further information about accessing this database, contact:

> Youth for Britain, Higher Orchard,
> Sandford Orcas, Sherborne
> Dorset DT9 4RP
> Tel/fax: 01963 220036

The British Trust for Conservation Volunteers (BTCV) is the largest UK conservation charity. It offers opportunities for volunteers to participate in environmental projects in the UK and abroad. International conservation working holidays take place in most European countries, and there are occasional opportunities further afield, in Turkey, Japan, or Africa, for example. Contact BTVC at:

> 36 St Mary's Street
> Wallingford, Oxon OX10 0EU
> Tel: 01491 839766 Fax: 01491 839646
> e-mail: information@btcv.org.uk
> or www.btcv.org.uk

> Acorn Projects
> PO Box 538, Melksham
> Wiltshire SN12 8SU

is a branch of the National Trust dealing with outdoor conservation projects.

If you want to work on outdoor projects in Scotland then you should write to:

> The National Trust for Scotland Thistle Camps, 5 Charlotte Square,
> Edinburgh EH2 4DU; or

> The Scottish Conservation Projects Trust,
> Balallan House, 24 Allan Park,
> Stirling FK8 2QG

For Northern Ireland there are two addresses:

> National Trust, Northern Ireland Region
> Rowallane House, Saintfield, Ballynahinch
> County Down, BT24 7LH; and

> Conservation Volunteers (Northern Ireland)
> 137 University Street, Belfast BT7 1HP

Organisations offering voluntary work can increasingly be found via the Internet. A useful site which provides links to volunteer organisations in the UK and abroad is the Advisory and Counselling Centre at the University of Central Lancashire:

> www.uclan.ac.uk/other/student/advisory/acad.../volinfo

I would like to sample a completely different type of culture

One way in which you could get experience of a society and culture which are completely different from your own is by volunteering to work in a kibbutz. Kibbutzim, of which there are hundreds throughout Israel, give you an opportunity of living and working in small communal societies. A kibbutz is a small independent agricultural community whose members do not receive any wages but who work in return for the provision of basic needs. Volunteers are accommodated in wood cabins and eat in communal dining rooms. Some kibbutzim have a bar, and perhaps even a disco. You would receive a small allowance, but you would be responsible for your own travelling costs.

The minimum period for which you can go to a kibbutz is eight weeks, and on some schemes you can spend up to a year there. You have to work hard, for eight hours a day, six days a week — it's no holiday! — and the conditions can sometimes be rather basic and uncomfortable. However, most volunteers find the experience highly rewarding and enjoyable. You can find out more by writing to:

> Kibbutz Representatives
> 1a Accommodation Road
> London NW11 8ED
> email: enquiries@kibbutz.org.il

If you are even more adventurous, you might like to go on an expedition with:

> Raleigh International, Venturer Division
> 27 Parsons Green Lane, London SW6 4HZ
> Tel: 020 7371 8585
> www.raleigh.org.uk

which organises ten-week expeditions to remote places in the world and to challenging locations like mountains, deserts and glaciers. The aim of the expeditions is to help young people between the ages of 17 and 25 stretch themselves physically and mentally, and develop their self-confidence and leadership skills. Each expedition consists of about 100 people, but you are split into small groups to undertake projects — anything from helping to construct buildings or bridges, to conducting scientific surveys. You have to be in good health and able to swim . . . and you have to raise £2,995 to cover the costs of your participation. Participation in one of the expeditions depends upon a rigorous and challenging selection process which takes place over a weekend.

> The Project Trustt, Breacachadh Castle
> Isle of Coll, Argyll PA78 6TB
> www.projecttrust.org.uk

offers you an opportunity of sampling life and work overseas, particularly in the developing world. The work is mostly teaching or community work, for which you would be given some basic training by the Project Trust before you left; and there are also placements available on sheep and cattle stations in Australia, and on farms in Thailand. Most opportunities are open to both young men and young women, although opportunities in Jordan, Egypt, Vietnam, Malaysia and Pakistan are limited to males only, as are also the Outward Bound type exercises in Hong Kong. The first round of the selection process is an interview and if you pass this, you are invited to a four-day selection course on the Hebridean Isle of Coll. As with the Raleigh International projects, you have to be physically fit, and you have to raise about £3,000 (of which at least 5% must be earned by you).

The main drawback of these schemes would initially seem to be the necessity to raise close on £3,000. However, both organisations say that volunteers do not usually experience great difficulty in raising the money, which is done by seeking sponsorship and putting on a variety of fund-raising events. There are books mentioned in the **Appendix** which offer suggestions on how to raise money for expeditions.

The British Universities North America Club (BUNAC) is an organisation which offers work and travel programmes worldwide, making it possible for students and young people to live and work abroad, sampling the working life of a country together with exciting travel possibilities — their Work Australia programme, for example, includes a a flexible 18-month round-the-world flight, a two-day stop in Bankok on the way from London to Sydney (or four nights in Hawaii if you were to leave from Los Angeles), help with getting a visa, and the security of knowing that you would not be on your own once you were in Australia because there would be a representative of the organisation on hand to help with jobs, travel and accommodation in the event of an emergency. You would be met at Sydney airport and provided with guaranteed accommodation for the first two nights, and the opportunity to meet up with other world travellers like yourself. In addition to Work Australia, they have Work America, Work Canada, Work New Zealand, Work South Africa, Work Ghana, and Work Jamaica options, together with an OPT (Overseas Practical Training) programme in the USA which allows you to spend between three and eighteen months receiving structured career-related training in the States in a range of subjects including business, management, law, leisure and entertainment. It costs £4 to join if you are a student, and this gives you access to all their programmes. Each BUNAC programme has specific eligibility conditions, so visit their website at www.bunac.org where you can check out the possibilities and order a brochure online. Or write to

> BUNAC, 16 Bowling Green Lane,
> London EC1R 0BD
> Tel: 020 7251 3472

Again, these are just examples of the opportunities available; for fuller details you should consult *A year between*, or some of the other publications mentioned in the **Appendix**.

I would like an opportunity to practise my languages

If you intend ultimately to do a language course it would be a pity to waste an opportunity of improving your languages — or even of trying to pick up a new one.

One of the most popular ways of spending some time abroad experiencing a foreign way of life at first hand in a family and to earn a little money is by working as an *au pair*. Although in theory *au pair* posts are open to men and women, there are many more opportunities for women. An *au pair* lives as a member of the family (not as a servant) and looks after any children, undertakes light housework, prepares simple meals, does the shopping, and so on. In return he or she receives board and lodging and some pocket money. There is usually a fair bit of time for social activities (and perhaps some studying, or a part-time language course?), with one full day and two or three afternoons per week free.

If this is an arrangement which interests you, then you should contact one of the reputable *au pair* agencies of which there are many in the UK, for example:

> Academy Au Pair and Nanny Agency
> 42 Cedarhurst Drive, Eltham
> London SE9 5LP; or

> Students Abroad Ltd, Whitehorse Chambers, Whitehorse Street
> Baldock, Hitchin, Herts SG7 6QQ.

If you are not afraid of hard work you might like to consider paid work in holiday or ski resorts.

> Canvas Holidays, 12 Abbey Park Place,
> Dunfermline, Fife KY12 7PD

employ young people as members of a 'flying squad' to set up and equip tents on camp sites in Austria, France, Germany, Italy, Spain and Switzerland. Workers are needed for this job from the end of April to the beginning of June; and there are opportunities again in September/October when the tents need to be taken down, cleaned, and put away for the winter. You would have your outward travel paid, and your return fare would be paid on condition that you had fulfilled your contract satisfactorily. You would live in self-catering tented accommodation, and would receive a salary. The same organisation also offers employment to couriers for their campsites — as well as looking after the campers and organising activities for them, the job includes domestic work, like cleaning. Another organisation offering similar employment is Eurocamp — if you are interested, contact:

> The Courier Department, Eurocamp
> Canute Court, Toft Road, Knutsford
> Cheshire WA16 0NL.

> Jobs in the Alps Agency
> PO Box 388, London SW1X 8LX

can organise for you employment in hotels in Alpine ski resorts in France, Germany or Switzerland. You would need to speak French or German reasonably well, and be prepared to work hard for very long hours. There are opportunities from December to April, and from June to September as waiting staff, bar staff, chambermaids, kitchen helpers, receptionists and night porters. The salary is fairly good, board and lodging is provided, and just occasionally cheap ski passes are available.

If you want to go abroad on a language course or some other study course, then there are a lot of private firms which can organise this for you. See *How to study abroad* by Teresa Tinsley (details in the **Appendix**) for some of the options.

I would like the opportunity to teach English as a foreign language

Teachers of English are in demand since English is one of the most widely spoken languages in the world, and is the international language of business, science and technology. If the idea of going abroad to teach English appeals to you, there are some language schools and organisations which will employ school/college leavers. There are some books in the 'Gap Year' section of the **Appendix** which will give you some addresses to write to.

The Project Trust and Gap Activity Projects Ltd (addresses given above) both arrange teaching placements throughout the world. Gap placements are for six months. You would have to pay a fee of just under £500, your fares and insurance, and in return your board and accommodation would be provided (and perhaps a little pocket money). Project Trust placements are for a year, and the Trust would expect you to raise about £3,000 (as explained above), but your fares, insurance, accommodation (and probably meals) would be paid for, and you would get a small monthly allowance. The selection process for Project Trust teaching placements is similar to that for their expedition programme.

One of the specialists in training in TEFL (Teaching English as a Foreign Language) for Gap year students is:

> i to i International Projects Ltd.
> 1 Cottage Road Leeds LS6 4DD
> Tel: 0113 217 9800.

They also send young volunteers to teach English in Sri Lanka, India, Russia, Romania and Cuba (as well as arranging conservation projects in Australia). You would have to raise your air fare and project costs.

The Central Bureau's Junior Language Assistants scheme is of particular relevance to those going on to higher education courses in French, German or Spanish. Junior Language Assistants work in a French, German or Spanish school under the direction of the teachers of English, helping small groups of pupils to practise their spoken English and to learn about the British way of life.

Because the number of posts is limited, competition is strong and you should apply in good time (by 1 June for France, 31 March for Germany, early September for Spain) and be prepared to attend a selection interview in London. Posts in France and Spain are for six-month periods, from January to June; and in Germany (where very few posts are available) for periods of six or nine months, starting in September. You would have to pay your own travel costs, but board, lodging and a monthly allowance are provided. If you would like to do this (and six months in the country would do wonders for your French, German or Spanish!) you should write for details to:

> The Assistants Department
> The Central Bureau for Educational Visits and Exchanges, 10 Spring Gardens
> London SW1A 2BN
> www.cbeve.org.uk

If you live in Scotland, there is a branch at:

3 Bruntsfield Crescent
Edinburgh EH10 4HD;

and in Northern Ireland at:

1 Chlorine Gardens
Belfast BT9 5DJ.

How will I be able to afford the travel costs?

There are several ways in which young people can get reductions on travel costs — many of which you will probably already know about.

A Young Person's Railcard, which you can get at the ticket office of your nearest railway station, will give you a discount on your fares in the UK. It is worth having one of these railcards during your period in the sixth form, so that you can travel fairly cheaply if and when you are invited to an interview or Open Day.

An Inter-Rail pass, costing about £300, gives you one month's almost unlimited access to the rail network of Europe. Inter-Railers can get on-board couchettes or reclining sleeper seats at cheaper rates, and special rates on Eurostar and on some ferry crossings, too. An Inter-Rail pass is available from major railway stations.

There is a huge variety of rail passes for Europe. You can, for instance, also buy individual country passes, a few of which not only give you cheaper travel, but also discounts on museums and other sights. A good website which lists the rail passes available is www.railpass.com — although primarily intended for Americans visiting Europe, many of the offers apply to Europeans too.

National Express Coaches give you 30% off your fares in the UK if you buy a National Express Coach Card which costs £8 for a year and is obtainable from any National Express or Caledonian Express agent. You can also get discounts off coach travel in mainland Europe with this card. Eurolines (www.eurolines.co.uk) operate coach services to a wide range of European destinations.

If you need to travel by air there are various standard methods of getting cheaper flights. You may also be able to get special youth fares which offer a large reduction on the cost of a standard economy fares to European destinations and a few other places. Two useful websites which give information about economy air travel in Europe are www.eurairpass.com and www.europebyair.com. And the section below on the studentuk website will help you find cheap flights.

Round-the-World (RTW) tickets also represent good value for money if you intend going by air to several destinations — they last for a year and enable you to make at least three stopovers. You have to plan your trip in advance, because when you buy your ticket you have to say which countries you are going to visit, and how long you intend to stay there.

And finally, www.budgettravel.com is a US site providing a huge list of further links to companies which offer low-cost travel by land, sea and air in every country in Europe, as well as right across the world. It gives the most comprehensive list of worldwide rail, coach and air transport information anywhere on the Web, with links to websites in each country, enabling you to get details of all the up-to-date timetables and ticket prices so that you can plan your journey.

www.studentuk.com

All students have free access to the Internet through their school, college or university, and www.studentuk.com is the students' own website. It is the online guide to all aspects of student life, linking students across the UK and, through its internet links, across the world. It provides answers to any academic, health, welfare, entertainment, financial and work questions you may have, and a forum for you to communicate with other students. It has a very effective search facility, enabling you to access just about anything you could want to know. It provides, for example, quick on-line access to a wide variety of gap year possibilities. It also has a regularly updated section which covers all aspects of travel opportunities, with links to sites such as www.budgettravel.com.

Taking time out: the gap year
Checklist

1 There are many good reasons for taking a year out after the sixth-form: you should gain in maturity and self-reliance; you can gather experience and skills related to your future course or career; you could travel; you could get fluent in a language; you could perhaps earn some money; and you stand a good chance of enjoying yourself!

2 It gives you time to reassess what you want out of your course or your career. A few young people even change their minds about the course they wanted to do, or the future they had planned.

3 If you want to go on to a higher education course after your gap year, you can either apply for a deferred place in your final year at school/college, or you can apply during your gap year.

4 Universities are under no obligation to allow you to defer your entry — although most are in favour provided that you have a satisfactory reason.

5 Sponsorships are available to promising students. A number of industrial companies and professional and government organisations sponsor selected university students and offer them a year in employment before they start their course.

6 There are several organisations which can arrange voluntary work for you in different parts of the world.

7 You could really change your ideas by travelling to a part of the world which is completely different from where you live now, or you could stretch yourself physically and mentally by doing something really adventurous.

8 If you intend to use languages in your career you could spend part of your year abroad, improving your language skills and experiencing a foreign way of life.

9 There are opportunities to go abroad and teach English — either within the EU, or in a wide range of countries around the world.

10 There are several ways in which young people can get reductions on the cost of travel.

Section 6

Making your choice

Finding a course

Getting in

Interviews and Open Days

Finding a course

Why am I applying for a higher education course?

You must think seriously about your reasons for wanting to do a higher education course.

Here are seven bad reasons for doing so:

- your school/college seems to expect it of you;
- you think your parents would like you to get a degree;
- your brother/sister/cousin is already at university;
- all your friends are going on to higher education;
- you can't think what else to do;
- you don't want to decide on a career yet;
- you will give it a try to see if you like it.

If these are your main reasons for applying, then you had better think again.

To make a success of any course, you need to be really motivated, and in the case of a language course that motivation has got to last you four years. You might ask yourself how committed you are to your school/college work at the moment. Do you actually enjoy studying? How well do you think you would get on if you didn't have your teachers to push you along a bit? Teachers in higher education are far less likely to keep a continuous eye on your progress, so your motivation will have to come from within yourself, rather than from outside.

The decision you take now is a very important one — possibly the first real decision of your adult life. Your decision to go on to higher education must be made for positive reasons, and reasons which are important to **you** and **your future**.

High on your list of reasons should be the satisfaction and enjoyment you think you will derive from studying your chosen subject.

You will no doubt also wish to have a useful qualification at the end of your course, so you must assess how the experiences you are likely to gain on the course, and the qualification you will get from it, will fit in with and advance your career plans.

If you can't think of any positive reasons why you are applying, then you should consult your careers advisers about other routes into a career. There are many routes to a successful future which do not involve studying at a university or a college of higher education.

On the other hand, if you think you have the ability and the motivation to go on to higher education, then go for it!

Doing the groundwork

The most important thing is to do your research carefully. This will take you some time, since it will involve sifting through careers literature and university and college prospectuses, consulting computerised databases, making a list of courses and institutions you are interested in, going back to check prospectuses again, tentatively selecting some courses and eliminating others as you narrow down your choice to the six courses you will put down on your UCAS application form, writing away or telephoning for more information, talking to teachers and careers advisers and others who may be in a position to help and advise you, perhaps modifying your choice of a course, or even changing your mind completely, visiting institutions, filling in forms . . . and later on in the selection procedure, using interviews or open days as part of the process which enables you to select or eliminate.

In choosing a course you will probably already have a subject or subject area in mind — a subject you are doing at the moment, or one which is related to one of your present subjects. It may be that you have a career in mind, in which case there is probably a subject or a course you must take in order to qualify.

Diploma courses tend to be mainly linked to specific careers. Some degree courses are vocational, or semi-vocational in nature — law or business studies, for example — and you will go for one of these courses, if you have a particular career in mind. On the other hand, very many employers who recruit graduates do not specify any particular subject area — there are plenty of careers open to graduates of any discipline.

The important thing is not to think too narrowly, either about a degree or diploma subject, or about a career. For the first time, probably, in your life you can take your own decisions about what you are going to do and where you are going to live.

And you have a wonderful opportunity to lay very important foundations for the sort of career you want and for the rest of your life — don't waste it!

When you start to choose a higher education course, make a rough list of the subjects you might study, and the careers you might enter. This is just a starting point. How about trying to expand the range of subjects and/or careers which may be of interest to you? One of the easiest ways to do this is to use one of the computerised databases, or by visiting the UCAS website — www.ucas.ac.uk — which has an interactive course search facility. In this way you might find a course or a subject you did not know about, and which really seems to suit you and your career plans.

How do I make my choice?

What you will have realised from your search through the prospectuses is that there is an abundance of courses to choose from, assuming you are likely to get the minimum grades laid down by the universities. This means that the potential for making mistakes is very great, so it is important to do your homework thoroughly and well in advance.

What grades will I need?

You will need to ascertain that you are in with a chance of getting on to the courses for which you intend applying. It doesn't make sense to waste choices by applying for courses requiring higher grades than you can manage.

The current edition of *University and College Entrance: The Official Guide*, published by UCAS, will give you a fairly good idea of the standard 'A' level grades required for all of the degree and diploma courses at UK universities and colleges of higher education. These might be expressed as grades (like BCC) or as a points' score (where A=10, B=8, C=6, and so on). Requirements are also expressed in terms of Advanced GNVQ, Scottish Highers, and the International Baccalaureate. Individual prospectuses usually give information on offers, too.

Which course should I choose?

The reasons students put forward for choosing a programme of study are extremely varied, ranging from enthusiasm for the course itself to simply having heard that the music scene at such and such is brilliant!

In this section the emphasis is on the nature of the institution and the course rather than the social backdrop, since it is impossible for others to decide for you what choice you should make, since this is an area which is largely subjective.

The first decision you must make is the **combination of subjects** you wish to take, the **balance** of one subject against another, their possible **integration,** and how the **assessment scheme** operates.

In a languages degree, it is also important to find out how much time you are expected to devote to **language acquisition** and whether it is intended that the performance should be to near-native standard — both written and spoken — or whether the language is regarded mainly as a means of getting to grips with another discipline (such as literature, history, etc).

Combination of subjects

It will be apparent from reading the prospectus of the university or college what combinations are possible. There has been a spectacular increase in recent years in multidisciplinary degrees and there is no reason why a foreign language should not run alongside **any** subject or combination of subjects, since it can serve equally well as a vehicle for natural science, mathematics, social science or humanities. The fact that it is the last two of these categories that one normally finds in combination with a language is peculiar to this country. Scientists and mathematicians in other countries know they will have to be competent linguists too if they are to succeed in their profession. To be fair, in some universities in this country, a highly developed modular scheme now makes it possible for a student of virtually any discipline to take a language module as part of the course.

Balance of subjects

A foreign language may occupy most of the curricular space, or an infinitely small part of it. It is important to know where the limits are. If you are an enthusiastic linguist, you do not wish to find that your options run out before you thought they would. But you must expect to do a lot more than learn to speak the language if you are to take a 'languages degree'. A modern languages graduate will always have studied, either theoretical components of the language (i.e. linguistics), or another discipline alongside.

Integration

Integration is the extent to which two or more disciplines intertwine. For example, in a degree in languages and law, are the legal concepts explained or discussed in the foreign language, or is the foreign language learned totally free of legal content? There can be little integration in a modular scheme between languages and specialist disciplines such as law, since students from all over the university can opt for the same language module. Engineers may be learning German side by side with the lawyers: they have no interest in learning legal terminology, nor do the lawyers particularly want to learn the vocabulary or concepts of mechanical engineering. The language that will be taught will be that of generic social or business situations, therefore, not integral to the discipline. That does not mean there will be no possibilities for integration somewhere about. There may well be a Language Centre where students can access computer-based materials in their own discipline, in their own study time. You should ask about this when choosing a course.

Experience tells us that students are attracted by modular schemes because of the range of **choice** they offer. Such schemes can make extra demands on students, however, in that they have to decide between quite complex sets of alternatives so there has to be lots of advice available from the course managers. In addition, the connection between one part of the course and another — which is usually quite obvious in an integrated 'package' designed to have internal consistency — may be less obvious in a modular scheme, where the connection has to be made by the student. To take a simple example, if the history of twentieth century France were to be studied side by side with the French social novel it could well be easier to understand both components. If you chose to study one but not the other, you would arguably have to work harder to make sense of that particular module.

Assessment

Check on the methods of assessment, too. Is there a continuous assessment component, based on essay and project work? What percentage of your final assessment depends on continuous assessment? Would you have exams every year? Do they all count towards your final assessment? Or is your course assessed entirely by exam performance in your final year? If you go abroad to study, does the work you do there count towards your final assessment? Can you substitute a dissertation/extended essay for one taught course in your final examination?

These questions may be especially relevant to you if you are a particularly good, or a particularly bad examinee, for instance. If you suffer from exam pressure, then a course with a large measure of continuous assessment and/or a dissertation component could suit you very well. If, on the other hand, you usually do well under examination conditions, and continuous assessment makes you feel uncomfortable under scrutiny all the time, then a course assessed mainly by written examinations could be the one for you.

From what we have said already, it should be obvious that choosing a course is not an easy matter. Mistakes can be expensive and difficult to rectify. Students vary enormously in background, intelligence, sensitivity, motivation and personal qualities. Parents and relatives usually do not know enough about higher education courses in the subject to give good advice. It is up to you, therefore, to speak to those with some expertise, on whose judgement you know you can rely (teachers, friends studying in that university, careers officers), then attend an open day to see for yourself.

What questions should I ask when I visit the department?

Points you should ask about in the context of modern languages are:

- combination, balance and integration of the language(s) with other disciplines;
- method and weighting of assessment and examination;
- amount of teaching in the foreign language
- nature of the placement abroad, where relevant;
- career destinations of previous graduates;
- possibility of meeting some current undergraduates from the course;
- specialist facilities (books and journals, word processing, multimedia, open learning).

When I have found the course I want, what next?

Choosing a higher education course is about much more than studying a particular subject. You are, after all, choosing the environment in which you will be living and working for the next three or four years. It is important to choose your institution to suit the much wider ambitions, interests and preferences you have. Only you can make final decisions about these matters, so give them serious thought.

Where?

- How far away from your home?
- A large city or a small town?
- A large institution or a smaller one? A smaller institution may be friendlier, and easier to adapt to; but a larger one may have better facilities and more resources for learning.
- A single institution or one divided into colleges?
- An institution in a town, or set apart on its own campus?
- A place where you can pursue any special interests you may have, or perhaps take up new ones? For example if you are an aspiring mountaineer, you might give some thought to institutions in Wales or near the Peak District.
- Is it important to you to be near a place where there is plenty of cultural activity — concerts, theatres, art galleries, and so on?

What are the studying facilities like?

- How good are the libraries?
- Are there language laboratory facilities?
- Are there satellite links for language students?
- Are computers, interactive video and other forms of information technology widely used?

Most prospectuses will give you an idea of the learning resources available within the teaching department, as well as the library and other facilities for the general use of students throughout the institution.

If you are able to visit an institution it is worth visiting the library to find out not only what books and periodicals it holds which support the course you would be doing, but also what the atmosphere would be like to work in, what the opening hours are — can you work until quite late in the evening, for example? Is it open during the vacations?

What would the social life be like?

One of the best ways of finding this out is to talk to undergraduates. Perhaps there is a former member of your school/college at the institution, and you can ask him or her. Or perhaps you will take the trouble to discuss the matter with undergraduates if you visit the institution during term-time. You could find the students' union and have a look round. Take a look at the notice boards which will usually give you a pretty good idea of the clubs and societies, as well as the general 'feel' of the place. There may be an *Alternative Prospectus*, written by students, which you can get by writing to, or visiting, the students' union — this should give you information about social activities.

What accommodation is available?

It is sensible to give some consideration to accommodation — after all, it is going to cost you quite a bit of money to house and feed yourself over the next few years.

It could well be one of the factors you consider important when making up your mind about an institution.

Universities have thousands of students and are therefore unable to accommodate all of them within the institution. Many of the colleges of higher education, on the other hand, are small enough to be able to offer college accommodation to a much larger proportion of their students.

Most institutions will try to accommodate all first-year students in study bedrooms in halls of residence or hostels. These are usually on campus or not too far away — although those belonging to city institutions may be scattered around the city, and a bus-ride away from where you will be working. In some halls of residenc most of your meals will be provided; others have shared kitchen facilities so you can cater for yourself, or buy your meals at quite reasonable prices in student refectories or snack bars. Self-catering halls provide all the usual communal facilities like common-rooms and television, but they do not cost so much because you provide your own meals, and perhaps help out with some of the routine cleaning and the general tidiness of the communal facilities.

Some institutions own student houses. These are houses they have bought and converted into furnished accommodation. Each house will accommodate about a dozen or so students in single or shared study bedrooms, with communal cooking facilities like those offered by self-catering halls. A study bedroom in a student house will cost about the same as one in a self-catering hall.

If you do not have a place in institution-owned accommodation you have to make your own arrangements, although the university accommodation services will be able to help you. In some cities, particularly in London, it is difficult to find accommodation at prices students can afford.

After a year in institution-owned accommodation, some students club together to rent, or even to buy, a house or a flat. This can work out successfully if you all get on together, and it is usually pleasant to have your independence. However, independence brings with it responsibility, and privately-rented and privately-owned properties bring with them complications like contracts, tenancy agreements, the cost of repairs, electricity, gas and water bills, and so on.

If you do not wish, or cannot afford, to enter into a private arrangement like this, the other options open to you are 'digs' or a bedsit. 'Digs' are usually quite a satisfactory option, but since such accommodation is not always intended specifically for students, you should make sure that there would be adequate study facilities for you. In a bedsit you are fairly self-contained and cater for yourself, which is fine if you value your independence, but you could end up feeling very lonely, particularly if you are some way away from the university and other students — which can happen in a big city. Although the university accommodation service may send you lists of suitable places at affordable rents, they do not usually inspect the accommodation, so it is a sensible idea to go and have a look for yourself before committing yourself. Check out if there would be any extras to pay for, too, like heating in your room, or baths and showers.

Then, of course, there is one other option: living at home. Choosing an institution near to where you live can solve a lot of problems — although, on the other hand, you may not enjoy the freedom and the valuable experience of fending for yourself which comes from moving away from home.

Read the section on accommodation in the prospectuses. There is usually a lot of helpful information. But don't accept all the information at face value: question statements you may find like these:

- *'We have 2,400 rooms in halls of residence.'* (What is the total student population? What proportion of the rooms are reserved for first year students? Can they accommodate all their first year students in hall?)

- *'Almost 70% of our undergraduates are in university accommodation.'* (How does the cost compare with university accommodation at other universities? What proportion of the places in halls of residence are self-catering, and therefore cheaper?)

University accommodation offices provide an information and advice service, and there is no reason why you should not contact them to ask any questions you may have about the availability and cost of different types of accommodation. The address and telephone number is usually in the prospectus, but if not, ring up the university itself and ask. Finding a good place to live is an important factor in choosing your higher education institution.

The final six . . .

When you come to pick your final six choices to put down on your UCAS application form you need to bear in mind the grades you are likely to get in your 'A' level or other examinations. And you also need to consider the worst scenario! What would you do if you didn't get high enough grades? So, make sure that amongst your six choices there are a couple of suitable courses which normally accept people with lower grades.

When and if you get offers from your chosen six, and you have to narrow your choice down to two — your preferred course and an 'insurance' offer — you can hang on to one of the lower grade offers. In that way you will have some room to manoeuvre if the worst happens next August!

Finding a course
Checklist

1	Examine your reasons for applying. Be really sure you want to go on to further study.
2	Don't waste choices by applying for courses requiring higher grades than you can manage.
3	Researching your course properly is a long and painstaking process — but it is very important.
4	Don't think too narrowly about the choice of a course or a career. Use careers literature and databases to expand your ideas about the range of subjects and careers open to you.
5	Check on course content: combination and balance of subjects (including available options), integration across subject disciplines (where appropriate), teaching in the foreign language, pattern and weighting of assessment, possibilities of placement abroad.
6	Ensure that you visit the department and try to talk to students who are currently on the course.
7	Visit the library and any specialist facilities in the department while you are there.
8	Choosing where you are going to study is as important as what you are going to study.
9	Accommodation can be a critically important factor, too.
10	Include some courses which require lower entry grades in your final choice of six, so that you have some room for manoeuvre if you don't get the required grades for your first choice offer.

Getting in

The application process

Applications for first degree courses, DipHE courses, HND and some university diploma courses at all British universities and most colleges/institutes of higher education are administered by UCAS — the Universities and Colleges Admissions Service. You must apply through this agency.

You will be given an application form and UCAS Handbook by your school or college, or if you have already left you can get them from a careers office, or by writing to:

UCAS, PO Box 28
Cheltenham Glos GL50 3SA.

You apply for up to six courses on one application form and these can be all degree courses, all diploma courses, or a mixture.

During the course of the application process UCAS passes on to you the decisions of universities and colleges as to whether you have been given an offer, or have been rejected. It plays no part at all in the process of selection, though — that is entirely a matter for individual admissions tutors. UCAS also simplifies for you the procedure of writing to admissions tutors to accept or decline offers you have been made, by providing you with cards on which you can record your decisions and send them off.

Part of the 'package' you buy with your fee is the UCAS 'Clearing' service: at the end of the applications process in late August/early September, UCAS will try to find you a place on a course (provided you have the right qualifications) if you were rejected by all the courses you applied to, or if you declined any offers made to you, or if, after your examination results are announced, you find you have not met the conditions of the offer made to you, and are therefore without a place.

Electronic applications system

UCAS has introduced EAS — the electronic applications system — which allows you to complete your application form on a PC, and then submit it to UCAS via the Internet or on a floppy disk. You still have to go through your school or college, or through a careers service — the EAS facility is not available to you on a personal basis. There are a number of benefits — it is easier to make corrections (without crossings out!); you can word-process your personal statement and then paste it on to the form; useful notes and instructions are included in the package so that they are there at the touch of a button, and you don't have to sift through a lot of paper instructions; and it speeds up the processing of applications by UCAS. The EAS software will be available at your school or college.

How can I make myself irresistible?

This is perhaps a bit of a tall order, but you can try to create the right impression. It is worth taking the trouble to make your application look not just good, but outstanding. This is important because your UCAS form is the first (and perhaps the only) contact you have with the selectors.

So here is a checklist for you:

Create a good impression

- If you do not use the EAS system, don't fill in the actual form without first making a rough draft . . . perhaps several rough drafts, improving all the time.

CiLT

- Make sure the selector will be able to read it. You are asked to complete the form in black ballpoint pen — not felt-tipped pen or roller-ball because they do not photocopy well. You may type or word-process your form, but if you do, make sure that the cartridge in your machine is new enough to print clearly and boldly. Your form will be photocopied and reduced to half-size before the selectors see it, so if your handwriting is poor, cramped or untidy, or if your typescript is too faint, then it doesn't really matter what you have put in your application because they won't be able to read it anyway! Most selectors have hundreds of forms to read, so they may be forgiven if they don't spend much time trying to decipher the illegible ones.
- Check meticulously for spelling mistakes and other errors. Remember that you are trying to create a good impression in the reader's mind. Sloppy presentation and carelessness will not convince the selectors that you are a serious candidate.

What will the selectors be looking for?

As you fill in your UCAS form this is the question you should keep at the back of your mind. Clearly they will be hoping to choose the best, and the most interesting students.

- They will be looking, first and foremost, for academic potential . . . so they will look to see if you have good grades in a broad range of GCSEs (or equivalent). Make sure you include all your grades, even in subjects where you got low grades, because this will indicate the breadth of your studies.
- They will pay a lot of attention to what your school/college says about you as a student. The reference which goes on p4 of the form is the single most important piece of evidence that the selectors have at this stage that you are suitable (or not) for the course you have chosen.
- The reference will contain predicted grades for your forthcoming examinations/assessments. The selectors will be very interested in these predictions and in how they match up to the grades that they would expect successful applicants to get.

But by the time you come to apply for a higher education course you are not really in a position to do anything to change your GCSE results, your reference or your predictions. However hard you intend to work this year, the results of your GCSE year and your first year of sixth form work are as water under the bridge.

But where you can improve your chances of getting a place is by filling in your 'Personal Statement' (Section 10 of the UCAS form) in a way which demonstrates how very suitable you are for your proposed course. Applying for a place in higher education is unfortunately very like entering a competition, and Section 10 could be seen as the tie-breaker, which selectors use to choose between candidates who have similar academic backgrounds.

Since selectors have found that a candidate's personal qualities are very significant in determining future success, they are looking for two things in the Personal Statement which will give a more rounded picture of you:

- They want to see signs of interest in, knowledge of, and commitment to the subject for which you have applied. They want to know **why** you have applied for the course, and, especially if you have chosen to do something you have not studied before, that you have taken the trouble to find something out about it. You could mention any reading you have done, work experience you have undertaken, taster courses you have attended, travel, study visits, etc, that are related to the course you want to do.
- They would also like to see evidence from your non-academic achievements that you are capable of taking something to a higher level than most people do — to set you apart as an individual. This can be anything from sporting achievement or musical prowess, to community work, family or other responsibilities, travel, an interesting hobby, or an unusual job.

What areas should I cover in my Personal Statement?

- State the reasons for your choice of course. If you are choosing something completely different from the subjects you are currently studying, explain why.

- Are you applying for two different sorts of course? Explain why.

- Or do your six chosen courses contain a mix of subjects? This is not generally a good idea, since it may not indicate the necessary commitment to any one course. However there may be good and sensible reasons for a split choice, and it is in this section of the form that you should explain them. (It is perfectly acceptable to put down the same subject area at different levels — for example four degree courses and two HND courses in travel and tourism — particularly if you are a borderline candidate for a degree.)

- Try to give some idea of the type of career you might eventually wish to follow — even if you have only a very general or hazy idea at present.

- Say what part of your current course(s) have particularly interested or inspired you — especially if you want to do a related HE course.

- Mention any relevant private reading, travel, work experience, holiday jobs, Saturday jobs, writing, drama . . . that you have done.

- Include anything else relevant to your chosen course — for example, work with children for a B.Ed course, time spent abroad for language courses, specific practical experience for a whole range of media- and performance-related courses, visits to law courts for law or sociology courses . . .

- Include your social and sporting interests, especially where they have involved positions of responsibility.

- List any useful skills (if they are not included elsewhere on your application form) such as computer literacy, driving, experience of organising things . . .

- If you have lived or travelled abroad, give details.

- Include anything else (which is relevant, of course) which you think makes you **special.**

- If you have any special circumstances (recent serious illness, difficult family circumstances . . .) you may wish to mention them, although it would be advisable to discuss this with your tutor, or whoever is responsible for compiling your reference, since such matters might be better dealt with in the school/college reference. There is no point in using up valuable space on the form by saying the same thing twice. (NB: you must mention any disability or medical condition in Section 8. This is so that special arrangements can be made for you if necessary. It will not count against you as a candidate in any way.)

- Mention if you have secured sponsorship. This could attract the interest of the selectors.

Marketing yourself

You should now have plenty — if not too much — to say about yourself. So you will need to edit what you write very carefully. You may wish to ask your tutor for advice about what to include, and what to leave out.

Try to angle your information in order to highlight your 'plus' points and to conceal anything which is unlikely to appeal to the selectors. But don't tell lies — you may have to substantiate your claims if you get an interview!

Try to arrange what you write in a clear and logical way — to show the selectors that you have a clear and logical mind! You could perhaps use headings if you think it would be easier for the selectors to read.

Of course, if you have a Record of Achievement, you should use it to help you compile Section 10 (as well as to prepare yourself, later, if you are invited to an interview). It is unlikely that extracts from your

Record of Achievement would be suitable for your UCAS form as they stand, because you need to 'target' a particular readership on the UCAS form. Moreover, some selectors may be interested in seeing your Record of Achievement (or just the summative statement) as well — you may be asked either to send it on to them, or take it to an interview.

Put your finished draft away for a day or so before reading it through again. How do you think your application will strike the selector? Are **you** impressed? If not, see if you can improve on the first version. Remember how important Section 10 is — it is worth spending time and effort on it.

And finally . . .

Get someone to read your final draft to check it for expression, and, in particular, spelling.

When you come to fill in the actual UCAS form, make sure that you create the impression that you care about getting a place — the form should be clean, neat, and not dog-eared.

Finally you will of course read through the form to make sure you have made no silly mistakes and that you have left nothing out that is important. Don't forget to sign your form. And don't forget the £12 fee!

Keep a copy of your form for future reference: it is important to know what you wrote if or when you have an interview. Keep it in the folder with all the correspondence connected with your applications. You can be in trouble if you lose important slips of paper — it pays to be efficient.

Good luck!

Getting in
Checklist

1. Applications for degree and diploma courses in higher education have to be made through the UCAS scheme.

2. It is worth taking the trouble to make your application look not just good, but outstanding.

3. Create a good impression by writing clearly, legibly and accurately.

4. Selectors will be looking at your form for signs of academic potential, and will pay a lot of attention to what is said about you in your reference.

5. They will also be looking for signs of commitment to your proposed course. You should try to demonstrate this in your Personal Statement in Section 10 of the UCAS form.

6. Include in your Personal Statement your reasons for your choice of course, your interests and anything you have done which is relevant to this course. If you have lived or travelled abroad, give details. Include anything which makes you special.

7. Edit what you write very carefully in order to highlight your 'plus' points.

8. Start a folder in which you keep together all the correspondence connected with your applications.

Interviews and Open Days

What is the interview for?

Interviews serve a two-way purpose:

On the one hand they give an opportunity for the selectors to meet you, to answer the questions they had in mind after reading your application form, and to decide whether they will give you an offer of a place, or not.

On the other hand — and it is important to realise this — it gives you an opportunity to find out if experience matches up to what is described in the prospectus, to meet people who might perhaps teach you next year, to ask any questions you want about the course and the institution, and to decide whether you want to go there, or not. Ask yourself afterwards . . .

- Were the people I met the sort I would like to spend the next three or four years with?
- Was I made to feel welcome?
- Did they value my opinion? . . . answer my questions? . . . were they interested in me?
- Is the course they offer really the one I am looking for? Will it motivate me?
- Was I asked about my career aspirations? . . . does the department seem interested in the careers of its graduates/diplomates?
- What were the facilities like? . . . libraries? . . . computers? . . . satellite TV? . . . arrangements for self study? . . . learning other languages?
- Did the place look as wonderful as in the prospectus? (Probably not, but does it matter to you?)
- What were the social facilities like?
- What arrangements will there be for me to pursue my sporting/musical/other interests? . . . to take up new interests?
- Do I want to live in this place for the next few years?

Do all departments interview?

No. Not long ago most suitable applicants for a degree course were interviewed, but, given the recent expansion in higher education, departments find that there are just too many applicants for them to be able to give the time to interviewing them all. If you have applied for a teacher training course you will definitely be interviewed, since it is a statutory requirement that you be seen before being given a place.

Don't think that it is a bad sign if you are not called for interview. You may be sent an offer without an interview.

Among those departments which do interview, there is a range of different policies for doing so:

- some only see the applicants they regard as borderline candidates (perhaps they have a lot of average candidates they cannot choose between, or they think your predicted grades are low);
- some only interview those they are seriously thinking of giving an offer to;
- some only interview the really good candidates they want to attract;
- others believe that the interview is an essential part of the selection process, both for them and for you, and will try to find the time to interview all those they consider to be serious candidates.

CiLT

Are there different types of interview?

Yes, several — and, as we have said before, it is worth asking about the purpose and the format of the interview before you go.

As far as the purpose is concerned, you need to find out if it is to be a formal interview, which will decide whether or not you are given an offer; or an informal interview, where the department has already decided that they will make you a standard offer but would just like to meet you. Even if it is to be a formal interview, they may not sit behind a desk — they are likely to try to make the occasion as relaxed and 'non-threatening' as they can.

As far as the format is concerned, what is called an 'interview' does not always follow the traditional pattern of you facing one interviewer or a panel of interviewers. It could be of the following types:

- a one-to-one interview — you and a single interviewer;
- an interview where you are questioned by two or more people;
- a group interview — you and one or two other applicants are seen together;
- a discussion or a team-task involving you and other applicants — especially if you have applied for a course where you have to work a lot in groups;
- a practical exercise — especially if you are applying to do one of the performance arts.

And, of course, if you want to do languages you can expect to have to converse in your main language at some time during your interview — unless you are intending to study a new language from scratch.

There might be a short written exercise or other form of test as well, but you will usually be told this in your letter of invitation. In fact, most departments will make it quite clear what the purpose and format of the exercise are when they write to you, but if you are in any doubt you should ring up to check.

I have been invited to an Open Day

If you do not have to attend an interview, you may be invited to an Open Day. Some institutions or departments have a policy of not interviewing (because they simply have too many applicants), and feel, in any case, that an Open Day gives you a better opportunity of looking around, meeting staff and undergraduates, hearing about the course, and asking all those questions you need to ask in a more relaxed setting than an interview room.

There is a difference between the sort of Open Day which usually takes place in the late spring or early summer, where prospective students, their teachers, and sometimes their parents, descend in cars and coaches to have a look round and generally find out more about the institution . . . and the Open Day which takes place from the autumn onwards, which is usually a departmental Open Day, to which you are invited by name. This is often a cross between an interview and an Open Day, where you spend a day which may include a short interview, as well as opportunities to meet undergraduates, to explore the facilities, and to ask the questions you need before deciding definitely if you want to choose that course and institution.

> On arrival at the university all the students who had come for the Open Day were shown to one of the language rooms to have coffee and biscuits and a chat with some of the members of staff there. The atmosphere was very relaxed and the staff were extremely helpful.
>
> We were then given a talk explaining in detail the different parts of the course. This lasted for about 45 minutes. We were then split up into groups of about eight or nine and were shown to the refectory by a few 4th year students who were coming to the end of their course . . . we had been given luncheon vouchers to subsidise the meals. We were able to chat to the students during the meal and found out quite a bit about university life.
>
> After a very thorough tour of the campus we went back to the modern languages department to be allocated times for our interviews.
>
> My interview consisted of a very pleasant chat with one of the French teachers. It was extremely informal and it was really up to me to ask the questions, not him. The interview only lasted about fifteen minutes because by this time of the day we all had a very good idea of what the course entailed and of other aspects of university life.
>
> Everyone we met throughout the day was very friendly and willing to talk.

Of course, not all events follow this exact pattern. There are bound to be differences from department to department, and from subject to subject. Often the interview is more searching and demanding; or sometimes people are seen in small groups.

Sometimes you are invited to an Open Day, and you are not sure if there is to be a short interview or not. If it is not made clear in your invitation, it would be a good idea to ring up the department to check; and if there is to be one, you could ask what form the interview will take. Is it to be an advisory interview, for example, where you can ask questions to find out all you need about the course and the institution; or is it to be a selection interview, where the selector will be finding out about you, and coming to a decision about whether to make you an offer or not. It is as well to find out in advance so that you can go prepared!

Just occasionally the Open Day experience is not so enjoyable and relaxed. But remember they are not just choosing you, you are also choosing them. Even a negative experience can be a valuable one — you can, after all, eliminate that institution from your list of places to go!

Must I attend the interview or Open Day?

If you are invited to an interview or an Open Day, you would be well advised to accept — unless you already have some offers, of course, and have decided what institution you want to go to.

A few departments will not make you an offer if you do not accept the invitation. And even departments which have already decided to make an offer have been known to lower it a little if they take a particular liking to you. If you cannot manage the date they suggest, they will usually offer an alternative date if you contact them in time.

If you are given an offer without being invited to an interview or an Open Day, you really should ask if you can go and have a look round before deciding to accept or not. After all, you wouldn't accept a job in a distant town without first going to see where you would be living and working. It is really important that you find out about the place, and whether you think you could be happy living and studying there for three or four years — especially since this may probably be your first time away from home.

Is it going to cost a lot of money?

Travelling around to interviews and Open Days can be an expensive business. Some schools/colleges and even some local education authorities may be in a position to help the genuinely needy student financially.

Universities and colleges of higher education will usually be understanding, too, if the interview involves a long journey which will cost more than you can easily afford. Sometimes, if you have two interviews on different days at institutions which are quite close to one another, but at the other end of the country from where you live, one of the institutions may be able to rearrange its date to coincide with your visit to the other one. They may even be able to give you a bed for the night.

Don't be afraid to ring up and explain any difficulties you have; or to discuss them with someone at your school/college who may be happy to ring up on your behalf.

If you don't have your own transport, or a parent, relation or friend cannot take you to the interview, going by coach is probably your cheapest way to travel. And if you buy a National Express Coach Card you will get a reduction on your coach fares.

If it is more convenient for you to go by rail, you can get a Young Person's Railcard which will give you a discount on most rail fares for one year. Get it at the ticket office of your local railway station. You can also get cheaper rail travel on some journeys by booking in advance.

How can I get the best out of an Open Day?

Your task at an Open Day is to find out as much as you can about the place as possible. You will do this by listening to what is said to you, by observation, and by asking questions.

You will probably find that the day is very structured. Is this just because there are a lot of visitors to organise? Or are they trying to hide anything? Are you allowed free contact with students? Or are they just giving you the 'official line'? Ask lots of questions to find out what you need to know! Are you being shown everything you need to see? The library? Word processors? Computers? Language lab? Are they freely available to all students? (See if you can ask current students how much they actually get to use these things.)

Is the library big enough to cater for everyone they teach? (Have a look to see if there are long queues.) Try to have a look at the section in the library that caters for your subject.

What is the food/student accommodation/campus . . . like? How much does a cup of coffee/a meal cost? Is there a bookshop/bank/laundrette . . . close by? If not, does it matter to you?

How can I compare one institution with another?

As soon as you can after your visit — whether it has been to an interview or an Open Day — write down your impressions. It is surprising how quickly you can forget things, and how difficult it is to remember which of the places it was that you saw all those good private study facilities . . . .or that fantastic drama studio.

Try to record if you had a good experience or not, and what it actually was that made you like or dislike the place or the people. See if you can establish some common criteria against which to judge all the places you are trying to choose between, and rate each of the places you visit according to these.

If the interview was not a good experience, or if the Open Day did not reveal very much, try to identify why. Write down anything you did which you would do differently next time! Use this information so that your next interview or Open Day goes better.

Interviews and Open Days
Checklist

1. Remember that the interview is a two-way experience — for the selector to find out about you, and for you to find out about the course and the institution.

2. Not all university/college departments can find the time to interview all applicants. Some prefer to invite you to an Open Day.

3. Try to find out beforehand whether your interview is to be formal or informal, an individual or group interview, and whether there will be any kind of test.

4. Don't accept the offer of a place without visiting the institution first. If you have not been invited to visit, try to find an opportunity to do so.

5. Prepare for your interview so that you can really do yourself justice; and see if you can have a 'mock' interview before you go.

6. It is impossible to predict the questions you will be asked, but remember that by their questioning interviewers are trying to select intelligent people with the enthusiasm and motivation to work hard and succeed. They are probably asking themselves: 'Do I want to teach this person?'

7. Expect to have to speak the language you intend to study (unless you are hoping to study it from scratch).

8. Have some questions ready to ask them.

9. To get the best out of an Open Day, keep your eyes and ears open, and ask lots of questions.

10. Record your impressions after your visit, and see if you can establish some common criteria against which to judge all the places you have to choose between.

Appendix

Where to go for more help — a list of further resources

Here is a selection of books (plus some videos and computer software) which are available to help you research the options open to you.

Many of them will be on the shelves of your school/college careers library; or you will probably find them at your local public library or careers office.

If you would like to have your own copy of any of them, you should be able to find most of them at any large bookshop, or you could ask any bookseller to order the publication you require. A few publications should be ordered directly from the organisation which produces them, and where this is applicable, addresses are given.

NB: higher education institutions frequently update and modify their courses and introduce new ones, so **it is important to consult the most up-to-date publications you can** — many are published annually.

1 General information about courses, institutions, basic entrance requirements, etc

The big official UCAS guide to university and college entrance
published annually (UCAS)

> Essential for researching your subject, course, and place of study; also lists 'A' level, 'AS', International Baccalaureate, Scottish Highers, SCOTVEC, BTEC and GNVQ requirements for degree and HND courses, entry statistics, and estimated grades and offers.
>
> Also includes **Studylink UK,** the official CD-ROM multimedia guide to HE.

Entrance guide to higher education in Scotland
published annually (UCAS; distributed by John Smith, Glasgow)

> Profiles of all HE institutions in Scotland, details of all degree and HND courses available in them, and Scottish Higher and 'A' level entry requirements.

The Potter guide to life at university and college
by Sheila Potter and Philippa Clare. Published annually (Dalebank Books)

> An overview of HE institutions, and the facilities they offer, together with information on course structures and teaching quality assessments.
>
> Also available on CD-ROM.

The complete degree course offers
edited by Brian Heap. Published annually (Trotman)

> Comprehensive guide to entry requirements for degree courses, plus other useful additional information. Also available on the *ECCTIS* CD-ROM (see below).

ECCTIS

> Database on CD-ROM of all further and higher education courses in the UK. Widely available in schools, careers offices, and at many FE and HE institutions.

ASET Directory of sandwich courses
(Association of Sandwich Education and Training, ASET)

> Details of all advanced level sandwich courses in higher education.

Getting into Oxford and Cambridge, 6th edition
Book and video (Trotman, 1999)

> Useful information on how to choose a college and a course, and go about applying for an Oxbridge place.

How to complete your UCAS application form
Book, video, and software by Tony Higgins, Chief Executive, UCAS. Published annually (Trotman)

> Help with filling in your application form — including 'How to . . . and 'How not to . . .' examples.

A life of knowledge
Video produced by UCAS

A look at student life through the eyes of students, graduates and lecturers, and including information about a range of topics, such as choosing what and where to study, getting in, teaching and assessment, accommodation, welfare, finance, and overseas opportunities.

What do graduates do?
Published annually (Hobsons in association with AgCAS) **now discontinued**

Statistics, by subject, of the career destinations of a sample of those who have successfully undertaken degree and HND courses, together with a useful general introduction, and case studies.

2 Information about specific subjects and career routes

Careers using languages, 8th edition
by Edda Osterhild (Kogan Page, 1998)

Offers comprehensive guidance, including case studies, on career opportunities using languages. Includes discussion of study paths and qualifications, working abroad, sources of further help.

Degree course guides
Published biennially (CRAC/Hobsons Publishing plc)

Guides by individual subject to degree courses, together with useful information on course content, teaching methods and career prospects — including the following language titles:

French with linguistics
German with Dutch and Scandinavian studies
Hispanic studies and Italian
Russian and Oriental studies
Politics and European studies

Getting into languages
(Trotman, 1995)

Clear, concise advice on all aspects of continuing to study languages once you leave school/college.

Great careers for people interested in ... languages
by Joanna Grigg (Kogan Page, 1998)

Case studies of the range of careers, both expected and otherwise, open to students of languages.

Which degree
(CRAC/Hobsons Publishing plc)

Useful information, arranged alphabetically by title and institution, to help you narrow down your choice before looking at prospectuses. Four volumes grouped by field of study:

Art, humanities, languages
Engineering, technology, geography
Sciences, medicine, mathematics
Social sciences, business, education

Handbook of initial teacher training in England and Wales
Published annually (NATFHE; distributed by Linneys ESL)

Details of the full range of undergraduate and postgraduate teacher training opportunities.

3 Studying and work placements abroad

Socrates-Erasmus — the UK guide for students entering higher education
Published annually (ISCO Publications)

Gives useful information on the range of Erasmus-supported courses at UK institutions, and examines some of the issues arising from studying at a foreign institution.

How to study abroad, 3rd edition
by Teresa Tinsley (How To Books, 1998)

Advice and information on study opportunities abroad, qualifications necessary, accommodation, finance, travel and visas, health and insurance.

Getting into Europe
(Trotman, 1995)

An examination of the study and work opportunities in continental Europe.

Europa world year book: a world survey
Two volumes (London: Europa)

4 A year out/holiday jobs

NB: for some of the jobs listed in the following publications you need to be over 21.

A year between — the complete guide to taking a year out, 3rd edition
(The Central Bureau for Educational Visits and Exchanges, 1997)

Details of placements in industry, research, business, teaching, community service and youth work, together with ideas for study and adventure.

A year off... a year on? 3rd edition
(Hobsons Publishing plc, 1998)

Ideas of what to do to make the best of a year off, together with details of how to apply.

Opportunities in the gap year, 12th edition
Edited by Anna Alston (Independent Schools Careers Organisation)

Useful advice, and details of what is available to do in a year out (ISBN: 0901936 52 9).

Taking a year off, 3rd edition
Book and video by Val Butcher (Trotman, 1997)

Information and advice to help you plan your year out, including work experience relevant to a course, voluntary work at home and abroad, learning a new skill, and foreign travel.

Spending a year abroad, 3rd edition
by Nick Vandome (How To Books, 1996)

Details of the numerous options available, together with practical advice on short-term employment opportunities and travel.

Working holidays — the complete guide to seasonal jobs
Published annually (The Central Bureau for Educational Visits and Exchanges)

Details of holiday job opportunities in the UK and right across the world, together with advice on work permits, travel, health, insurance and accommodation.

The directory of summer jobs abroad *
edited by D Woodworth. Published annually (Vacation Work)

Details of vacancies in over 50 countries for sports instructors, bar staff, holiday company reps, Kibbutz volunteers, English teachers, tour guides, farm hands, archaeologists, fruit pickers, etc, plus advice on work permits, health insurance and cheap travel.

The directory of summer jobs in Britain *
Published annually (Vacation Work)

Details of vacancies in the UK for a range of seasonal jobs such as fruit picking, hotel work, child care, holiday camps, archaeological digs, voluntary work.

* **May supplement to** *summer jobs abroad/ in Britain*

It is worth getting this supplement which is published by Vacation Work at the beginning of May to include information received from employers too late to be included in the two books which are published in November. You should contact Vacation Work, 9 Park End Street, Oxford OX1 1HJ; Tel: 01865 241 978.

Summer jobs USA
Published annually. (Peterson's Guides)

Available through Vacation Work

Information about summer jobs for students in North America (including Canada), together with advice on legal requirements, visas, etc.

Discovering Germany — a guide to work and study opportunities for young people
(The Central Bureau for Educational Visits and Exchanges)

Information and advice for young people planning a visit to Germany, together with guidance on travel, accommodation, work opportunities, German language courses and long-term study, and holiday and leisure activities.

Live and work in Japan
by David Roberts (Vacation Work, 1999)

The au pair and nanny's guide to working abroad, 3rd edition
by Susan Griffith and Sharon Legg (Vacation Work, 1997)

Sensible guidance on finding posts in Europe, North America and Australasia.

Working in ski resorts — Europe and North America, 4th edition
by Victoria Pybus (Vacation Work, 1997)

Useful advice on finding seasonal work in ski resorts — as, for example, ski instructors, ski technicians, couriers, chalet girls, resort reps, couriers, au pairs, shop assistants, office workers, disk jockeys, snow clearers . . .

Teach abroad — the complete international guide to teaching opportunities overseas, 2nd edition
(The Central Bureau for Educational Visits and Exchanges, 1999)

Guidance on a wide range of teaching opportunities abroad, including teaching English as a foreign language, short- and long-term posts, exchanges and voluntary placements.

Teaching English abroad, 4th edition
by Susan Griffith (Vacation Work, 1999)

A guide to short- and long-term opportunities for both trained and untrained teachers to teach English as a foreign language abroad. It includes the ways in which English speakers can find work in countries worldwide, lists language schools which hire English teachers, and provides information on how to become a qualified EFL teacher.

Working in tourism — the UK, Europe and beyond, 2nd edition
by Verite Reily Collins (Vacation Work, 1999)

Information on seasonal and permanent employment as guides, company reps, drivers, cabin crew, child minders, sports instructors, etc in the tourist industry across the world.

Workplace — the complete guide to work experience placements
(The Central Bureau for Educational Visits and Exchanges, 1996)

Practical advice on organising work experience, work shadowing and work observation, together with information on funding, health and safety, insurance, accommodation and travel.

Home from home — the complete guide to homestays and exchanges
(The Central Bureau for Educational Visits and Exchanges)

Advice on homestays, exchanges, home exchanges, farm stays and term stays across the world.

Volunteer work — the complete guide to voluntary service
(The Central Bureau for Educational Visits and Exchanges)

Details of projects worldwide, qualifications and skills required, conditions of work, plus advice on preparation, development issues, travel and health.

International directory of voluntary work, 6th edition
edited by Victoria Pybus (Vacation Work, 1997)

A guide to short- and long-term volunteer opportunities in the UK and abroad.

How to do voluntary work abroad — a practical guide to the opportunities worldwide
by Mark Hempshell (How To Books, 1994)

Details of opportunities available, together with skills and qualifications required, case histories, and checklists of essential information.

Kibbutz volunteer, 6th edition
(Vacation Work, 1996)

Full details of Kibbutzim, together with details of short-term work in Moshavim, in hotels, on conservation projects, archaeological digs, fruit farms, or as an au pair.

The voluntary agencies directory, 15th edition
compiled by the National Council for Voluntary Organisations (1996)

Available from NCVO Publications, Regent's Wharf, 8 All Saints Street, London N1 9RL.
Tel: 020 7713 6161

Details of the voluntary agencies in the UK — useful if you are planning to do voluntary work somewhere in Britain.

Adventure holidays
edited by Victoria Pybus. Published annually (Vacation Work)

Details of opportunities for all age groups for activity holidays in the UK and in countries throughout the world.

Expedition planners' handbook and directory
by S Winser and N McWilliam
(The Expedition Advisory Centre, 1992)

Available from the publisher at
1 Kensington Gore, London SW7 2AR.
Tel: 020 7581 2057

Comprehensive information on all aspects of planning an expedition. Some sections of this book may be bought separately — and therefore more cheaply — as individual booklets, for example:

Fund-raising for expeditions
Insurance for expeditions
Reference sources for expeditions

5 Other useful publications

The alternative guide to the sixth form
(Trotman, 1994)

Information to help you plan for the future, including sponsorships, taking a year out, employment and finance.

Students' money matters, 5th edition
Book and video by Gwenda Thomas
(Trotman, 1999)

> Useful advice on managing your money, including students' costs, budgeting, sources of finance for undergraduates and postgraduates, sponsorships, working abroad, work experience, a year out and travelling.

Into higher education 2000
(Skill: National Bureau for Students with Disabilities, 1999)

> Information for people with disabilities who are applying for higher education.

Sponsorship for students (Springboard)
Published annually (CRAC/Hobsons Publishing plc)

> Details of sponsorships offered annually by employers and professional bodies to those doing degree, HND, and other comparable courses.

The international guide to qualifications in education, 4th edition
Compiled by NARIC (Mansell, 1995)

> Information about international education qualifications and their acceptability as entrance qualifications for courses and professions.

6 Free publications

Student grants and loans: a brief guide for higher education students
(DfEE)

> Available from your local education authority, or from Department for Education and Employment, Publications Centre, PO Box 6927, London E3 3NZ

> Similar information for students in other parts of the UK can be obtained from:

Student Awards Agency for Scotland
Gyleview House
3 Redheughs Rigg, South Gyle
Edinburgh EH12 9HH

Department of Education for Northern Ireland
Rathgael House, Balloo Road,
Bangor, Co. Down BT19 7PR

Welsh Office Education Department
FHEI Division, Cathays Park
Cardiff CF1 3NQ

Loans for students — a brief guide
(DfEE/Scottish & Welsh Offices)

> Available from DfEE and Scottish, Northern Ireland and Welsh Offices (addresses above) or from your local education authority or careers office.

Ten ways to fill the gap ... Ten ways to work and travel ... Ten ways to discover the world
Free leaflets

> Available from the Central Bureau for Educational Visits and Exchanges, Information Unit, 10 Spring Gardens, London SW1A 2BN. Tel: 0171 389 4880. Fax: 020 7389 4426

A parents' guide to higher education

> Available from UCAS, Fulton House, Jessop Avenue, Cheltenham, Gloucestershire GL50 3SH

... and, of course, the **Prospectuses** and **Alternative Prospectuses** of individual institutions — available in your school/college careers library and your local careers office, but you can also get your own copies free by contacting the institution concerned.